SECOND EDITION

CURRICULUM WEBS

Weaving the Web into Teaching and Learning

CRAIG A. CUNNINGHAM
National-Louis University

MARTY BILLINGSLEY
The University of Chicago Laboratory Schools

Boston   New York   San Francisco
Mexico City   Montreal   Toronto   London   Madrid   Munich   Paris
Hong Kong   Singapore   Tokyo   Cape Town   Sydney

Senior editor: Arnis E. Burvikovs
Editorial assistant: Kelly Hopkins
Marketing manager: Tara Kelly
Manufacturing buyer: Andrew Turso
Cover designer: Rebecca Krzyzaniak
Production coordinator: Pat Torelli Publishing Services
Editorial-production service: Stratford Publishing Services
Electronic composition: Stratford Publishing Services

For related titles and support materials, visit our online catalog at www.ablongman.com.

Between the time web-site information is gathered and published, some sites may have closed. Also, the transcription of URLs can result in unintended typographical errors. The publisher would appreciate notification where these errors occur so that they may be corrected in subsequent editions.

Many of the designations used by manufacturers and sellers to distinguish their products are claimed as trademarks. Where those designations appear in this book, and Allyn and Bacon was aware of a trademark claim, the designations have been printed in initial or all caps.

To obtain permission(s) to use material from this work, please submit a written request to Allyn and Bacon, Permissions Department, 75 Arlington Street, Boston, MA 02116 or fax your request to 617-848-7320.

ISBN: 0-205-45940-4

Printed in the United States of America

10   9   8   7   6   5   4   3   2   09   08   07   06

CAC: To Cheryl

MB: To my parents

BRIEF CONTENTS

CONTENTS

CHAPTER FOUR
Laying Out an Effective Web Page   70

CHAPTER TEN
Constructing Interactivity   196

CHAPTER ELEVEN
Evaluating and Maintaining Curriculum Webs   222

FIGURES

PREFACE

This book helps teachers, curriculum developers, and informal educators to utilize the World Wide Web as a central resource to facilitate learning.

The title of the book refers to curriculum webs. A curriculum web is a web page or pages designed to support a curriculum, or a "plan for a sustained process of teaching and learning" (Pratt, 1994, 5). This book describes the process of building curriculum webs from the early planning stages through to design of the web pages, and using the finished product in classrooms. It also includes discussion of WebQuests, a simple form of curriculum web that makes it easy for teachers to begin to use the Web more effectively with their students.

The contents of the second edition of this book reflect our updated understanding of what preservice and inservice teachers and other educators need to learn how to create curriculum webs. This understanding arises from eight years of experience training teachers in the Web Institute for Teachers, an intensive summer professional development experience hosted by the University of Chicago.

The effective use of the Web to support teaching and learning requires ongoing attention to explicit reflection and planning. Only such reflection and planning will produce desired learning outcomes—knowledge, skills, and attitudes—in diverse students in a rapidly changing world. A successful teacher or other web-based curriculum developer understands the phases of curriculum development and routinely considers a range of issues involved in building web sites to support the needs of learners while taking advantage of the ever-expanding possibilities of the Web. He or she also pays careful attention to how the curriculum web is used by learners, and makes ongoing modifications in order to help a range of learners to reach desired outcomes. Through participation in this cycle of creation and reflection, he or she exemplifies what it means to be a professional educator.

On the companion web site, *curriculumwebs.com*, you will find example curriculum webs that can serve as an inspiration to you as you work toward creating your own curriculum web, as well as a series of Hands-On Lessons that will teach you the basic steps of creating a curriculum web using several popular web-page editors.

WHO SHOULD READ THIS BOOK?

Anyone who wants to increase student learning will want to learn how to build curriculum webs.

This book will be helpful to teachers in schools and those who are learning to teach, curriculum developers working for educational organizations such as school districts and museums, and parents who are homeschooling their children. Our greatest hope is that this book will help individual teachers or groups of teachers who want to create webs to support unique or locally significant learning activities, or educators who want to take advantage of variably occurring "teachable moments" that crop up continuously in their local community or in the global village. We also hope that nonschool curriculum developers, who create web-based learning materials for federal, state, and local agencies, nonprofit organizations, historical sites, parks, and museums, will read this book and use its concepts and procedures to produce more effective materials.

We believe that every teacher should know how to build web pages to support their ongoing teaching as well as the unexpected learning needs and specialized interests of their particular students. A basic familiarity with computers, a willingness to put time and energy into planning and design, and this book are all that is required.

We use the words *teacher*, *planner*, *developer*, and *designer* more or less interchangeably in this book. The only difference between the first and the other three is that teachers may be developing the curriculum knowing that they will actually be using it with their students, and so we expect teachers to be the most diligent, careful, and effective curriculum developers and web designers of all.

HOW TO USE THIS BOOK

This book includes all the information you need to plan effective learning activities on the Web. The Hands-On Lessons found on the companion web site at *curriculumwebs.com* provide software-specific instructions that guide you through the actual process of constructing the pages of your curriculum web.

The best way to use this book is to read it from beginning to end, doing the activities along the way and completing the appropriate Hands-On Lesson after reading each chapter. In a series of professional development workshops or a college course the participants could read one chapter and complete one Hands-On Lesson per week. If you are using the book on your own, you might want to read all of the chapters first, and then cycle back to the Hands-On Lessons, referring to the book again to learn more about general principles and procedures related to the lessons.

Each chapter includes several features designed to help you learn:

- *Overview:* provides a summary of what will be covered in the chapter.
- *Activities:* solidify your understanding of key concepts or procedures along the way.
- *Questions for reflection:* helps you to think about the content of the book in terms of larger questions having to do with professional and personal growth.
- *Your next step:* suggests how to use the Hands-On Lessons that accompany the book and prepares you for subsequent chapters
- *Chapter summary:* reviews what was covered in the chapter.
- *For further learning:* guides you to additional print and web resources. Full citations are listed in the References at the end of the book.

In addition to the chapters, this book contains a number of features that will help you:

- The *Appendix* (An Overview of Web Technologies) tells you everything you need to know about web servers, bandwidth, filenames, and other technical aspects of using the Internet. Read this appendix if you find yourself at sea with some of the terms or concepts that we assume of our readers.

■ The *glossary* contains definitions for words that appear in **boldface** the first time they are introduced in the book or in the lessons. A lot of nontechnical terms are also included here as a way of demystifying some philosophical and pedagogical concepts found throughout this book.

■ An extensive set of *references* includes citations for all the sources consulted in preparing this book. Citations in author-date format are given through the text.

■ An extensive *index* is useful if you want to use this book as **hypertext** (you'll find a definition in the Glossary); that is, if you want to use it as a reference tool rather than read it from cover to cover.

Don't forget to use the companion web site—*curriculumwebs.com*—to find links relevant to many of the topics in the book, to access additional information about HTML and cascading style sheets (CSS), to download the Hands-On Lessons and related resources, to see example curriculum webs, or to contact the authors.

WHAT THIS BOOK IS AND WHAT IT IS NOT

This book covers the entire process of planning curriculum, creating web pages, and using web pages to support teaching, so readers will be able to benefit from this book even if they have never created a web page or used the Web with students.

Successful use of this book has several prerequisites. We assume that you are computer literate. The book therefore does not cover basic computer skills such as saving, copying, and deleting files, installing hardware or software, or connecting your computer to the Internet. We assume that you are already familiar with operating your computer, creating folders or directories, saving and moving files, and browsing the Internet. (For some background on these topics, see the Appendix.) We also assume you are comfortable and excited about learning new approaches to using the computer (even if you are a little intimidated). You do not have to know anything at all about building web pages.

We provide detailed guidance and step-by-step procedures for using popular web-page editors such as Macromedia Dreamweaver, Microsoft FrontPage, and Mozilla Composer throughout this text and in a series of Hands-On Lessons, available at *curriculumwebs.com*. These lessons tell you exactly what buttons to press or what menu choices to select—in all of these software programs—to produce the essential design elements of curriculum webs. We do not cover every function of the more advanced software packages, but the lessons cover numerous procedures and include advice for learning more.

Even if you are a computer wiz, fully versed in web design, you can still benefit from our coverage of curriculum planning, learning activities, assessment and evaluation, and using the Web with students. Web-page designers can use this book to help them reflect on and design better learning environments.

The book itself does not include any click steps, and only a few addresses of web sites. The Web is evolving so rapidly that web site contents and addresses often change or become obsolete. We want this book to remain useful even as specific resources change or become unavailable. We have included a few web sites that have maintained their same address for at least two years and are maintained by established organizations and are thus likely to remain stable. You can find many additional links to relevant online resources on our companion web site at curriculumwebs.com. We encourage you to send us additional resources if you find them useful.

ENHANCEMENTS IN THE SECOND EDITION

This new edition of *Curriculum Webs* includes several important enhancements that reflect the feedback from our readers and what we have learned from our ongoing work with teachers and others who are developing curriculum webs. The order of the chapters has been changed to reflect better the sequence of steps that the developers of curriculum webs actually follow when they work. A new chapter (Chapter Two) has been added covering WebQuests and other activity formats for using the Web to enhance teaching and learning. Greater attention has been given throughout to the importance of teacher reflection and continuous improvement. Each chapter includes one or more Questions for Reflection to encourage this important process. We've included more examples throughout the book and on the companion web site at *curriculumwebs.com*. We've added many new activities to support the application and practice that will truly teach you how to create a dynamic and effective curriculum web. The Hands-On Lessons have been completely rewritten to reflect our new sequence of topics and procedures, and to incorporate changes in the software. All of the content has been updated to reflect current technologies. We pay a lot more attention to CSS, and have included a CSS reference on the companion web site. Our HTML Reference has been moved from the book to the web site to make it easier to use and to allow more space in the book for discussion of streaming audio and video and new approaches to interactivity. The References have been updated and expanded, as have the Glossary and the Index.

We believe the second edition is a stronger and more useful book. We hope you agree.

ACKNOWLEDGMENTS

Many people have made this book possible. The authors take full responsibility for any remaining errors or inadequacies.

This book initially arose out of the Web Institute for Teachers (WIT), a professional development program for teachers held each summer from 1997 through 2004 at the University of Chicago, when we could not find a suitable text. The single most important person in making WIT possible is Professor Don York, noted astronomer and director of the Chicago Public Schools/University of Chicago Internet Project (CUIP). Don's astronomer-like attention to detail, combined with his persistence and vision, have connected numerous schools, teachers, and children to the Internet. His work exemplifies the moral responsibility of universities in a democratic society.

Mitchell Marks, technical coordinator extraordinaire for CUIP and WIT, made it possible for us to have a reliable and easily configurable server for WIT and for the development and hosting of curriculumwebs.com. Mitch exemplifies the technical support that universities can provide to the public schools. Russ Revzan, a veteran teacher in a Chicago public school and longtime WIT mentor, became an expert in FrontPage while helping to produce and revise the Hands-On Lessons. Sharon Comstock, another WIT mentor and a youth librarian, provided us with important insights and useful suggestions for incorporating the concepts of inquiry and reflection into the second edition. Tamar Friedman and Janet Gray-McKennis (also former WIT mentors) made detailed suggestions for the second edition. Christie Thomas (another WIT mentor), Caitlin Devitt, and Janet Geovanis provided useful feedback and suggestions as the first edition of the text was initially written.

Arnis Burvikovs, our editor at Allyn & Bacon, has been optimistic yet helpfully critical of our work at every stage. Susan Walker of Stratford Publishing Services ably and cheerfully pulled everything together for the second edition. The following reviewers made helpful comments about the first edition of this book: Robin Burke, DePaul University; Ralph Cafolla, Florida Atlantic University; Maria Teresa Fernandez, United States International University; Diane McGrath, Kansas State University; Jean Morrow, Emporia State University; Catherine M. Ricardo, Iona College; and Paula Zeszotarski, UCLA and ERIC Clearinghouse for Community Colleges. Finally, we received detailed and valuable advice from the following as we prepared this second edition: Karen Kusiak, Colby College; Diane McGrath, Kansas State University; and Jean Morrow, Emporia State University. Of course, none of these reviewers share our responsibility for what you now hold in your hands.

Most of all, we want to thank the hundreds of teachers who have been mentors and learners in WIT during the past eight years. These teachers have taught us much about the nature of teaching and learning, and about how to use the Web as a teaching tool.

ABOUT THE AUTHORS

Craig Cunningham is associate professor in the Technology in Education program, National College of Education, National-Louis University, and is founder and director of the University of Chicago's Web Institute for Teachers. Before joining the National College of Education, he was research associate at the Center for Urban School Improvement, University of Chicago, and curriculum director for the Chicago Public Schools/University of Chicago Internet Project (CUIP). Craig has a Ph.D. in philosophy of curriculum from the University of Chicago. He has taught at Northeastern Illinois University, the School of the Art Institute of Chicago, DePaul University, Chicago State University, the University of Chicago, Hyde School (Bath, Maine), and the Hyde Leadership School of Greater New Haven, and has published papers on moral education and technology integration. See Craig's web site at *craigcunningham.com*.

Marty Billingsley chairs the computer science department at the Laboratory Schools of the University of Chicago, where she has taught for 10 years. She has a B.S. in computer science from Montana State University, and has worked as an engineer for Hewlett-Packard and Tektronics. In 1999–2000, Marty served as assistant director and webmaster of the Web Institute for Teachers, and she was a mentor again in 2003. See Marty's web page at *mbillingsley.com*.

The two authors come from different backgrounds that intersect in this book. Craig's background in teaching and in the philosophy of education has prepared him to look with a critical eye at contemporary educational structures, practices, and innovations, and to be constantly on the lookout for new possibilities and potentialities for learning. As a teacher, researcher, and reformer, Craig has always seen technology as tool rather than an end in itself. Marty, however, comes from a background as a software engineer. Her primary interest has been computer science—not the application of computers for productivity, but on how computers themselves work and their application in problem solving. This is the focus of her ongoing learning and also what she is most passionate about teaching to others. When Craig's interest in educational improvement is combined with Marty's interest in how computers work, the result is a stereoscopic view on how computers can be used to support teaching and learning. We hope you find our dual perspectives helpful.

Let us know how you like the book, and tell us about the curriculum webs you make! You can contact us at *curriculumwebs.com*.

CHAPTER 1

PLANNING CURRICULUM FOR THE WEB

Overview

This chapter introduces you to the concept of curriculum webs, explores why they might support teaching and learning, and offers initial guidance on how to build—and use—them. This chapter also acts as an invitation to reflect on your own use of computers both within and outside of the classroom; to reflect on your own teaching; and to, perhaps, revisit some of your assumptions about what "works" in your classes.

WHAT IS A CURRICULUM WEB?

As educators, most of us have a pretty good notion what "curriculum" is. For our purposes here, we are defining a **curriculum*** as "a plan for a sustained process of teaching and learning." It describes a coherent set of intentions, subject matter, activities, and methods for determining whether students have learned (Pratt 1994). A curriculum usually consists of a number of different learning activities, linked together in a coherent sequence that builds toward a defined set of learning objectives.

A **curriculum web** is a **web page** or **web site** designed to support a sustained process of **teaching** and **learning.** Generally, a curriculum web includes instructional guidance for students; thoughtful and relevant information that may include text, images, or other multimedia; and external **links** to other valuable resources. A complete curriculum web includes the following components:

- A carefully developed *curriculum plan* that defines the purposes and learning activities of the curriculum;
- A front or *home page* that is the main entry point into the curriculum web;
- Student *activity pages* that describe specific learning activities for students and lead them to appropriate resources;
- A *teaching guide* that contains information useful to the teacher (and which includes elements of the curriculum plan);

---

*Words printed in **boldface** in this book are defined in the Glossary, beginning on page 257.

- Online **rubrics** and *self-assessments*, so students can test—and reflect on—their new knowledge or understanding;
- *Feedback mechanisms* so students can communicate with the teacher or curriculum creator, allowing for enhanced engagement and individualization; and
- *Selected links* to relevant web sites that have been carefully evaluated and determined to support learning.

See Figure 1.1 for a screen shot of a typical curriculum web home page. This curriculum web, "Beaks and Feet," is designed to support an inquiry into biological diversity by English–language learning kindergartners and their third-grade buddies.

Every curriculum web is based on a **curriculum plan.** It should come as no surprise that the more elaborate the curriculum web, the more elaborate the curriculum plan that lies behind it. In fact, the key to creating successful learner-centered activities that harness the power and excitement of the **World Wide Web** is careful forethought and ongoing **reflection.** Our experience has been that we never really "finish" a curriculum web: we plan, create, reflect, and revise throughout—before, during, and after the learners use it. This book stresses the importance of reflection and **planning** during the entire **development**—and implementation—process. We encourage you to create a written curriculum plan that serves as a blueprint for the curriculum and the curriculum web you are building. Effective plans will have a common set of **elements** that we describe in detail in this book. Writing this plan during the curriculum development

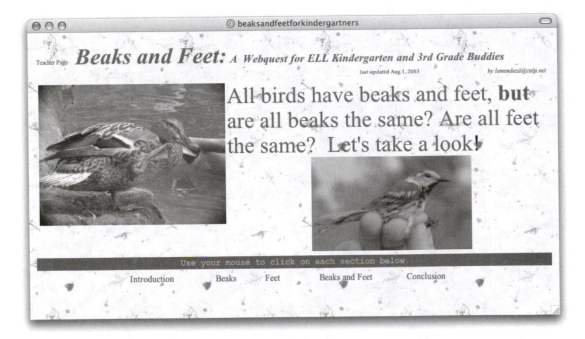

FIGURE 1.1   A typical curriculum web front page.

Source: Courtesy of Laura Mendoza, *cuip.net/~lemendoza/beaksandfeetforkindergartners.html*

process helps you to organize the many factors that influence the structure and content of the curriculum web.

Don't think that the curriculum plan is somehow set aside once you start building your curriculum web. The written plan you've created during development of the curriculum web then becomes an online **teaching guide** in the final curriculum web, providing helpful suggestions for the teacher or other users (much like the annotations given in the teachers' edition of a textbook). The teaching guide is especially helpful for other teachers using your curriculum web who were not personally involved in its development, offering a window on the curriculum's assumptions, goals, and structure. The teaching guide can also prove invaluable to parents, students, and administrators, by enabling them to see the thinking behind the curriculum web: how the web site *reflects the planning*. The teaching guide also serves as an opportunity for you to reflect on your own curriculum building process as an artifact of what you have learned during the process.

Each curriculum web discussed in this book (or linked on *curriculumwebs.com*) includes a teaching guide that has all of the elements listed in Table 1.1. Again, the teaching guide is not an add-on created after the curriculum web has already been developed; rather, it emerges directly out of the curriculum plan that is produced before and during development.

Well-planned curriculum webs embody *both* an effective curriculum plan *and* a well-designed web site that supports that plan. In this book, we take you through the development of both. We cover the process of planning your own curriculum web, discuss aspects involved at each stage in planning, and describe principles and procedures for designing an effective web site to support your plan. Of course, we also provide many specific examples in the book and on the companion web site at *curriculumwebs.com*.

TABLE 1.1   Elements of a Complete Curriculum Plan and Teaching Guide

An *introduction* that provides an overview of the curriculum web (optional for the curriculum plan; necessary for the teaching guide)

A summary of the developer's broad educational *goals*

Description of the target *learners* and their needs

Description of *subject matter* or content

A listing of the expected *prerequisites* for successful use of the curriculum

A list of specific *learning objectives*

A concise statement of *aim* or purpose

A *rationale*, justifying the aim

An *instructional plan* (describing how to use the web site with students), including a list of the equipment and *materials* necessary

A plan for *assessment* of learning and for *evaluation* of the curriculum web itself

Contact information for the author, and *acknowledgements* of sources utilized in building the web site

WHY BUILD CURRICULUM WEBS?

As stated before, a curriculum web is a tool for using the **Web** to enhance teaching and learning. Like all tools, it is good for some tasks but not for others. Here are some of things curriculum webs may be good for, and some compelling reasons why teachers may want to learn how to create and use them:

- Curriculum webs can guide **learners** to resources that have been preselected for having high educational value relative to the desired learning objectives. This avoids the mindless **surfing** students sometimes engage in when given access to the Web.
- **Teachers** can provide information or instructions to individuals or small groups of students when the students are ready for that communication, without having to repeat instructions or other information for each student or group. Each student accesses a given page in the curriculum web only when he or she is prepared to utilize it, that is, "just in time."
- Different individual learners or groups of students can work through the curriculum web at their own pace, and the teacher can focus on helping individual students or groups of students to master the specific challenges they face. This capacity to differentiate instruction is one of the most compelling features of curriculum webs.
- It is also possible to use web pages for whole-classroom activities in which all the students are accessing a web page or web site together, using a computer **projector** connected to an **instructor station** or over a computer **network.**
- A curriculum web can become a replacement for—or an enhancement to— workbooks, textbooks, chalkboards, slide projectors, overhead projectors, calculators, certain manipulatives, software, trips to the library, and (through **streaming** of video over the Web) film projectors and VCRs.
- Developing curriculum webs involves many tasks that teachers already engage in: lesson planning, giving instructions, providing examples, and assessing learning. Thus, it does not take much additional work to move from traditional media to the Web.
- Curriculum webs are easy to make, given a basic understanding of curriculum development and mastery of the basics of web page creation. Once a teacher or other curriculum developer has produced a few simple curriculum webs, he or she will be ready to incorporate increasingly sophisticated technical and pedagogical techniques. Curriculum webs provide a natural pathway for teacher growth and professional development, while helping the teacher to keep up with technological and curricular changes.
- A teacher well versed in building curriculum webs can respond to "breaking news" or local events by quickly creating a relevant lesson or curriculum on the Web. The capacity to respond to the unexpected enhances schooling enormously. Traditional textbooks could never be used for this purpose; book libraries could help with background materials; newspapers could provide news summaries. Now, with the Web, teachers can immediately incorporate breaking news stories, background information, maps, images, video, and sound into the

daily lesson, thus making learning more interesting, immediate, and relevant to the students' lives.

- Curriculum webs can allow individual students to pursue their own interests within wider curriculum goals. Webs can be structured in such a way as to allow individual choice of particular topics or resources to be used for learning activities. This is especially useful when dealing with gifted or advanced students—or students with special needs—within the regular classroom.

- Curriculum webs can save money. Obviously, schools must undergo the large expense of getting connected to the **Internet,** purchasing adequate computers, and accessing sufficient electrical power. But once these are in place, curriculum webs can cut down on the costs of schooling by replacing textbooks, workbooks, paper, and other consumables.

- Curriculum webs can be effectively integrated with real world experiences. Clearly students also need to practice the sorts of things that people actually do, such as getting around in the world, and maintaining one's body/mind/spirit through participation in real physical, emotional, and social experiences. The Web cannot replace these experiences, but it can make them more educative, by providing background information and facilitating communication and understanding before and after the experiences.

- Since web pages can sit on **a web server** indefinitely, they become a perennial resource for schools and teachers. And because their developers can quickly, efficiently, and naturally update their curriculum webs, they provide ongoing support year after year while eliminating (at least the appearance of) yellowed index cards.

- Curriculum webs do not usually require special software or hardware to be used. Rather, all that is needed is a **web browser** and an Internet connection, and occasionally one or more widely available and free **plug-ins** to access special content. Indeed, curriculum webs can be easily accessed using any Internet-linked computer, whether the computer is a Macintosh or PC. This nearly universal compatibility is not often the case with commercially available educational software.

- Curriculum webs help schools and teachers to meet national, state, and local **standards** for technology integration in the curriculum. For example, the National Educational Technology Standards for Students (NETS-S), produced by the International Society for Technology in Education (ISTE), call for students to "use technology to locate, evaluate, and collect information from a variety of sources," including the Internet. (See page 9 for more information about the relationship between curriculum webs and standards.)

- Parents can participate more actively in the education of their children. They can see the curriculum, try out the activities, understand teacher expectations and intentions, and communicate more freely with the teacher.

- Students can communicate with one another and with the teacher, even when everyone has gone home or is on vacation. The simplest way of facilitating student-to-student communication is by providing them with e-mail, although other options, such as web-based chat rooms and bulletin boards, can also be used. But curriculum webs also eliminate the limitations of place, time, or physical materials. Students who are homebound or temporarily unable to participate in the classroom, or who have lost their book, worksheet, or assignment, can access the curriculum web from home or anywhere else with Internet access. This helps these students to keep up with missed work, and provides a way for teachers to support students who, for various reasons, are learning at a different pace than the rest of the class. (Curriculum webs are, of course, especially useful for **distance education,** where they are already widely used.)

- Schools and school districts can manage student learning. When curriculum webs are woven together on a school web site, they form a "school web," which can facilitate participatory and cooperative learning among all the students of the school, at every grade level and in every subject. Schools do not have to start out with the ambitious goal of creating a complete school web. One teacher or group of teachers can start building a section of the school web at any time. The technology of the Web is not going away; time is certainly on your side!

- Students can build curriculum webs as a **culminating project** to a learning unit. We all know that teaching something is one of the best ways to really learn it. If students have the opportunity to consider the many factors that go into the creation of an effective curriculum web, especially if they design the curriculum web for a group of younger students or other learners who will actually use the curriculum web, they will come to a better understanding of the underlying concepts and structure of the subject matter, and may also gain increased motivation for learning the material at a high level.

In addition to these benefits, perhaps the most significant effect of curriculum webs is their effect on the teacher or curriculum developer who builds them. We believe that teachers can improve their teaching through the ongoing creation of curriculum webs. Building an effective curriculum web is pretty good preparation for teaching an effective curriculum unit. Teacher involvement in curriculum development and web design fosters improvements in teaching and in teachers. We are not saying that this is the only way teachers can improve, but it is one way, and it is one that is timely and increasingly available to teachers in schools and in colleges of education. Building a web site for learning is itself a process of learning in which meaning is created. Meaning consists of associative relations among concepts or experiences. As people learn, these relations, or meanings, intertwine in complex mental webs that are built in the medium of ongoing experience. Designing a web site is like creating a web of meaning around a set of experiences. In order to design the site, the developer/designer/teacher who creates a meaningful curriculum web becomes at the same time a more knowledgeable and effective teacher, with a more sophisticated mental map of the subject and enriched ideas about how to foster learning.

The availability of information on the Internet and World Wide Web leads to a new role for teachers. In the classroom, teachers who develop their own curriculum webs can become facilitators of learning experiences specifically designed for their students, based on a careful **assessment** of the students' needs, rather than standardized deliverers of information or skills training. By engaging in the process of curriculum reflection and planning, teachers grow as teachers and as learners, modeling the process for the students as they grow.

This is not to say that traditional schools will easily accommodate this new role for teachers. As Brunner and Tally (1999, 7) write:

> Schools need to be wired humanly even more than they need to be wired electronically; that is, schools need to be supported by better, more informed, and more trusting relationships between parents, teachers, students, administrators and community members. Technologies can help create the conditions for these relationships and these conversations to happen, but a school's rules, norms, and values—especially those around who gets to speak, to whom, and for what purposes—are the more important preconditions.

Teacher **habits**—whether good or bad—are often fostered or maintained by the organizational realities of schools. Different aspects of schools interrelate in ways that are mutually reinforcing. For example, tracking students by ability in math often causes them to be tracked effectively in other subjects as well. In another example, the decision whether to give students **e-mail** accounts at school affects other decisions about instructional planning and student empowerment.

Perhaps the biggest obstacle to changing the role of teachers through the use of curriculum webs is time. Because teachers were traditionally expected only to deliver curriculum created by others (mostly textbook publishers), schools are not well organized to encourage teachers to create and maintain curriculum webs. Especially when they are just learning how to use a web-page editor, teachers also need a lot of technical and pedagogical support. This is why we believe the best way to encourage use of curriculum webs is to bring teachers to the school or other setting during the summer to work for several weeks on their first curriculum web, under the guidance and support of experienced mentor teachers. This is the model we have followed in the Web Institute for Teachers (WIT) at the University of Chicago. (More information about WIT can be found at *webinstituteforteachers.org*.)

SOME EXAMPLE CURRICULUM WEBS

To help you to better understand what a curriculum web is and how it works, we have created three example curriculum webs. These examples can be examined online by visiting *curriculumwebs.com*, and clicking on "Example Curriculum Webs." We refer to these three examples throughout the book, and it would be a good idea for you to spend some time looking at them.

The three example curriculum webs are:

- "Our United States," a curriculum web designed for middle school students. It takes them on an exploration of the relationship between geography and economic and recreational activities. See Figure 1.2 for a screen shot of the home page of this curriculum web.
- "Who Am I?," a curriculum web designed for high school students to explore self-identity while learning about how to use the Web to support research and writing. See Figure 1.3 for a screen shot of the home page of this curriculum web.

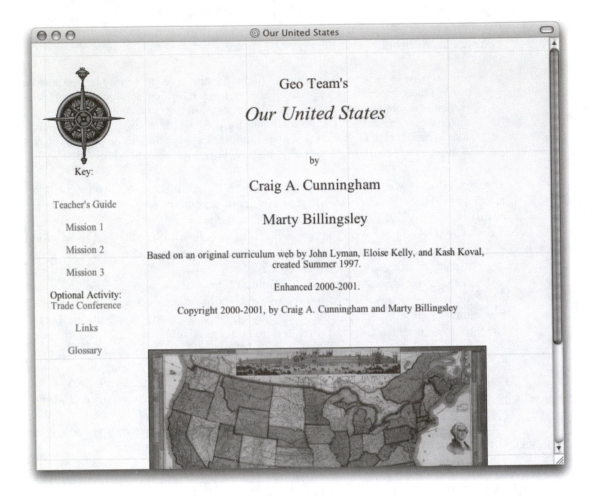

FIGURE 1.2   "Our United States" curriculum web.

- "Building a Curriculum Web with Dreamweaver," a curriculum web designed for adults (teachers) to help them learn how to use the web-editing software Dreamweaver to build curriculum webs. See Figure 1.4 for a screen shot of the home page of this curriculum web.

As you look at these three curriculum webs, you will notice that they share a few common features:

- A home page or **entry-point** that introduces the curriculum web and provides links to all the activities and resources within the web site.
- A consistent look and feel within the web site that makes navigation easy and that distinguishes the curriculum web from other web sites.
- A teaching guide that contains the elements listed in Table 1.1.

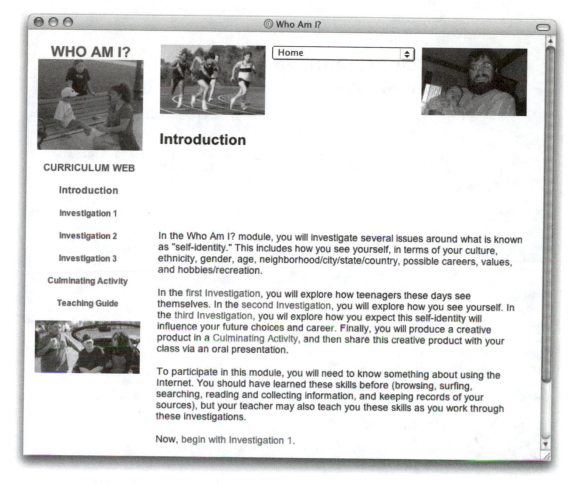

WHO AM I?

Introduction

CURRICULUM WEB

Introduction

Investigation 1

Investigation 2

Investigation 3

Culminating Activity

Teaching Guide

In the Who Am I? module, you will investigate several issues around what is known as "self-identity." This includes how you see yourself, in terms of your culture, ethnicity, gender, age, neighborhood/city/state/country, possible careers, values, and hobbies/recreation.

In the first Investigation, you will explore how teenagers these days see themselves. In the second Investigation, you will explore how you see yourself. In the third Investigation, you wil explore how you expect this self-identity will influence your future choices and career. Finally, you will produce a creative product in a Culminating Activity, and then share this creative product with your class via an oral presentation.

To participate in this module, you will need to know something about using the Internet. You should have learned these skills before (browsing, surfing, searching, reading and collecting information, and keeping records of your sources), but your teacher may also teach you these skills as you work through these investigations.

Now, begin with Investigation 1.

FIGURE 1.3   **"Who Am I?" curriculum web.**

- A set of **learning activities** designed to lead the learner to the **learning objectives** listed in the teaching guide. These activities sometimes take the learner into the wider Web by including links to sites that have been previously selected to be relevant to the curriculum web.
- A mechanism for the learner to contact the curriculum web developer or the teacher to submit work, give feedback, or ask questions.

Any curriculum web you develop should share these basic features.

STANDARDS AND CURRICULUM WEBS

The most significant development in education during the past twenty years—besides the widespread availability of personal computers and the Internet—has been the

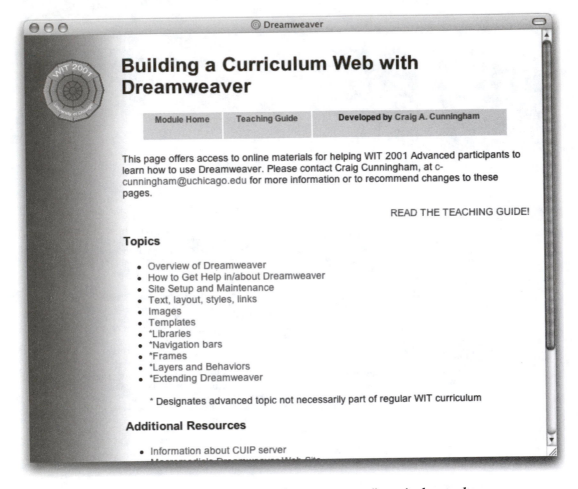

FIGURE 1.4   "Building a Curriculum Web with Dreamweaver" curriculum web.

development of educational standards by almost every state and by many national and international organizations such as the National Council of Teachers of Mathematics and the American Association for the Advancement of Science. These standards are designed to create shared expectations of what students will learn in each grade and subject area, so that teachers and schools will know what to teach as well as how to assess whether teaching and learning have been effective.

In Illinois, for example, the state board of education coordinated the development of the Illinois Learning Standards in 1997 and subsequently organized the development of performance descriptors and classroom assessments tied to the standards. The performance descriptors describe the kinds of tasks that students will be able to do when they have reached certain stages in meeting the standards, and are designed to help schools and teachers to develop curriculum that will move students through 10 stages in developmentally appropriate ways.

For example, Illinois Learning Standard 1A for grades 1–5 is "Apply word analysis and vocabulary skills to comprehend selections." The general performance descriptor for this standard is "Students who meet the standard can apply word analysis and vocabulary skills to comprehend selections." Notice that at this general level, the performance descriptor is just a restatement of the standard in terms of what students can do. However, Illinois also provides detailed descriptions of the stages of development students are likely to progress through in meeting the standard. The detailed descriptions include specifics on the use of phonics, root words, synonyms, meaning in context, and the use of additional resources. Teachers or others who are developing an elementary school language arts curriculum can look at the standards and performance descriptors to determine the appropriate learning objectives (and often, learning activities) for a given audience of students in any subject area. Although the assignment of "standards" to lesson plans is often treated as a routine activity without a lot of careful thought, it is our experience that spending real time reading and reflecting on these documents can truly help teachers to focus on what has been carefully selected as important for students to learn. We will say more about this process in Chapter Three on identifying educational goals, beginning on page 35.

In addition to subject area standards, curriculum webs also provide ideal opportunities to meet standards related to student use of technology. Many states have developed or adopted technology standards for their students. We believe that these standards are best learned (and applied) in the learning of subject matter and content that goes beyond technology itself. For example, word-processing skills may be learned best while engaging in activities in the language arts, social sciences, and even science and math, rather than learned separately in so-called computer class. Curriculum webs devoted to a variety of educational goals will—by their very nature and the ease of including web-based resources—help to meet these technology standards.

The most comprehensive and widely followed set of technology standards for students has been developed by the International Society for Technology in Education. Known as the National Educational Technology Standards for Students, or NETS-S, these standards may be considered *the standard* (so to speak) for student technology standards. In addition to standards for student learning, NETS-S also provides a list of the essential conditions that schools must create for effective student learning (these conditions are listed in Table 1.2), and profiles that illustrate what students should be able to do on meeting the standards. The profiles include performance indicators that serve a similar function to the performance descriptors described above.

The NETS-S themselves are organized according to six categories—basic operations and concepts; social, ethical, and human issues; technology productivity tools; technology communication tools; technology research tools; and technology problem-solving and decision-making tools—and are given in four grade-level ranges: preK–2, 3–5, 6–8, and 9–12.

For example, prior to grade 2, NETS-S call for students to "gather information and communicate with others using telecommunications, with support from teachers, family members, or student partners." By the end of grade 5, they should "design, develop, publish, and present products" (including web pages), "collaborate with peers, experts, and others using telecommunications," and "research and evaluate the accuracy, relevance,

TABLE 1.2   The Essential Conditions of School Technology Use, as Defined by the International Society for Technology in Education

Vision with support and proactive leadership from the education system

Educators skilled in the use of technology for learning

Content standards and curriculum resources

Student-centered approaches to learning

Assessment of the effectiveness of technology for learning

Access to contemporary technologies, software, and telecommunications networks

Technical assistance for maintaining and using technology resources

Community partners who provide expertise, support, and real-life interactions

Ongoing financial support for sustained technology use

Policies and standards supporting new learning environments

Source: http://cnets.iste.org/students/s_esscond.html.

appropriateness, comprehensiveness, and bias of electronic information sources concerning real-world problems." Before graduating from grade 8, students should be able to "use content-specific tools, software, and simulations" (including web tools) "to support learning and research," as well as "design, develop, publish, and present products" (including web pages), in addition to meeting the goals set for the end of grade 5. Finally, before finishing high school, students should be able to "routinely and effectively use online information resources to meet needs for collaboration, research, publications, communications, and productivity" (ISTE 2000a).

ACTIVITY 1A ■ Exploring NETS-S

1. Visit the NETS-S web site at *cnets.iste.org*
2. Using a word-processing program or spreadsheet, create a table of the performance indicators listed on that page.
3. Structure the table so that you can compare them by grade level.
4. Choose 1 of the 10 performance indicators and examine the changes in the indicator as you move from preK–2, through 3–5, 6–8, and 9–12 grade levels.
5. For the performance indicator you have selected, make an ordered list of what students will have to master in order to demonstrate that they have mastered the performance indicators at each grade level.
6. Brainstorm the kinds of learning activities that students will have to complete as they move through a school system that helps them to meet the standards.

The International Society for Technology in Education has also developed a set of standards for the training of teachers in technology. These National Educational Technology Standards for Teachers (NETS-T) set forth what teachers should be able to do at three levels: before starting their student teaching; after their student teaching and internship; when they are ready to take over their own classroom; and at the end of the first year of teaching. The list of proficiencies is long. It includes broad familiarity with technology and resources and how to use them with students. (You can find the NETS-T at *cnets.iste.org/teachers*.)

The NETS-T note that there are three "foundations for effective use of technology" by teachers. These can be thought of as the prerequisites for teacher utilization of technology in schools. They are:

- Basic computer/technology operations and concepts
- Personal and professional use of technology
- Applications of technology in instruction

The best way for teachers to learn the first two of these skills is by using computers themselves while they are students. The third foundation will probably be laid only in the preservice teacher education program itself, either integrated into early methods classes or in a separate course on educational technology. (Some research suggests both a separate course and integration into methods courses is most effective. See Bielefeldt 2001.) Once the teacher has mastered these foundations, he or she is ready to learn how to teach with the technologies in schools. Somewhere along the way, the teacher will learn how to (among other things):

- "Engage in planning of lesson sequences that effectively integrate technology resources and are consistent with current best practices," and
- "Plan and implement technology learning activities that promote student engagement in analysis, synthesis, interpretation, and creation of original products" (ISTE 2000b).

These and the other skills outlined in the NETS-T are precisely the ones that can be furthered by having teachers develop their own curriculum webs:

- Critical thinking
- Data collection
- Ethical behavior
- Assessing and selecting resources
- Planning effective learning activities aligned to standards
- Developing methods for getting hardware, software, and technical support
- Arranging for equitable access for students
- Creating assessment activities to generate information that can help to improve instructional planning, management, and implementation of learning strategies
- Using technology tools to collect, analyze, interpret, represent, and communicate data for the purposes of instructional planning and school improvement.

We're not suggesting that curriculum webs are a panacea. In order for teachers to be able to create and use them, they not only need the skills that can be learned through this book, but the conditions listed in Table 1.2 need to be fulfilled in your school. Computers (in classrooms or **computer labs**), Internet access, electrical upgrades, and technical support all have to be paid for and maintained. (See Chapter Twelve for discussion of some of these essentials.) Superintendents, principals, colleagues, parents, and even students need to be convinced that new approaches to teaching and learning are wise and effective. Inequitable access to resources remains a huge obstacle to educational quality (and one of the great moral issues of our times), and this must be addressed through the political process. In the meantime, we expect curriculum webs to be used by more and more teachers, in more and more schools, where the conditions and supports are present.

EASING INTO BUILDING CURRICULUM WEBS

Fortunately, it does not take much to design and create web pages that are useful for teaching and learning. The actual creation of the pages themselves is a straightforward and simple process, once the curriculum has been planned. Web-page editing software is easy to use, especially for the moderately computer-literate person who has used a variety of computer software and who has ready access to a computer to practice new skills. Most people will need to invest some time up front to learn the software, which is often best done (using this book) as part of a course in preservice teacher education or as a series of inservice workshops after school or during the summer. Once the software and the process of building curriculum webs is mastered, the teacher or curriculum developer will find the creation and use of curriculum webs to be second nature, and they will wonder how they ever did their jobs before!

In this book, we will take you through many of the steps necessary to create a curriculum web using **HTML** (HyperText Markup Language), or "raw code." However, most web developers use specially designed software—web-page editors—to create and maintain their web sites, using HTML only for tweaking the code created by the software when it won't do exactly what they want it to do. We cover the code in the book because of its universality—HTML is HTML no matter how it is created—and because we believe everyone who creates web pages should have at least some familiarity with what goes on "under the hood." In the Hands-On Lessons available on *curriculumwebs.com*, we also show you everything you need to know about using three popular web-page editing packages: Macromedia's Dreamweaver, Microsoft's FrontPage, and Mozilla Composer. By the time you finish this book, you will be able to create almost any web page that you can envision. (One thing we don't cover is the creation of complex graphics or **animations.**)

The most challenging part of building curriculum webs is, we think, to tie curriculum reflection and planning together with web creation. These processes are usually treated separately, with web design sometimes handled by techies rather than educators. But this need not be the case, and we believe that reflective planning and implementation by educators is crucial for the success of a curriculum web. Enabling teachers to master and combine both of these skills is our goal in this book.

If you are a teacher who wants to use the Web in your teaching, you do not need to jump in with both feet. There are ways of easing into Web use. The first stage could be using the Web as a resource to support you as you develop lessons that will be delivered using traditional media. You can begin by familiarizing yourself with materials that are available on the Web already, and the tools required for accessing these materials. Your school librarian or media specialist may be willing to help you with this process. He or she may help you to use a search tool such as *yahoo.com* or *google.com* to look for materials. Simply typing "Causes of the Civil War" or a similar phrase into a popular **search engine** can give you a sense of the kinds of resources available on any given educational topic. For many topics, a search will generate a large number of links to a huge quantity of information. Some of these links will be useful to you, while a lot of the material will have nothing to do with the topic. Winnowing the information becomes an important skill. Again, your librarian will know how to help. By searching and browsing the Web, or collaborating with a librarian to collect materials, you can learn a lot about a given subject in preparation for teaching about that subject. Such preplanning is not only a great starting point for building a curriculum web, but it's also a good way to prepare yourself for teaching any subject in any medium, with technology or not. (With time and practice, you can improve your searching skills, and learn to find resources that are more relevant and useful. We discuss effective searching and winnowing techniques in Chapter Seven.)

A second stage for teachers is to visit one of the many explicitly educational sites on the Web. Included on most of these sites are lesson plans, generated by teachers on many topics and available to be copied and sometimes modified for use. A number of educational sites specifically designed for students can facilitate a teacher's first use of the Web in the classroom. Our companion web site at *curriculumwebs.com* lists some links to excellent sites, where teachers can find well-organized information related to a wide variety of subjects and learning objectives.

A third stage, slightly more complicated, is for a teacher to create a page for students that contains a list of web sites relevant to a particular topic, giving the students a starting point for further **inquiry.** The list of starting points, or links (sometimes called a "hotlist") can be created automatically during the process of the teacher's own Web search. We will show you how to do this in Chapter Seven and in the Hands-On Lesson that accompanies that chapter.

At a fourth stage, teachers can create a simple web-based lesson, involving just one or a few web pages. This is a good way to learn and practice the skills required in building larger web sites. In Chapter Two we introduce you to WebQuests, a fairly simple structure for creating curriculum webs that has proved to be the most popular approach to building web-based lessons.

Once you've built one or more WebQuests, you are ready to build a complete curriculum web. That process is covered in the remainder of the book.

OVERVIEW OF CURRICULUM PLANNING

Following Ralph Tyler's classic *Basic Principles of Curriculum and Instruction* (1949), we think of curriculum planning as involving four fundamental questions or phases (plus a fifth one we'll add below). The four questions are:

- What educational purposes should your curriculum seek to attain?
- How can learning activities be selected that are likely to be useful in attaining these objectives?

- How can learning activities be organized for effective instruction?
- How can the learning that results be assessed?

Developers of curriculum webs need to keep these questions in mind throughout the planning process, and also while designing the web site to support their curriculum plans.

It is possible to think of the process of curriculum planning for traditional media as a linear process, in which the curriculum planner first answers the first of the questions listed above, and then moves on to the second question, and so on; however, we know that in actual practice these questions are intertwined with one another. Planning for assessment, for example, can inform the choice of learning activities or the order in which you want students to complete them. Or, you may decide to embed assessment into learning activities, thus changing the nature of the activities themselves.

When the issues and procedures of designing a web site to support a curriculum are considered, the process is even less likely to resemble a step-by-step linear process. For example, you may discover that there are resources available on the Web that you had not previously considered, causing you to rethink your selection of learning activities. Or you may discover that the Web's capacity to support nonlinear navigation opens the possibility of a less traditional manner of sequencing activities. In our experience, building a curriculum web is more **iterative** than linear. Later aspects of the process often result in adjustments to decisions made earlier. Plus, a curriculum web is never really finished. The developer—especially if the developer is a teacher—will be tempted to improve it again and again as new groups of learners use it and provide feedback on what works and what does not work, and as new resources appear on the Web or emergent technologies and greater skills at web design open new possibilities.

For this reason, we suggest a fifth fundamental question to add to Tyler's famous list:

- Do the learning activities you have selected inspire your students toward further learning?

This question is at the heart of teacher reflection, which we define as the process of considering whether selected actions have led to desired consequences, and what to do about that. Reflection was critical to the philosophy of John Dewey, who believed that **educative experience** is a combination of action and reflection in which reflection contributes toward a refinement of action so that subsequent actions are more and more likely to lead to desired goals. This theory was further developed by Donald Schön in his 1983 book on the reflective practitioner. Schön differentiated between reflection-in-action, which occurs during the implementation of a plan and attempts to understand what is going on in light of prior experiences, and reflection-on-action, which is retrospective and takes place after results or consequences have actually occurred, allowing for deeper consideration of the wider causes of results and often leading to new approaches or theories. Both types are required by teachers (and by curriculum developers who actually pay attention to the ways their curriculums are used by learners), and both are essential to the effective development, implementation, and refinement of curriculum webs. Reflection examines not only the direct consequences of actions, but also their personal, ethical, and political implications, and often goes beyond consideration of any one event or experience to consideration of the effects of institutions or cultural practices. For individual teachers, reflection represents the single most important source of professional development: the creation of an evolving sense of meaning and purpose to one's actions that tie them together into a coherent and motivated whole. For this reason, we believe that the reflective teacher is by definition the effective teacher.

On a less profound level, any curriculum web will be successful to the extent that the teacher or developer can keep up constant interaction among curriculum planning, web design, and the learning that actually occurs when learners use the curriculum web. This is one of the reasons we want teachers to learn how to build curriculum webs: teachers, above all people, understand the challenges and possibilities of curriculum development and are in the best position to build effective web sites to support teaching and learning. It is also why we support the need to assess student learning—so that teachers and curriculum developers can see whether or not their curriculum plans are effective in practice and use that information to improve them. Teacher-developed assessments (discussed further in Chapter Six) that are used during and immediately after the students' learning experiences are often better instruments for determining whether students have met objectives than more universalized and standardized assessments mandated by state and federal law. Because their results are often available immediately to a teacher or other developer of a curriculum web, they can be used to make quick modifications to a curriculum web so that other students will benefit. (Teachers may wish to avoid the tendency to "wait until next year" to make improvements, so that they can reflect on assessment results and make modifications while the experience of using the curriculum web is still fresh in their minds.) In general, we believe, the entire process of web-based teaching, from determining student needs, to developing curriculum plans and curriculum webs, to facilitating learning with the curriculum webs, to assessing learning and revising plans and web sites, should be teacher-driven. This reveals, perhaps, our not-so-secret agenda for educational reform: to put the teacher in the center of curriculum development, not the textbook companies or impersonal testing organizations. Curriculum webs represent one important strategy toward that goal.

ACTIVITY 1B ■ Reflecting on Reflection

Robert Greenaway (2004), an expert on outdoor education, has examined a large number of models of the role of reflection in learning. Whereas many writers prefer fairly complex models of the process, Greenaway makes a strong argument for a simple, three-stage model of "Plan, Do, Reflect." This simple model can inform the process of developing curriculum webs.

Read about Greenaway's work at *http://wilderdom.com/experiential/elc/Experiential LearningCycle.htm* or via a link at *curriculumwebs.com*. Write a short summary of his reasons for preferring a three-stage model over the more complex models he describes. Do you agree or disagree? Why or why not? If you are using this text as part of a course, discuss this with your class.

Chapter Summary

This chapter:

- Gives reasons for using the Web as part of teaching and learning. Specifically, the Web has multiple *resources*, can support a variety of kinds of learning *activities*, enhances *communication*, and is conducive to *critical thinking and analysis* skills.
- Talks about our vision for how teaching and learning will change with the incorporation of the Web into education.
- Suggests that teachers should plan, develop, implement, and reflect on their use of curriculum webs.
- Describes a sequence of stages that teachers can go through in becoming more proficient in using the Web to support teaching and learning.
- Describes the four traditional phases of curriculum planning, and the iterative nature of the process of developing curriculum webs, and suggests adding a fifth phase focused on teacher reflection.

Questions For Reflection

Have you ever participated in an individualized or highly differentiated process of learning, in which you got to choose or select learning experiences or topics rather than doing what everyone else was doing? If you can't think of an example from your schooling experience, think about nonschool educational experiences such as athletics, music, or community service. How was this individualized learning experience different from, or better than, standardized learning experiences? What was the role of the teacher or teachers, and how did that differ from other situations? How does your consideration of these questions affect your motivation to learn and to use curriculum webs in your teaching?

Your Next Step

If you have not already looked at the example curriculum webs on *curriculumwebs.com*, then do so now.

Also, it is time to choose a web-page editor and begin to learn how to use it. Download Hands-On Lesson 1 and either read it on your screen or print it out. Once you know which package you are going to use, download a trial version of that software or purchase and install the full package. You will begin to learn how to use the software in Hands-On Lesson 2, after you have read the next chapter.

For Further Learning

- - - - - - - - - - - - - - - -

- See *curriculumwebs.com* for some links pertinent to the topics in this chapter.
- These are excellent books about curriculum development and planning: Pratt 1994, Ornstein and Hunkins 1998, Tanner and Tanner 1985, Jackson 1992, and Wiles 1999.
- To learn more about the uses of computers in instruction, see Druin and Solomon 1996, Provenzo et al. 1999, Jonassen 2000, Schofeld and Davidson 2002, and Bruce 2003.
- Several authors (besides us!) have written good books about designing web-based teaching and learning materials for K–12 learners. Our favorites are Harris 1998 and Warlick 1998.
- See Rubin 1996 for a nice overview of how educational technology can facilitate inquiry-based learning.
- See Burbules 2004 for a discussion of the role of reflection in evaluating educational quality.
- See Clandinin and Connelly 1992 for a discussion of teachers as curriculum makers.
- See Krough 1990 for a very different conception of the meaning of a "curriculum web," as a framework for developing nonlinear lesson plans for early childhood education.

CHAPTER 2

- - - - - - - - - -

CREATING A SIMPLE CURRICULUM WEB

Overview

This chapter provides an overview of the process of building a curriculum web by introducing you to WebQuests, a well-structured, easy-to-create form of curriculum web. After reading this chapter and completing Hands-On Lesson 2, you will better understand the concepts and processes involved in constructing more elaborate curriculum webs. In addition, you'll be able to use many of the page-editing features of your web-editing software.

ACTIVITY FORMATS FOR THE WEB

Curriculum webs represent the epitome of web-based learning approaches. A complete curriculum web, designed to support a unit of instruction, can contain many pages, links, resources, activities, and assessments. Most people will not want to start their creation of web-based lessons with such a curriculum web. Fortunately, curriculum webs can be much simpler, containing perhaps two or three activities and about 10 total web pages.

Simpler still are web-based lessons, which usually contain one activity or a closely related set of activities, designed to be completed in one or at most three or four class sessions. A variety of approaches to constructing web-based lessons has been developed. (See March 2001 for a thorough discussion.) These include:

- *Topic Hotlists:* These are a set of links, usually annotated, and related to a topic, allowing for guided student exploration of the topic in preparation for another activity, or as a supplement to activities using more traditional **media.** Often a teacher will create a hotlist, post it to a web site, but then provide instructions to students through a handout or worksheet. In Hands-On Lesson 7 we will show you how to convert your bookmarks, or favorites, into a hotlist.
- *Multimedia Scrapbook:* This is a collection of links, pictures, audio, or other media files related to a topic, allowing students to choose content that is relevant to their particular project. These differ from a hotlist in that the learners use the listed resources to build something on their own, not only to explore the topic. For example, the students may create their own **multimedia** projects using a software

program such as Hyperstudio or eZedia. Rather than have them find resources on their own (which can take a lot of time), the teacher collects the resources in advance, linking them to a web page.

- *Treasure Hunt:* In this format, the teacher not only collects relevant resources or links, but also provides a structured activity, on the web page itself, that leads students to examine the collected resources. Having an exciting or interesting question that inspires the students to learn is the key ingredient. One approach is to include a number of factual or opinion-based questions that lead to a larger, overarching question that culminates the activity.
- *Subject Sampler:* Here, you also collect relevant resources, but they are ones that serve as a sampler of the kinds of information, resources, topics, and media that pertain to a particular subject. This is a great way to start a new unit, by having students explore several different perspectives or topics that will come later within the unit. The best Subject Samplers appeal to student emotions and interests, inspiring curiosity.

To experiment with these activity formats, visit our companion web site at *curriculumwebs.com.* We have collected some examples and other resources for each format.

The line between the simple activity formats listed here and curriculum webs is the difference between a lesson and a curriculum unit, which is more sustained. A sustained experience takes place over a period of time that is longer than one to three sessions. We also consider curriculum webs to extend beyond web-based lessons not just in terms of time spent, but also how deeply they go into a topic or a problem. A curriculum web should encourage learners to consider multiple perspectives, tools, issues, theories, or solutions, rather than just one, and to apply multiple modes of thinking, such as re-stating, summarizing, comparing, simplifying, or evaluating facts or points of view. A curriculum web should also appeal to a wider range of learning styles.

A WebQuest is a form of web-based lesson that begins to transcend the limitations of a single lesson and move into the kinds of possibilities that come with a curriculum web. Therefore, we turn to them now as a transitional form that can be simple or complex, as needed by your subject matter, as appropriate to your learners, and as fitting to your own emerging web creation skills.

WHAT IS A WEBQUEST?

WebQuests were originally developed by Bernie Dodge and Tom March of San Diego State University as an easily adaptable lesson format for structuring student learning around inquiry. Dodge and March have refined the format tirelessly to make it easy for teachers to create and implement WebQuests, and have helped spread the concept through a variety of approaches, including conducting workshops and building an online library of existing WebQuests, templates, and other resources. Due to their influence—and the ease of creating and using them—WebQuests are the most popular approach to building web-based lessons. See Figure 2.1 for a screen shot of a very well-designed WebQuest.

FIGURE 2.1   A WebQuest with a very compelling activity.

Source: Courtesy of Belinda Davis, *http://webinstituteforteachers.org/~bdavis/webquest.html.*

Although WebQuests can be designed as either short-term or long-term activities—that is, as units of instruction ranging from one class session to a curriculum unit covering many weeks—most WebQuests are created on the short-term model, with activities designed to be completed in one to three class periods. The length of time it takes learners to complete a WebQuest depends on the complexity of the task and the process necessary to complete it. Long-term WebQuests—examples of which are hard to find—require more elaborate web sites than short-term ones that can be contained within one web page. Long-term WebQuests are curriculum webs that incorporate the WebQuest standard structure and approach while allowing for unique modifications to suit learners, subject matter, or available resources.

WebQuests are organized around a question, issue, case, or problem that requires students to use web resources to complete an inquiry or investigation involving **higher-order thinking.** A well-designed WebQuest guides students to make comparisons, evaluations, or syntheses of existing information, resulting in new theories, creative solutions, or custom-designed products.

All WebQuests embody a similar structure, or set of elements, which makes it easy to use **templates** in the construction of new WebQuests. A variety of templates exist that allow teachers or other novices the option of basically filling in a form to create a WebQuest. Some of these templates and a huge array of additional resources about WebQuests can be accessed on our companion web site at *curriculumwebs.com* or directly at *webquest.org*.

The basic elements of a WebQuest are:

- *Introduction* (a statement that sets up the problem, putting it in context, and often includes an **essential question**)
- *Task* (a statement of what is to be done to complete the WebQuest)
- *Process* (a detailed step-by-step guide to completing the WebQuest)
- *Evaluation* (an explicit statement of how any products resulting from the WebQuest will be judged, often in the form of a rubric or rubrics)
- *Credits* (links to web-based resources and citations to print-based resources that will be used by the learners to complete the WebQuest)
- *Conclusion* (a statement that ties the WebQuest together, perhaps leading to additional questions or encouraging learners to continue to increase their understanding of the subject matter)
- *Teaching Guide* (information for teachers about the purposes and structure of the WebQuest, including the elements discussed throughout this book)

You can see links to each of these elements in the WebQuest pictured in Figure 2.1.

ACTIVITY 2A ■ Examining Some WebQuests

Visit *curriculumwebs.com* and navigate to the resources related to Chapter Two. We've provided links to some example WebQuests. Examine the WebQuests to get a sense of how the various components work together. Think about how you might use these WebQuests with your students. What hardware and other resources would be required? What prior training in use of the Web or other tools would your students need to be successful with these WebQuests? How do the WebQuests compare to paper-based learning materials?

THE IQ WEBQUEST: AN ELABORATED EXAMPLE

To explain the components of a WebQuest and describe how they work together to create an effective learning opportunity, we have created a WebQuest about WebQuests, called "Measuring IQ: The Inquiry Quotient of WebQuests," or the "IQ WebQuest" for short. By completing the IQ WebQuest, you will experience firsthand the way that WebQuests foster higher-order thinking, while also learning more about WebQuests and preparing to create your own WebQuest in Hands-on Lesson 2.

You'll find the IQ WebQuest—complete with links to the necessary resources—on our companion web site at *curriculumwebs.com*. We've also included most of the IQ WebQuest (without live links, of course) in this chapter, so you can follow along with our description whether or not you are sitting at a computer. You'll find two different forms of the WebQuest on the companion web site: a one-page version in which all of the elements are contained on one page with a menu at the top of the page containing links to the elements, and a multipage version with each element on a separate page, each linked to a home page. Generally, the one-page format is more suitable for short-term WebQuests and the multipage format for long-term WebQuests, although it is really a matter of personal preference as well as the sophistication of your web-editing software and skills.

Note that the Teaching Guide is a component that is often missing from WebQuests. We believe that this is a fundamental mistake. As we discussed in Chapter One, the Teaching Guide is useful not only to any teachers who use the WebQuest with their students, but is also the natural outgrowth of a systematic process of planning during the construction of the WebQuest. Since the process of construction requires attention to the **aims,** goals, **objectives**, subject matter, **audience, prerequisites,** instructional plan, and assessment of learning, it is smart to create an explicit description of these components, as a blueprint for the construction and as the eventual Teaching Guide included with the completed WebQuest. Here, we reproduce the IQ WebQuest Teaching Guide and include some annotations that will help you to understand the planning process that went into creating this WebQuest. We also reproduce most of the WebQuest itself, again with annotations. (We don't include the Resources section here, because these **URLs** may change and the book—unlike the companion web site—cannot be easily updated. You will find a current version of the Resources section on the companion web site at *curriculumwebs.com*.)

If you prefer, you can read the WebQuest online, rather than in the book, in preparation to completing Activity 2B on page 33. However, if you do read it online, be sure to read our annotations (available in the online versions by pointing your mouse to the word *note* in the margin of the pages).

The IQ WebQuest Teaching Guide

Note: Remember that the teaching guide starts as a curriculum plan, and later is repurposed and included in the finished curriculum web as the teaching guide.

Introduction.   This WebQuest is designed to introduce teachers to WebQuests by focusing on the question of what makes WebQuests different than other forms of lesson plans. Specifically, the WebQuest helps teachers to ask what features or qualities in a WebQuest lead students to inquiry.

Note: The introduction to the teaching guide provides an overview of your curriculum web so that readers can quickly get a sense of the whole.

Aim.   This WebQuest introduces teachers and other potential developers of curriculum webs to WebQuests and specifically to the challenges involved in creating learning activities based on inquiry.

Note: Like all aim statements, this one states very concisely *who* will be taught *what*. See page 64 for more about aims.

Rationale.   Because WebQuests are easy to create from templates, and because they are so popular, there are many, many examples of WebQuests available on the Internet. (In September 2004, a simple Google search for "WebQuest" revealed 444,000 references.) For many teachers, WebQuests are the first type of web-based lesson or unit that they create. Some sites make it incredibly easy to set one up with web-based forms and templates. (See, for example, *landmark-project.com/slate.php3*, which suggests that a WebQuest can be designed and created in about 45 minutes.) This means that many WebQuests have not emerged out of much careful thought or effort. Even a cursory look at some of the WebQuests that have been created and posted to the Web reveals many that are unlikely to lead to higher-order thinking by the students. Many simply ask students to fill in the blanks on worksheets, or to make simple lists, or to complete a relatively simple task that is taught directly or through a set of examples. It seems that some teachers who create WebQuests don't fully understand what it means to construct or facilitate an inquiry, as opposed to the mere collection of facts or mastery of fairly low-level skills. The IQ WebQuest is an antidote to this lack of understanding. We hope that teachers who have completed this WebQuest will build their own WebQuests with careful regard for what it takes to include inquiry as a learning activity.

Note: Rationale statements outline the reasons why a particular aim is important. Thus, they are written to defend the aim against any skeptics, and also to draw in the learner by describing the benefits of meeting the learning objectives. See page 65 for more about rationales.

General Goals

- Introduce the structure of WebQuests and their promise as an approach to learning how to construct curriculum webs
- Emphasize the importance of curriculum planning
- Expose the reader to a variety of activity formats including WebQuests and curriculum webs
- Engage the learner in an inquiry that explores the qualities of inquiry-based learning

Note: General goals provide a context for the curriculum web by outlining the larger purposes of the teacher, classroom, or course. See page 38 for more about general goals.

Subject Matter Description

- The structure of WebQuests
- The features of inquiry
- The construction of rubrics for evaluating complex situations

Note: Subject matter descriptions state the kinds of knowledge, skills, and attitudes around which the curriculum web is focused. See page 45 for more about subject matter descriptions.

Learner Description.   Readers of *Curriculum Webs* who are preservice or inservice teachers, or others who wish to design instructional plans that incorporate web-based resources. Expectations for those learners are described in this book's Preface.

Note: **Learner descriptions** describe the audience or audiences of the curriculum web, including any special features of the learners. See page 42 for more about learner descriptions.

Prerequisites

- Facility with a web browser
- Familiarity with the basic structure and purposes of WebQuests and curriculum webs
- Interest in learning how to build effective curriculum webs
- Understanding of the content of Chapter One and Chapter Two of *Curriculum Webs*

Note: The statement of prerequisites lists the knowledge, skills, and attitudes that are assumed to be present in the learners. Sometimes, this section will also list ways the curriculum web can be modified for those who do not meet the prerequisites. See page 61 for more about prerequisite statements.

Learning Objectives.   On completing this WebQuest, learners will be able to:

- Describe the purpose of each component of a WebQuest
- Be able to list at least five qualities or features of inquiry-based learning activities
- Create a rubric that can be used to distinguish inquiry-based learning activities from other forms
- Describe inquiry in general terms that help others to distinguish inquiry from other modes of learning

Note: **Learning objectives** state precisely what learners will be able to do on completing the curriculum web. See page 55 for more about learning objectives.

Materials

An Internet-linked computer with a web browser

The IQ WebQuest, found at *curriculumwebs.com*

The web-based resources listed in the IQ WebQuest Resources section at *curriculumwebs.com*

Note: This section lists the web-based, print, and other materials and equipment necessary to complete the curriculum web. See page 131 for more about lists of materials.

Instructional Plan.   This WebQuest is designed to allow the learner to use it on his or her own, without the assistance of a teacher or facilitator. So, the "instructional plan" is that the learners will access the WebQuest and follow the directions they find there. The activities that learners will follow include:

- Developing a working definition of inquiry
- Developing a rubric that can be used to evaluate the "inquiry quotient" of a WebQuest
- Using the rubric to evaluate 10 existing WebQuests
- Revising the rubric
- Developing a WebQuest task that exemplifies the features of inquiry that have been discovered
- Using Hands-On Lesson 2 to create a complete WebQuest built around the task that has been developed

Teachers who are in a position to facilitate learners' experiences with this WebQuest can do any of the following:

- Lead a group discussion about the qualities of good working definitions. You might start with an example that is somewhat easier than inquiry, for example "education" or "learning."
- Lead a group discussion about the features of inquiry as a learning activity. You will find a lot of background material for this discussion in the web sites listed in the Resources section of the WebQuest.
- Collect several examples of WebQuests that do a good job of incorporating inquiry, and discuss these with the group. You will find some very good ones at *webquest.org* in a variety of subject areas.
- Collect several examples of good rubrics and discuss the features, including the criteria, categories, and scoring. Some excellent examples of rubrics can be found using some of the web sites listed in the Resources section of the WebQuest.
- Use the tasks that are developed in step 5 of this WebQuest to foster a discussion of how inquiry can shape learning. Ask the learners to brainstorm other activities, besides inquiry, that can support thinking as well as, or better than, inquiry.

Note: The instructional plan contains a description of the activities necessary for learners to complete the curriculum web, from the perspective of the teacher who will be supporting the learning. See page 129 for more about instructional plans.

Plans for Assessment and Evaluation.   Learning that results from this WebQuests is assessed through an evaluation of the products that the learners produce. This WebQuest requires four products: a working definition of inquiry, a rubric that can be used to evaluate the inquiry quotient of existing WebQuests (which is revised later), an evaluation using that rubric of ten existing WebQuests, and a newly developed "Task" for a new WebQuest that meets the criteria in the revised rubric. The evaluation criteria for each of these products are found in the Evaluation section of the WebQuest itself. Because we want to illustrate alternative forms of evaluation, each product is evaluated in a slightly different way.

This WebQuest can be evaluated by the learners by having them submit a feedback form, a link to which is found at the bottom of the Conclusion section. (It was reviewed and critiqued by several teachers and non-teachers prior to publication.)

Note: This section spells out how learning will be assessed, and how the curriculum web will be evaluated. See page 134 for more about plans for assessment and page 222 for more about plans for evaluation.

The IQ WebQuest: Measuring the Inquiry Quotient of WebQuests

Note: This is the text of the IQ WebQuest itself. You will also find this at *curriculumwebs.com*; the online version also includes numerous links and interactive features.

Introduction.   WebQuests are the most popular form of web-based lesson because of their simple yet adaptable structure. Teachers can easily create them by filling in templates provided on the *webquest.org* portal and elsewhere.

Ideally, WebQuests are designed to foster inquiry in which students do not just collect existing information or resources from the Web, but use those resources to solve problems or develop new theories or products.

Unfortunately, the ease of creating WebQuests does not guarantee consistently high-quality products. Although extremely compelling inquiry-based tasks can be found, many more examples exist that do not require higher-order thinking at all, and in fact that primarily involve mere regurgitation of already existing information.

This WebQuest facilitates examination of the question, "What features or qualities makes a WebQuest effective, in terms of whether it fosters inquiry and higher-order thinking as opposed to mere regurgitation?" To answer this question, we first need to ask "What is inquiry?".

Note: This introduction begins by talking in general terms about WebQuests, and describing the problem that many WebQuests do not seem to use inquiry as the basis of student learning. It poses the question of what features WebQuests should embody in order to foster inquiry and higher-order thinking, and raises a larger, essential question—what is inquiry?

Essential questions are not an original feature of WebQuests; rather, they were added to the structure later by Tom March, probably because he realized that the inclusion of such questions made it more likely that the creators of a WebQuest have considered inquiry as a mode of learning. Wiggins and McTighe (2000) provide a good overview of essential questions and their construction. Among the qualities of good essential questions are:

- *They have actually been asked (and continue to be asked) by experts in the discipline or area of study.* Essential questions are perennial questions, the asking of which is central to the pursuit of understanding in a given discipline. For example, the essential question here, "What is inquiry?", is a question that has been addressed in detail by philosophers beginning with Plato and Aristotle, through Hume and Kant, to the present day.

■ *There is no one right answer.* The reason these questions keep popping up through history and continue to be asked is because different answers can be given—and justified—depending on the assumptions under which the question is asked and the state of the discipline at different points in time. The questions themselves are subject to interpretation and argument about what is being asked and what kind of answer is sufficient (March 1998b). Because "inquiry" has been analyzed by so many philosophers and other thinkers, there are many different answers to the question, "What is inquiry?".

■ *They go beyond what is given.* One cannot go out on the Web and "find" the answers to essential questions. Rather, they require the student to think beyond what he or she finds, to analyze, synthesize, or evaluate information. Thus, essential questions require students to think for themselves. Our question, "What is inquiry?", might lead some learners to simply copy a definition from a book or web site, but because the IQ WebQuest requires not simply a definition but a rubric that can be used to evaluate other WebQuests, applying the rubric to the evaluation of some WebQuests, and revising the rubric in light of what they learn, it will almost definitely require learners to think beyond what they find.

■ *They inspire learning.* Essential questions will stick in the mind of learners, provoking them toward thinking and inquiry, not just during their participation in a WebQuest, but continually, motivating lifelong learning. Because most participants in the IQ WebQuest will be teachers or others engaged in developing curriculum, we expect that the question of what inquiry is and how the inquiry quotient of a learning activity can be evaluated will become a central question throughout their careers (or at least we hope so!).

Task.   Develop a working definition of inquiry and use it to construct a rubric for evaluating existing WebQuests in terms of whether they contain no inquiry, contain some qualities of inquiry, or exemplify inquiry. Evaluate 10 WebQuests using the rubric. Revise the rubric based on what you've seen. Then, use the rubric as a guide to the development of your own WebQuest Task that embodies the best qualities of the tasks you've seen.

Note: The task here has been carefully designed to ensure that it cannot be completed simply by copying a definition of inquiry from a dictionary or from the Web. The learners have to not only develop the definition, but need to operationalize it into a rubric that can be used to evaluate WebQuests in terms of whether they embody inquiry as a mode of learning. In order to ensure that the rubric can actually be used for this purpose, we ask the learners to apply it to a number of existing WebQuests, and then revise it based on what they learned during this application. Finally, to ensure that the rubric is not simply an academic exercise, we ask the learner to use it to construct the task of his or her own WebQuest, to be further developed in Hands-On Lesson 2, as a stage in learning how to build a curriculum web.

Process.   The process consists of six steps, as follows:

1. Develop a working definition of inquiry that can be used to evaluate whether any given learning activity is based on inquiry. Examine the web sites listed in Resources under "About Inquiry." Paying close attention to the criteria of good working definitions found in the Evaluation section, write a definition that successfully distinguishes inquiry from other types of learning activities.

2. Develop a rubric for evaluating the inquiry quotient of existing WebQuests. Pay close attention to the web sites listed in the Resources section under "About Rubrics." Your working definition may provide enough criteria for the rubric, or it may not. You may need to add additional features of inquiry in order to have a suitable rubric. The goal is to be able to differentiate among WebQuests using the rubric.

3. Use your rubric to evaluate the IQ (inquiry quotient) of 10 existing WebQuests found in the Resources section under "Lists of Existing WebQuests." You should select WebQuests that address the same subject area—preferably a subject area you are familiar with and have taught or will teach. For each WebQuest, rate each criterion on your rubric, and compute a final score, or "Inquiry Quotient." Then rank-order the WebQuests from highest Inquiry Quotient to lowest.

4. Revise your rubric in light of what you've seen in the best WebQuests you've evaluated, and in light of what you learned about your rubric by following the procedure described in the Evaluation section. If necessary, revise your ranking.

5. Develop a new WebQuest task that embodies the highest possible Inquiry Quotient. Choose a topic and grade level that you will actually teach soon, either the same as the WebQuests you've already evaluated or a new topic.

6. Create a complete WebQuest built around the task you developed in step 5. The technical steps necessary for this process are explained in Hands-On Lesson 2, found on the companion web site at *curriculumwebs.com*.

Note: The process provides details on how to complete the task.

Resources.   Note: The resources for this WebQuest are listed at *curriculumwebs.com*. We don't list them in the book because many of the URLs are likely to change.

Evaluation.   As you complete the IQ WebQuest, you will produce four products: a working definition of inquiry, a (revised) rubric for evaluating the Inquiry Quotient of existing WebQuests, an evaluation and ranking of 10 existing WebQuests using your rubric, and a task for a new WebQuest.

Note: Because this WebQuest is designed not only to foster inquiry about WebQuests but to exemplify various approaches, we've included four different evaluation approaches here. The first lists a set of **criteria** for determining whether your working definition of inquiry is a good one. The second is a set of questions for determining whether your rubric is well designed and likely to be effective. The third relies on the development of an alternative measure of Inquiry Quotient that is then used to test the results of scoring WebQuests according to your rubric. The fourth simply applies your revised rubric to the evaluation of the WebQuest you create in Hands-On Lesson 2.

Evaluating the Working Definition of Inquiry.   Good working definitions:

- Say what kind or type of thing it is as well as what distinguishes the particular thing from others of its kind or type. (For example, to define computer, you would need to say that it is an electronic device—the type of thing it is—but also that it is programmable—because that distinguishes it from other electronic devices.)
- Are concise. Good definitions define the term using as few words as possible.
- Are clear. Good definitions make sense, and do not confuse the reader.
- Are complete. Good definitions encompass multiple meanings of words and do not leave out meanings that are found in common usage.
- Are distinct. Good definitions show how a particular word is different from other similar words.
- Can be used to determine whether the word applies to a variety of situations. This is what makes a definition a "working" definition; that is, the definition can "do work" in the real world. In our case, we want the definition to work to distinguish inquiry from other forms of learning activities.

Now, using these criteria, evaluate your working definition of inquiry:

- Does your definition say what kind or type of thing inquiry is?
- Does your definition say how inquiry differs from other things of its kind or type?
- Is your definition concise? Is it as short as you can make it without becoming unclear?
- Is your definition clear? Does it make sense to others? Ask a few people to be sure.
- Is your definition complete? Does it encompass multiple meanings of the word inquiry? (One way to test this is to examine 10 examples of the appearance of the word inquiry on the Web, and see if your definition encompasses them all.)
- Does your definition distinguish inquiry from other similar words such as research, investigation, inquest, question, examination, scrutiny, exploration, review, or study? (It could be that some of these are real synonyms for inquiry, and that they cannot be distinguished.)

If your working definition meets all of these criteria, then it is a candidate for a good working definition. The next step is to see if it can distinguish inquiry from other learning activities. Does your definition provide criteria for distinguishing the following activities from inquiry?

- Fact-finding, such as finding specific answers to close-ended questions
- Responding only to questions raised by the teacher and not to one's own questions or the questions of other students
- Activities that are solely of "academic" interest, without any correlation to activities undertaken in the real world, or connection to student interests
- Activities that are constrained to just one discipline or subject area

- Activities that can be completed in minutes
- Activities that can be assessed using simple check-off sheets or whether the answer is "right" or "wrong"
- Selecting examples of a thing or type of thing
- Creating artistic works that meet certain criteria
- Presenting information or concepts created by others
- Communicating information to others
- Mimicking the activities of others or creating similar products
- Giving opinions that do not contain carefully selected evidence
- Comparing two scenarios or situations without creating general principles that can be applied to new situations
- Accepting information or opinions without careful examination of the reasons that a particular person or organization would have that point of view
- Using technologies without paying attention to whether they are appropriate to the task

Evaluating the IQ Rubric.   To evaluate your rubric, ask yourself the following questions.

Does the rubric relate to whether the WebQuest is centered on inquiry, rather than some other criterion? The rubric should not address aspects of WebQuests that are extraneous to the question of whether they involve inquiry.

Does the rubric include developmental levels that allow for a comparison of different WebQuests? Does the highest level actually describe the ideal WebQuests, containing the highest level of inquiry, even if no existing WebQuests reach that level?

Are the distinctions among various levels in any given criteria clear and easy to apply? Are multiple people applying the same rubric likely to come up with the same score?

Can the rubric be understood by teachers and other developers of WebQuests? Can it be explained without using jargon or concepts that are even more complicated than inquiry?

Is the rubric too time-consuming to be useful? Can a WebQuest be scored in a fairly reasonable amount of time—certainly less than 20 minutes? Are there redundancies or omissions that need to be corrected before the rubric is used?

Do the ratings that result from the rubric correspond with intuitive or alternative means of evaluating the Inquiry Quotient of a WebQuest?

Evaluating the Evaluation of Existing WebQuests.   Once you have rank-ordered the 10 WebQuests, it is time to compare the results of using your rubric to another measure of each WebQuest's use of inquiry as a learning activity. It is up to you what alternative measure you will use. One option is to ask a few of your colleagues to rank-order the WebQuests according to their own criteria of whether they involve inquiry. Another option is to have a classroom full of students rank the WebQuests. A third is to compare your ranking to the rankings produced by the rubric created by another student in your class. A fourth is to find an existing rubric that evaluates inquiry and compare the results of that rubric to your own.

If there are discrepancies between the ranking produced by the other measure and by your rubric, you will either want to revise your rubric or conclude that the other measure is not as good as your own (or both).

Evaluating the Inquiry Quotient of Your Task for a New WebQuest.   The best tool for evaluating the Inquiry Quotient of the Task you created in the final step of the Process for this WebQuest is the rubric you created in step 2 and revised in step 4. Use this rubric to evaluate your task. Is it at the highest level? If so, you have been successful.

Conclusion.   In this WebQuest, you explored the concept of inquiry and worked to develop a way of evaluating whether WebQuests embody inquiry or other forms of learning. Have you gained a greater understanding of the challenge of incorporating inquiry into your curriculum planning? Or, have you become so confused about inquiry and its use as an instructional method that you are about to give up on it? Either way, we hope you have also gained a good familiarity with the structure and functioning of WebQuests so that you are now about to consider creating one of your own.

Note: The Conclusion is a good place to raise further questions, to connect the topics covered in the WebQuest to further topics or further inquiries, or to go back to the Introduction and once again relate the WebQuest to the learners' prior experiences or skills.

ACTIVITY 2B ■ Complete the IQ WebQuest Now

If you can, pair with another teacher or reader of this book to complete this activity.

Go to *curriculumwebs.com* and complete the WebQuest according to the directions, except for step 6 of the Process, which you will do in Hands-On Lesson 2 following this chapter.

Chapter Summary

This chapter:

- Describes several activity formats that can be used for the creation of web-based lessons and discusses the differences among them
- Introduces WebQuests as an intermediary format between the typical web-based lesson and curriculum webs
- Discusses the Inquiry Quotient WebQuest Teaching Guide to exemplify the various elements of an effective teaching guide
- Uses the Inquiry Quotient WebQuest developed by the authors to illustrate the structure and components of a WebQuest and to highlight the challenges of creating WebQuests incorporating inquiry
- Prepares you to create your own WebQuest by helping you develop criteria for what makes an inquiry-oriented task

Questions For Reflection

Can inquiry become the primary mode of student learning in the K–12 curriculum? Can you imagine a school where inquiry takes place every day for every student, and where students never merely fill in worksheets or regurgitate information that others have produced? If so, what would have to change about the structure of schooling or the training of teachers?

Your Next Step

Download Hands-On Lesson 2 for your particular web-editing software package, and follow the directions found there for creating a one-page WebQuest based on the Task you developed in Activity 2B. Be sure to use what you have learned about WebQuests and about inquiry in this chapter. Seek to create a WebQuest that has the highest possible Inquiry Quotient according to the rubric you developed. Use your Inquiry Quotient rubric to evaluate your own WebQuest.

Once you have created your WebQuest, you will be ready to go on to the next chapter, which discusses in much more detail the identification of educational goals as the first step in planning a curriculum web.

For Further Learning

- See our companion web site at *curriculumwebs.com* for additional examples of WebQuests and for more information on essential questions and inquiry.
- See SBC Filamentality 2003 and March 2001 for discussions of a range of approaches to incorporating the Internet into teaching and learning, most of them simpler to create than WebQuests.
- See Harris 1998 and her companion web site at *http://virtual-architecture.wm.edu* for some very useful background theory about types of learning activities fostered by the Web.
- See Dodge 2001, and March 1998a, 1998b, and 2000 for lots of useful information about the purposes, structure, and varieties of WebQuests.
- See Bernie Dodge's WebQuest portal, at *webquest.org*, for many examples and articles about WebQuest creation and use.
- See CPS 2000 and Wiggins and McTighe 2000 for excellent discussions of the criteria for good rubrics.

CHAPTER 3

IDENTIFYING CURRICULUM GOALS

Overview

In Chapter Two we provided an overview of the process of constructing curriculum webs by considering the development of a simple form of curriculum web—a WebQuest—that incorporated all of the elements of a complete curriculum plan. However, we did not discuss each element in much depth. Now it is time to dig deeper into the process of planning by focusing on the first phase of curriculum planning: identifying curriculum goals. This chapter discusses this process as a sequence of activities that result in defining important elements of the curriculum plan:

- General goals
- Description of learners
- Description of subject matter
- Learning objectives
- Prerequisites
- Aims
- Rationales

Articulating these elements will prepare you to select learning activities and (eventually) to provide a useful teaching guide with your curriculum web.

A PROCESS FOR IDENTIFYING GOALS

The most important questions to address when identifying curriculum goals are:

1. What are your *general goals*?
2. What do you know about your *learners*?
3. What is the theme or the *subject matter* of your curriculum web?
4. What are your *learning objectives* for your curriculum web—that is, the skills, knowledge, and attitudes you want your learners to gain?

In our approach to building curriculum webs, these questions are initially answered while creating a written curriculum plan. The plan should include sections articulating your general goals, describing your learners, outlining the subject matter of the curriculum web, and listing detailed learning objectives. It should also include a list of the prerequisites for successful use of the curriculum web, an aim statement, and a rationale that explains why these learning objectives are important for these learners to achieve. These initial statements may be revised throughout the development and implementation of the curriculum web, but their early articulation can help you to make reflective decisions about the structure, depth, and presentation of your curriculum web during its development.

As we discussed in Chapter One, the written curriculum plan has two purposes. During development, the plan serves as a blueprint, shaping decisions about the structure and content of the curriculum web (and itself subject to change in light of what is learned during development). Once the curriculum web has been developed, the plan is repurposed as a teaching guide.

As you read through this chapter, you should begin to develop your own curriculum plan. A worksheet for this purpose in both HTML (web format) and **PDF** (portable document format) is included on *curriculumwebs.com* and can be found by clicking on the Chapters link and choosing Chapter Three. Our suggestion is that you either copy the HTML version into your own web editor, where you can add each element as you write it (instructions for this are found in Hands-On Lesson 3 at *curriculumwebs.com*), or print the PDF version and fill it out with a pen as you read through this and the subsequent chapters. The questions on the worksheet are reproduced here as Table 3.1. Additional elements of the teaching guide are discussed in Chapter Four and Chapter Six.

THE RELATIONSHIP BETWEEN ENDS AND MEANS

People often subscribe to a theory that places ends or goals as prior to and superior to means or methods. According to this theory, we decide what we want (that is, we select our ends) and *then* we decide how to get there (that is, we select the means appropriate to realizing those ends). This approach is reflected in Tyler's model of curriculum planning, described in Chapter One, where *purposes* or objectives are chosen first and then are used to select *learning activities* that can achieve those purposes. It is also the approach envisioned in the recent trend toward the development of curriculum standards: the standards are supposed to come prior to the development of learning activities, acting as overarching goals or purposes that can be met using a variety of approaches to be determined by schools or teachers.

We mentioned in our discussion of Tyler's model that we do not have to take his four questions as representing a linear approach to curriculum development. Rather, we can think of them as "phases" of development that intertwine and inform one another in an iterative process. John Dewey (1985 [1916]) suggests that ends and means are not easily distinguishable, because in fact any articulation of an end assumes that certain means are available, and any selection of means will tend to alter our ends. In addition, as

TABLE 3.1   Worksheet for Recording Ideas for Curriculum Plan

ELEMENT

YOUR GENERAL GOALS

In general terms, what are you trying to achieve with these learners?

You will fill in this section in Activity 3A.

DESCRIPTION OF YOUR LEARNERS

Include their age and/or grade level, and other relevant information such as their interests, future goals, and background.

You will fill in this section in Activity 3B.

DESCRIPTION OF YOUR SUBJECT MATTER

What subjects, topics, or issues are at the center of this curriculum web?

You will fill in this section in Activity 3C.

DETAILED LEARNING OBJECTIVES

List your desired outcomes in terms of changes in the learners' knowledge, skills, and attitudes.

You will fill in this section in Activity 3D.

EXPECTED PREREQUISITES

What relevant knowledge, skills, and attitudes do you expect your learners to have before they begin using this curriculum web?

You will fill in this section in Activity 3E.

AIM

In a short sentence or phrase, describe *what* you want to teach to *whom*.

You will fill in this section in Activity 3F.

RATIONALE

Justify the use of time or other resources to achieve the aim written above. Why should these learners reach your objectives?

You will fill in this section in Activity 3G.

Printable and editable versions of this worksheet are available at *curriculumwebs.com*.

we plan and then implement our plan for achieving any given ends, we will often modify our ends in light of what we continue to learn about our subject matter, students, or the context in which we are teaching. Therefore, we cannot forget about ends as we plan the means to attain them; rather, we will continually alter both ends and means as we pursue our evolving goals in the light of changing circumstances.

What's more, many teachers find that their ends shift from externally mandated curriculum standards or goals to humanistic or localized purposes that more adequately reflect the **needs** and experiences of their students. As teachers shift from an emphasis on traditional educational outcomes to concern with the lived lives of real children, they often begin to emphasize the qualities of experience rather than the consequences of those experiences; for example, they may pay more attention to engagement and participation than to whether the students have mastered a predetermined goal. When teachers begin to emphasize **inquiry** rather than traditional textbook-driven schooling, their priorities shift further to an emphasis on the dispositions necessary for inquiry. Thus, education becomes more a humanistic process of **individuation** and growth than an attempt to "produce" certain skills or knowledge in every student. (See Burbules 2004, who suggests that the most important educational aim is helping our students to question the aims of the education they are experiencing.)

It is sometimes hard to describe the interrelationship of ends and means in clearly defined procedural steps such as may be desired by preservice teachers in educational methods courses. ("Just tell me what I need to do on Monday" is a typical concern of many.) In this chapter and in the book as a whole, we try to strike a balance between a linear and procedural approach that is easy to teach and to learn and a more reflective and philosophical approach that emphasizes the complexity of teaching and learning and the iterative process of developing curriculum webs that are effective in real contexts. So, for example, while we discuss the process in a certain logical order in the book, we often caution our readers that they need to remain flexible about the actual sequence necessary in their particular situation.

GENERAL GOALS

Any lesson or curriculum unit that you develop will need to be compatible with your overall educational purposes. Articulating these overall purposes, and how the given lesson or unit serves those purposes, is an essential step toward planning your curriculum web.

It may be quite obvious to you how a given curriculum unit fits into your larger educational context and purposes, but it is worth taking a few moments to write down your understanding of those larger goals. This can help to keep you focused on what is really important about a particular unit, and keep you from getting caught up in details or skills that are not really very important to your learners or to their lives or futures.

Some common sources of educational goals are listed in Table 3.2. Your own *personal values and sense of purpose* as a teacher are (or should be) reflected in your general educational goals. Realistically, since you probably work for a school, district, and state with their own educational goals, you need to balance personal values with other sources of educational goals. The goals that teachers emphasize usually depend, in part, on the *expected academic goals* of the grade level and subjects they teach. These academic goals often crowd out social and emotional goals of earlier schooling, but teachers also have humanistic goals, such as their *vision of the unique potential* of each student, and writing these other goals down can help you to remember them when planning curriculum webs.

TABLE 3.2   Some Sources of General Educational Goals

The teacher's own personal values and sense of purpose

The expected academic goals of the teacher's grade level and subject

The teacher's vision of the unique potential of each student

The need to prepare students for subsequent schooling

Society's shared conception of the educated person

The need to reinforce traditions and customs

The need to emancipate students from traditions and customs or to free students' individuality

Widely shared goals for schooling (often stated as standards)

Psychological research into developmentally appropriate learning experiences

Felt needs of students and adults, including teachers

Moral or religious values

Because of the nature of institutional schooling as a progression of grade levels leading toward graduation and then often more schooling after that, teachers need to consider what the students bring from their previous grade as well as the need to prepare students for subsequent schooling. The content and skills teachers emphasize will depend on what they see as their students' needs, or the gaps between what the students know and can do and the knowledge and skills necessary for success in subsequent courses. But teachers need to remember John Dewey's words:

> The ideal of using the present simply to get ready for the future contradicts itself. It omits, and even shuts out, the very conditions by which a person can be prepared for his [sic] future. We always live at the time we live and not at some other time, and only by extracting at each present time the full meaning of each present experience are we prepared for doing the same thing in the future. (1991[1938], 29–30)

If the only purpose of a given course is to prepare the student for the future, the student will never learn how to live fully in the present. Keeping this in mind can help teachers and curriculum developers to remember the human lives and values that make any endeavor—school-based or not—worthwhile.

General goals also come from *society's shared conception of the educated person*. In the United States, schools have had two, sometimes conflicting, purposes. The first has been to pass along the traditions and skills of previous generations. This is certainly an important goal—especially for various cultures that share a strong sense of unique beliefs or histories. But modern society also values individuality and creativity. Thus schools do not aim only to teach the children what the adults think is important, but to free the students' individuality, giving them an opportunity for self-expression and self-realization. In addition, our society tends to value self-sufficiency, and so our schools strive to graduate individuals capable of making a living and providing for themselves and their families. The schools also want students to succeed, and so they tend to emphasize goals for schooling that are actually achievable, or learnable. Each of these interests or values helps to determine the educational goals of a given teacher, course, or school (Ornstein and Hunkins 1998).

Some teachers have limited freedom to define their own educational goals. Often, these goals are defined by widely shared national, state, or local *standards.* These standards often have the effect of predetermining the curriculum for teachers in every subject and grade level. In Illinois, for example, the Illinois Learning Standards set forth the goals that schools should seek to achieve at each grade level in each of the various subject areas. These goals have been further defined as a set of **benchmarks** that set forth the kinds of tasks that students should be able to do at the completion of each grade. Many teachers believe that they do not have time during the school year to do much other than to try to meet these predefined standards. Teachers who base their educational goals on such state or local standards do not have to worry about justifying these goals to educational leaders, who are themselves often being evaluated in terms of their schools' capacity to help students achieve the standards. But standards represent an impersonal statement of educational goals, and do not necessarily represent the individual teachers' goals, or the goals of a particular course in a particular school. Nor do they usually include nonacademic goals such as the formation of values, the development of dispositions, or such skills as teamwork and **self-regulated learning.** This is another reason why it is a good idea to write down your own educational goals as a way of protecting yourself from losing your own personal mission—or your personal sense of what is important—when planning curriculum for your students.

Another source of broad educational goals is *psychological research* into how people learn as well as the **learning theories** developed to explain that research. Recent research into very early learning, for example, has shown that infants and toddlers need exposure to language, music, and social interaction in order to develop their intellectual and interpersonal capacities. Similarly, increased understanding of the developmental needs of young adolescents (age 12 to 15) has served to promote the middle school movement, in which schools specifically designed for these youngsters utilize advisory groups, teacher teaming, and interdisciplinary teaching. Recent developments in "brain-based learning research" (which generally refers to research into how the brain works and how people learn) are sometimes used to justify certain educational approaches over others (see, for example, Caine and Caine 1991), but such direct linkages between research and practice are often tenuous and can be hard to justify.

Other educational goals arise from *felt needs*, that is, needs that are experienced directly by the teachers or the students. When enough people experience a felt need, educational leaders will often create curriculum to help bridge the gap. Drug and sex education are examples of this type of curriculum development. The aim of drug education programs in middle schools is not to prepare the student for success in high school drug education programs, but rather to help the student to deal with life experiences during middle school and after. There may be felt needs by some in your school or community. Because national or state curriculum development efforts may ignore some local needs, these areas may be the ideal place to focus your efforts in developing a web-based curriculum. Indeed, we urge you, if you have the luxury, to write a curriculum web on something truly controversial or on a unique need that you see in your local community.

Moral or religious values or other shared ideals and values represent another source of goals. Examples include securing students' allegiance to certain moral principles or rules, shaping attitudes toward immigrants or other groups, increasing racial tolerance, or exposing students to the rewards of community service. Within some communities, there is a consensus that everyone should have the same beliefs, participate in a defined set of rituals, eat certain foods and not others, dress modestly or according to traditional customs, or work toward the realization of certain ideals or values in the world. It is easy to see the impact of values in religious schools. But actually, all curriculums imply some sense of the kind of life we want students to lead. To this extent, all curriculum attempts to answer the question: "What is the good life?" (Even a curriculum unit reviewing the reduction of fractions implies the view that students who *know* how to reduce fractions will lead a better life than those who do not!)

Example General Goals

You will find one sample statement of general goals in the IQ WebQuest discussed in Chapter Two, on page 25.

In Chapter One we described three example curriculum webs, and said that we would be referring to these examples throughout the book. You can find the complete curriculum webs at *curriculumwebs.com*. Each of these examples was planned and developed within a larger educational context that help to define general educational goals. The following statements describe those contexts.

"Our United States" General Goals.   This curriculum web was developed by middle school teachers who were concerned that their students did not have sufficient understanding of geography. This concern was echoed by a report published in 1996 about the poor geographical understanding of American schoolchildren. In addition, these teachers were already focusing on the United States because of general expectations about what would be covered in their grades. They also wanted to introduce their students to using the Web to conduct research.

"Who Am I?" General Goals.   This curriculum web was developed by a group of teachers from Chicago high schools, who felt that their freshmen students lacked a sense of personal self, or direction, and that they were therefore overwhelmed by the size, complexity, and social pressures of high school life. They developed this unit as a way of encouraging reading, writing, and web-based research skills while helping students to remember, or define, who they are in relation to the wider culture.

"Building a Curriculum Web with Dreamweaver" General Goals.   This curriculum web was written by one of the authors of this book to introduce Dreamweaver into the Advanced Strand of the Web Institute for Teachers (WIT). Because most of the likely instructors in WIT did not know how to use Dreamweaver, the author decided to create this curriculum web. The curriculum web emerged out of the broad goal of helping teachers to learn how to integrate the Web into their teaching and the learning of their students. This goal was based on the belief that teacher involvement in curriculum development could improve learning. Because the audience for this curriculum web had been former participants in the Web Institute for Teachers, it does not talk about curriculum planning, but rather focuses on the technical issues involved in using Dreamweaver.

ACTIVITY 3A ■ Describing Your General Goals

Using a piece of paper, word processor, or web-page editor, write a short essay incorporating the requested information and answering the following questions:

1. Choose a course and grade level to concentrate on for this activity. (Teachers in self-contained elementary classroom should just choose a grade level.) The course should be one that you have already taught or that you expect to teach in the near future, and the one for which you are likely to develop a curriculum web.
2. What is the name of the course? Is there a published course description (for example, in a course catalog)? If so, what is the description? If there is no published course description, write one now. Include a broad statement of what the course or grade level is "about."
3. List or describe the general educational goals of this course or grade level. Be sure to consider all of the sources of goals listed in Table 3.2.
4. For each goal, discuss the source of that goal. Did it come from your own personal conception of an educated person? Does it come from a set of standards? Is it a result of a certain learning theory? Does it arise as a felt need for the students or teacher? Does it reflect social ideals?

LEARNER DESCRIPTIONS

The students who will use your curriculum web to support their learning—we call them simply "learners"—represent the most crucial factor in whether a given curriculum web will be effective. Many characteristics of the learners are potentially relevant to curriculum development, including their social or cultural backgrounds, learning styles and preferences, prior experiences, motivation, habits, **attitudes,** skills, knowledge, beliefs about themselves and about learning, and abilities. Each of these factors may be relevant to the most effective structure or content of a curriculum web.

To some extent, you have considered your learners (at least implicitly) in articulating your general goals. However, now is the time to think more explicitly about the learners, and about whether they possess qualities that should be considered during further curriculum planning. Your learners' age may be an important factor, because there are some activities that will not work well with students if they are too young or too old. If your students are eight or nine, it probably doesn't make too much sense to ask them to use a search engine to find web sites relevant to the U.S. Constitution. If you want them to learn about the Constitution, you should probably provide specific links that direct them to age-appropriate materials. Older students who have learned advanced search techniques may be more engaged if they find their own materials.

The French biologist and psychologist Jean Piaget can be credited with disseminating the idea that children learn differently at different stages of cognitive development. The specifics of Piaget's theory have been questioned in recent years, but most educators still accept the general idea that what may be an appropriate learning activity for elementary students will probably not be appropriate for high school students. Elementary students are oriented more toward concrete, sensory experience and with specific facts, while high school students are often more concerned with abstract or formalistic concepts or models that relate to a variety of contexts or situations. See Chapter Twelve for more about the impact of age on using curriculum webs.

Similarly, if a group of students is vision- or hearing-impaired, the curriculum developer will certainly need to know this and to take it into account. Vision-impaired students can use the Web if their computers are outfitted with text-to-speech capabilities. But it would probably not work to ask these students to decide, as a curriculum web on Fibonacci numbers does, which of a given set of rectangles is most "pleasing to the eye." If students are learning disabled or developmentally delayed, a curriculum web may have to contain simpler instructions or activities. See Chapter Eight for more about building web sites for special needs learners.

The characteristics shared by the students in your class are also relevant to deciding what kinds of activities and resources will be most effective. Students who have been tracked into lower-performing groups based on prior school performance or test scores may be more likely than a random group to have negative learning attitudes: for example, to consider themselves poor in mathematical ability. Groups of gifted children may be more likely to respond to activities that seem, at first glance, to be beyond their abilities. In schools that track their students, teachers will need to consider whether they need to develop alternative versions of the curriculum web for the lower and higher tracks. You should not assume that lower-track students are not interested in academic challenges. Some so-called lower-performing students are craving the high expectations that challenging activities represent. (See Oakes 1985.) With curriculum webs, teachers can shape learning activities that are both interesting to hard-to-reach learners and also rigorously connected to educational goals.

It may also be important to pay attention to your learners' cultural or ethnic background. African American students may be more likely to be interested in a curriculum web on the Jewish Holocaust if reference is made to similarities with the American slave experience. Hispanic students might be more interested in learning about geography if emphasis is given to countries that use the Spanish language. Students with roots in American Indian communities may have a different response to lessons on the history of westward expansion—or to education about the effects of alcohol—than students of European descent. These are generalizations that may or may not apply in every case, but they suggest factors that each curriculum developer will have to consider.

Local issues may also be relevant in describing your learners. If you are developing a curriculum web about environmental problems, for example, it may be helpful to know what environmental issues your students face in their daily lives, whether that is acid rain, lead paint, or increased dangers from ultraviolet sunlight. It may require different strategies to interest urban schoolchildren in a unit on the environmental effects of industrial farming than to interest those who live in rural communities. This illustrates again the need for taking an iterative approach to curriculum planning; the elements of your plan will interact and inform one another throughout the process. To the extent you can pay attention to these interactions and modify elements as you work through the plan and develop the curriculum web, your curriculum web is likely to be more effective with the specific learners who will use it. (The capacity of curriculum webs developed by teachers to adopt to such local conditions is one of their advantages over traditional textbooks.)

Example Learner Descriptions

When describing your learners, it is a good idea to include any information that distinguishes your group of learners and sets them apart from other groups of learners. Because you may have not yet decided on the specific subject matter focus or the activities of your curriculum web, include as much information as possible at this stage. If your curriculum web is designed for a wide range of students, such as "Fourth-grade students in Illinois" (in the case of a curriculum designed to meet the state goal of teaching all fourth-grade students about the history of the state), then it does not make any sense to be very specific in the learner description. In cases such as that one, designing your curriculum for as wide a group as possible may be more effective than to appeal to the specific preferences or backgrounds of a few learners. Our example curriculum webs have been generalized to be suitable for wide audiences, and so the learner descriptions are not very specific. (To see additional learner descriptions, including some that are more specific, visit *curriculumwebs.com*.)

As you work further on your curriculum plan, it may become clear that your curriculum could be extended to include a wider variety of learners than you originally intended. It is perfectly fine to come back later and revise your learner description, or to include notes to teachers about modifying the curriculum to suit different groups of learners.

You will find one example of a learner description in the Teaching Guide for the IQ WebQuest on page 26. Here are three more:

"Our United States" Learner Description.   The activities in this web are designed specifically for middle school students (grades six to eight). However, it can be used with younger, motivated students, or older students who have yet to develop a geographical understanding of the United States.

"Who Am I?" Learner Description.   The "Who Am I?" web was originally designed for freshmen students in urban high schools. The subject matter and activities are appropriate for any adolescents in almost any environment. Teachers of specific groups of students may want to enhance the curriculum by including activities related to issues of importance to their particular students. For example, an audience consisting primarily of Native American or Mexican American students might emphasize issues having to do with their particular cultural heritage.

Students who have not had much experience browsing the Web or working on their own may have trouble completing the activities in this curriculum web without additional preparation.

"Building a Curriculum Web with Dreamweaver" Learner Description. This module is designed for teachers and other adult educators who are comfortable using a computer for word processing and other basic applications, who have access to an Internet-linked computer, who are familiar with the process of building a curriculum web, and who are already motivated to learn Dreamweaver.

ACTIVITY 3B ■ Writing Your Learner Description

Using a piece of paper, word processor, or web-page editor, create a written description of the students who will be using your curriculum web. Be as thorough as you can. Consider the following characteristics:

- Age
- Grade level
- Gender (if relevant)
- Social and cultural background
- Ethnicity (if relevant)
- Special needs
- Learning styles
- Stage of cognitive development
- Skill level
- Prior experiences
- Motivation
- Physical, emotional, or behavioral issues (if relevant)
- Local issues (if relevant)

SUBJECT MATTER DESCRIPTIONS

Once the general goals that define the context of a curriculum unit are articulated and the learners who will use the curriculum web are defined, the next step in developing the unit is to write a description of the subject matter of the curriculum web. The subject matter is the *content* of the curriculum: the knowledge, skills, or personal dispositions that the unit will be about.

Outlining your subject matter will help you to see broad themes or categories that should be explored in learning activities, and to organize the content on the eventual web site. Articulating themes and categories in an explicit description of the subject matter can also help you find the right kinds of materials and resources to support the curriculum web. Your description will contain key words and phrases that can be used as search terms. It will serve as a map of the territory to be explored both in designing the curriculum web and during learning, and can help you develop a table of contents or index for your curriculum web. The more detailed and specific you can be in your description, the better. "The ecology of lead poisoning in Chicago" is better than "environmental studies"; similarly, "the political, social, cultural, and economic causes of the Civil War" will be more useful as a guide later than simply "the causes of the Civil War" because it will remind you to pay attention to each of the listed categories.

Subject Matters of Curriculum Webs

Ongoing human experience is holistic. Everyday events do not come to us in packets labeled "math," "science," or "social studies." Rather, an experience as simple as a walk through the woods may touch on diverse topics such as the relationship between sunlight and the color of leaves, the history of farming and forestry in a given region, the work of certain poets, the psychology of joy, and even the mathematics of time, distance, and acceleration. Yet schools often treat human experience as if these topics are completely independent of one another, and habitually break learning into discrete disciplinary chunks. This specification of the categories of subject matter is to some extent arbitrary. Where is the line, for example, between biology and chemistry? Does poetry count as an artistic or linguistic endeavor? Can we easily distinguish among political science, economics, and history? Each discipline has its own perspective on human experience, but the events and behaviors that they each analyze intertwine inseparably.

The chopping up of subject matter into disciplinary categories is sometimes useful, despite its arbitrary nature. For one thing, it allows teachers to specialize in particular areas of study. Math teachers do not usually have to worry about making sure that science or social studies are covered. Social studies teachers can concentrate on their subject area and let others become experts in art and physical education. The disciplinary categorization also provides an efficient (and by now entrenched) organizational scheme for high schools and colleges, making scheduling of classes more efficient and satisfying the requirement for certain numbers of Carnegie units distributed across subject areas. But as many teachers know, this disciplinary organizational scheme has its drawbacks. Many problems, issues, and skills are ignored when experience is carved up into pieces. Where, for example, do values, habits of teamwork, persistence and commitment, the ecological effects of industry, or effective searching of the Web get taught in the traditional structure of math, science, social studies, and language arts? Where in the curriculum are moral issues discussed, when these are so often interdisciplinary in nature and context? Where do the basic skills of life, including being a wise consumer, a good citizen, a caring and able parent, or a loving person come into the curriculum? These topics are often sidelined, treated as if they are outside the purview or scope of the school, and better learned more informally or at home. With some students, whose families or experiences do not share values or contexts with what is expected in school, the academic separation of subjects can lead to disaffection, alienation, or worse.

Curriculum webs represent a potentially powerful tool for overcoming the arbitrary divisions between subject areas. You can plan and implement curriculums that take in more of the holistic nature of experience, or create specific links between subject areas. But without fairly well-defined notions of your subject matter and clear learning objectives, there is the tendency to load up web sites with multiple links, unclear directions, or too many options for the learner. Careful articulation of the subject matter focus of your curriculum web can help to prevent this.

It is important to keep in mind that subject matter is not just facts or topics. Subject matter can be issues, problems, skills, values, processes, or the learners themselves. The entire breadth of human experience can become subject matter for curriculum. Table 3.3

TABLE 3.3   Subject Matter of Some Curriculum Webs Produced in WIT

"Pizza Garden," the origins of the ingredients of pizza for third-grade science students

"Fibonacci Sequence Around the World," numbers in architecture and nature for high school art and math students

"Who Am I?," self-identity and discovery for sophomore high school language arts

"Success Express," study skills for effective learning in high school

"The Solar System," introducing the planets to first-graders

"The Golden Ratio," about the many places the ratio appears in art and mathematics, for high school algebra students

"A Virtual Tour of the Cuisines of Europe," comparing food words for first-year language students

"Exploring the Decades: U.S. History 1900–Present," for fifth-grade students

"Our United States," about the relationship between physical geography and recreational and economic activities for fifth-grade geography students

"The Rhythm of Poetry," about how figurative language appears in popular music, for language arts students in seventh and eighth grades

"Our Colorful World," about color words, for kindergartners

"Put Your Foot Down and Drive," a driving safety and awareness curriculum for drivers' education in high school

"Design the Atomic Theory Exhibit for the National Museum of Science" (a hypothetical institution), for high school chemistry students

"Remembering the Holocaust," for high school social science students

"Portraiture," history and the creation of self-portraits, for elementary school art

"African Folktales in the Classroom," for elementary school language arts

"Wacky Whales," about the collection of data for research, for elementary school science

"Understanding My World," a curriculum about Chicago for first-graders

"Character Education Through Literature" for third- to fifth-graders

"Paper Please," about creating collages and origami, for second- and third-grade students

URLs for these and other WIT curriculum webs can be found on *curriculumwebs.com*.

lists the subject matter of some curriculum webs produced in WIT during the past eight years. As you can see from this list, the range of subject matters is as wide as the range of human experience, or the curriculum developers' imaginations. Some curriculum webs focus more on interdisciplinary than subject-specific study. The "Who Am I?" curriculum web, for example, addresses issues that go beyond traditional school subjects. Another curriculum web produced by participants in WIT focuses on the various artistic and mathematical applications of a sequence of numbers known as the Fibonacci sequence. Another addresses the mathematical skills necessary to handle everyday challenges such as finding a job, renting an apartment, and paying for college. Other curriculum webs could deal with interdisciplinary subjects such as "Bridges," "The East and the West," or "Setting Up Your Own Business."

Centering Your Curriculum Web

The first step in deciding on subject matter is to determine the curriculum web's focus, or center. This center—which usually can be described in a short phrase such as those found in Table 3.3—helps to determine the curriculum web's topics, materials, and activities, and can be of three general types. A curriculum web can be centered on (1) a subject area or discipline, (2) the learners themselves, or (3) some problem to be solved. We discuss each of these types in turn.

Subject-Centered Curriculum.   Most curriculums are focused on topics within subject areas or traditional academic departments. Topics such as "Factoring binomial expressions" or "The parts of a cell" fit well in traditional regions of subject matter such as math and biology. These topics seem to imply a predetermined instructional plan, similar to that found in the typical school textbook, with the subtopics arranged in logical order from general to more specific, or from simple to more complex.

The expansive nature of the Web helps teachers to design subject-centered curriculums that use real-world data and the results of new research. It is relatively easy, for example, to use census data or real-time meteorological measurements in a math unit instead of relying on hypothetical data. However, the intrinsic structure of the Web suggests possible structures other than the traditional, linear approach. If you want to create a curriculum web on a traditional subject-centered topic, consider whether the content lends itself to variations such as a **hierarchical** or **hypertextual** design. (These types of design are discussed in more detail in Chapter Eight.)

Broader subjects such as social studies allow for more interdisciplinary curriculum webs. Teaching students to understand the connections between economics, political science, sociology, and anthropology can result in a curriculum centered on comparing disciplinary approaches. The "Our United States" curriculum web shows how subject-centered curriculum webs can avoid the typically dry approach found in textbooks. Teachers can specify conceptual clusters, such as "Science, Technology and Society," "Darwinism," or "Rituals" as cross-disciplinary subjects for study. (A useful technique for "mapping" the subject matter of these types of curriculum focuses is concept mapping, discussed on page 55 under "Describing Your Subject Matter.")

A third way to organize a curriculum around a subject center is to focus on certain processes, strategies, or life-skills, such as problem solving, decision making, or teamwork. Each of these processes can involve a variety of subject matters, problems, and issues. For example, in a curriculum web on problem solving, students could start with very simple problems, then reflect on the process of solving the problem, then apply these reflections to a more difficult problem, and so on. If the curriculum web also includes ways for students to share their problem-solving strategies (whether online or not), the curriculum web could lead to the students learning quite sophisticated problem-solving techniques.

Finally, the Web itself can become the subject matter of curriculum. One of the most important educational goals for the information age should be to teach students to be discerning consumers of information and media. Students must be taught to realize that not everything they read is accurate or should be relied on in making judgments about the truth or the relative worth of ideas or programs. This is difficult for schools to do, because for many years schools have tried to teach students to believe everything they read in their textbooks and to regurgitate that information back to the teacher when asked to perform on quizzes and exams.

But the real world has always been messy—different sources of information have different value, and students learn from their parents and peers not to trust everything they hear outside of school. The problem is that many students make a distinction between something they hear on the street and something they hear or read in school. In order to use the Web adequately, they need to learn that just because something is published on the Web—just because it is printed and formatted nicely on the screen—does not mean it is true. This lesson, when learned, will be quite valuable for students and will, we hope, foster a greater emphasis on critical thinking than has previously been seen in our nation's schools (Apple 1991).

To summarize, subject-centered curriculum can be focused on traditional areas in the traditional disciplines, on interdisciplinary topics that touch on a wide variety of fields, on processes such as problem solving, or on the goal of teaching students to be critical consumers of information.

Learner-Centered Curriculum.   A curriculum can also be centered on certain aspects of the learners themselves. Learner-centered curriculum may explore the learner's own life or family history or local **environment**. For many students, these topics are intrinsically interesting. The ancient Greeks had two principles on which they based all of their educational endeavors. The first was "Know Thyself," and the second was "Become What You Are." These principles are still ultimately important, and need to be addressed through education, even if they seem somewhat lofty or too personal for school to address. The "Who Am I?" curriculum web, developed as an example for this book, demonstrates a learner-centered approach, while also fostering the development of language arts skills.

There are many examples of learner-centered resources already on the Web. Many social and governmental organizations provide web sites focused on topics of personal interest to teenagers. Such curriculum webs explore students' self-understanding, self-concept, personal responsibility, attitudes, behaviors, values, health habits, physical well-being, and many other qualities. Webs can be designed to foster self-discovery, creativity, hope, awareness, doubt or faith, wonder, awe, or reverence. Students who go on a learning-centered journey can be asked to reflect on what they have learned through writing or other forms of communication. Students' ideas and attitudes about the past, present, or future can be explored and compared to their classmates'.

Such topics may seem far removed from the kinds of subjects stressed in local and national standards. However, building in activities that require practice in writing, problem solving, and thinking can further the objectives of these standards, while giving students something they really need: better self-understanding. Also, while subject matter standards are by their nature limited to skills and knowledge that are easily categorized within a particular discipline, interdisciplinary or nonacademic goals—such as teamwork, persistence, problem solving, a work ethic, ability to learn on the job, and interpersonal skills—are often stressed in reports that focus on the development of a strong labor force (for example, U.S. Deptartment of Labor 1991 and CEO Forum 2001). Such valued dispositions lend themselves to learner-centered curriculum webs.

Problem-Centered Curriculum.   Problem-centered curriculum, or **problem-based learning,** organizes subject matter around a problem, real or hypothetical, that needs to be solved. Such problems can be defined by teachers in advance or they can be negotiated with students. The ease with which a curriculum web may be created or modified will encourage both teachers and students to pursue new avenues of inquiry in response to shared clarification or definition of problems.

Types of problems to be explored include:

- Life situations involving real problems of practice (buying a car; finding affordable housing; choosing friends; getting a job);
- Problems selected from local issues (justifying or critiquing urban renewal goals; creating comfortable public spaces; improving neighborhood relations; exploring ideas for new economic activity);
- Philosophical or moral problems (what does it mean to be virtuous?; how should society deal with guns or drugs?; should marijuana be legalized?; or what should the United States do to reduce exploitation of children or labor around the world?).

Other problems might revolve around life at a given school. For example:

- How can we redesign the school playground to maximize the enjoyment of students of different age groups?
- What modifications could be made to traffic flow in front of the school that would ease congestion before and after school?
- What kinds of activities could the school sponsor during the summer that would reduce the tendency of students to forget a lot of what they learned the previous year?
- What programs can we implement that will reduce intolerance among different groups of students?
- What can be changed in the menu of the school cafeteria to increase nutrition while appealing more to the students?

Problem-centered curriculum is inherently engaging and authentic, because the students have a real purpose to their inquiry: solving the problem. And while the problems listed above do not necessarily seem directly relevant to state and national standards, problem-centered curriculums can certainly incorporate standard learning objectives having to do with basic skills and knowledge.

One example of a problem-centered curriculum web is Real-World Math, produced by a Chicago Public Schools teacher who participated in WIT 2003. The teacher wanted to show his students that math is actually helpful in real life, so he created a scenario in which his students would solve some real-world problems using math. One problem he presents is "Finding a Job," a problem that interests his students mainly because of the implications the solution has in terms of income and lifestyle. In the first activity, students are randomly assigned a job and must discover what their likely salary is using web-based resources. Then they use this information to make decisions about where to live, what kind of car to drive, and how to create a budget. See Figure 3.1 for a screen shot from the curriculum web.

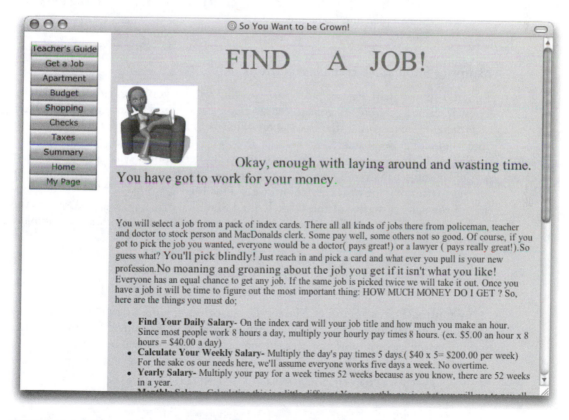

FIGURE 3.1   One of the pages in a problem-centered curriculum web called Real-World Math.

Source: Courtesy of Paul Goldsmith, *http://webinstituteforteachers.org/~pgoldsmith/StartLesson.htm.*

Problem-based learning is used extensively in the professional education of doctors, lawyers, and (increasingly) teachers, because it teaches students skills necessary to deal with data and perspectives that are sometimes conflicting and rarely neatly defined. Often, there is more than one solution possible, with differing consequences and benefits. Effective problem-centered curriculums allow for such messiness in the ways that problems are described and solved. Generally, problem-centered curriculums follow this sequence of activities:

1. The problem is first encountered, perhaps through a newspaper story or the presentation of the results of a poll, and then is more specifically defined by the students, resulting in a set of criteria for a good solution.
2. Students brainstorm resources and information that may be relevant to the problem and gather those they decide will be helpful.
3. Students synthesize the information they have gathered and propose possible solutions.
4. Possible solutions are tested against the selected criteria, and the best solution is presented to the class or to an authentic audience interested in solving the problem. (See Stepien and Gallagher 1993.)

Example Subject Matter Descriptions

The best subject matter descriptions are specific without getting caught up in details. They describe a discrete area of subject matter, an aspect of the learners, or a problem in sufficient detail so that decisions about what belongs in the curriculum and what does not belong can be made.

The best organizational structure for your description will depend on your particular subject matter. The traditional outline format might work to organize the subject matter of your own curriculum web. This format works well for the description of the subject matter of the "Our United States" curriculum web. Note that the outline is divided into "information" and "concepts and skills." Both are the subject matter of the curriculum.

You will find one example of a subject matter description on page 25 in the IQ WebQuest Teaching Guide. Here are three more:

"Our United States" Subject Matter Description.   This curriculum is centered on subject matter relevant to the relationship between geographical features of states and their primary economic and recreational activities. Topics will include:

INFORMATION ON REGIONS OF THE UNITED STATES

- Geographical Data
- Topology
- Rivers, lakes, and oceans
- Mountains
- Elevation
- Climate
- Major economic activities
- Major recreational activities

CONCEPTS AND SKILLS

- Interdependence of geography and economics
- Map reading
- Increased geospatial awareness
- Use of the Web to support research
- Information literacy

- Note taking
- Teamwork
- Presentation skills
- Division of labor
- Data collection
- Data analysis

"Who Am I?" Subject Matter Description.   We have chosen to represent the "Who Am I?" subject matter with a concept map because the curriculum is not linear but based on the complex interrelationships of ideas. See Figure 3.2.

Most teachers are familiar with concept maps, also known as semantic networks. Concept maps enhance brainstorming and provide a useful means of organizing related topics or themes. Some advocates of concept maps believe that they are similar in structure to the representation of knowledge in memory. They are easy to create (whether by hand or with a computer program), and enhance the capacity of students to understand the relationships among concepts, events, facts, or theories (Jonassen 2000, 58–59).

"Building a Curriculum Web with Dreamweaver " Subject Matter Description. This curriculum web is centered on using Dreamweaver to solve the problem of how to build a curriculum web, and so the subject matter description focuses on the skills that will help the learner to solve the problem.

Learning Dreamweaver involves the exploration and use of a number of components and procedures essential to building a complete curriculum web, including:

- Structure of the program and its components
- Simple web-site planning and design
- Site management
- Document setup
- Page layout
- Inserting tables
- Using frames
- Asset management
- Text formatting
- Inserting images and other media
- Editing HTML directly
- Linking and navigation
- Applying templates and library items
- Using layers
- Creating behaviors
- Building forms
- Publishing a site

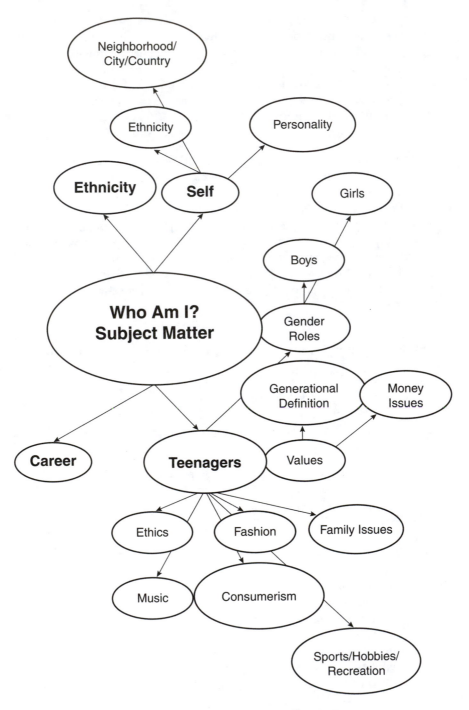

FIGURE 3.2   The "Who Am I?" subject matter description.

ACTIVITY 3C ■ Describing Your Subject Matter

Using a piece of paper, word processor, or web-page editor, create a subject matter description.

1. Decide whether your lesson or unit will focus on subject matter, the learners, or on problems, or some combination of the three.
2. List the important subtopics or skills that will be taught in your lesson or unit.
3. Decide on an organizational scheme for your subject matter description (either outline or concept map or some other format that works for you).
4. Write a draft description.
5. Ask yourself: "Would I be able to use this description to decide whether a given topic is included in my curriculum web?" If not, refine as necessary.

LEARNING OBJECTIVES

Once you have a sense of your general goals, and have defined your learners and your subject matter, you are ready to begin to write the learning objectives for your curriculum web. Learning objectives define in detail the knowledge, skills, and attitudes that you want your learners to gain from the activities in the curriculum web. They represent the specific purposes of the curriculum and later are used to define the **performance criteria** or indicators that will assess the learning that has resulted from use of the curriculum web. (We discuss performance criteria further in Chapter Six.)

For example, one of our general goals for this book is that readers will see the value of teacher involvement in developing curriculum webs, and will want to produce their own curriculum web or webs. This goal encompasses a set of more specific learning objectives:

- The reader will be able to give examples of how resources on the Web can be useful for teaching.
- The reader will be able to describe the special features of the Web that make it different from print media, relative to its use in education.
- The reader will be able to offer at least three reasons that teachers should be involved in writing their own curriculum webs.

Learning objectives serve as the criteria by which materials are selected, content is outlined, instructional procedures are developed, and tests or assessments are prepared. They are, therefore, of fundamental importance in curriculum planning.

In order to be most useful, learning objectives should be:

- Limited in number (because each objective takes time to achieve)
- Consistent among themselves and with general educational goals
- Worthwhile (according to the values or educational purposes that teachers and students share)
- Succinct and clear (so that teachers and students can understand them)

- Appropriate for the intended learners (so that teachers or students do not get too frustrated or bored)
- Logically grouped (so it is easier to keep track of them at each stage of the curriculum development process)
- Periodically revised (as students, teachers, and conditions change)

How to Write Learning Objectives

As you write a learning objective, you should consider both what you want the student to be able to do and what content or subject matter they will be able to do it with. For example, "Students will be able to solve problems" is an incomplete learning objective. Solve what kind of problems? A better objective might be "Students will be able to solve complex word problems involving rates of flow into and out of a container." Learning objectives often also state the conditions under which the learner will be able to complete the task. This might mean adding a phrase such as "using a scientific calculator" or "without referring to a map." Finally, learning objectives sometimes include a statement of the standard by which success will be measured: "at least 80 percent of the time," or "without more than one error."

So, to summarize, a learning objective consists of:

- The behavior or skill that the learner will be able to do or demonstrate;
- The content area that the behavior or skill applies to;
- (Optionally) The conditions under which the behavior or skill will be demonstrated; and
- (Optionally) the standard by which success will be measured.

A complete learning objective might be: *After reading this book and completing the Hands-On Lessons, readers will be able to use Dreamweaver to create a curriculum web of their own design that proves to be an effective learning environment for their chosen students.* This learning objective leaves open the question of how to tell if a curriculum web is "effective," but any further specificity would probably not be warranted given the wide range of possible topics and audiences of the curriculum webs produced.

Some learning objectives state precisely what students will actually be observed to do on completing a given curriculum. For many years, this was sort of a fad among U.S. educators, who were taught that all objectives must be "behavioral," that is, state an observable and measurable behavior in order to count as a worthy educational objective. This trend reflected the view that only what is observable and measurable "counts" as an educational outcome, a view that was supported by the reigning behaviorism that dominated the field of educational psychology. Some educators complained that this excludes objectives that are either open-ended or that concern the inner person rather than outward behaviors. Recently, most curriculum experts have allowed that objectives can be either open-ended or unmeasurable and still be worthwhile.

According to this more recent and more liberal view, there are at least six domains in which learning objectives can be defined, depending on the kinds of outcomes desired (Pratt 1994). Table 3.4 lists these types.

TABLE 3.4   Six Domains of Learning Objectives

- Knowledge—an objective based on the factual, empirical, or declarative capacities of students
- Skill—an objective based on the ability to manipulate materials or tools to produce new materials or other desirable effects
- Somatic—an objective based on changes in the physical body, such as health, fitness, and nutrition
- Attitude—an objective dealing with feelings, emotions, character, and the way students respond to various stimuli
- Process—an objective that obliges students to take part in a process requiring multiple steps to complete
- Experience—an objective that students will experience some event

Some objectives are met simply by having students go through a given experience. These are known as "process" or "experience" objectives. It might be the objective of a middle school advisory group that each student introduces him- or herself to every other student (a process objective). Or a high school English course might have as an objective that each student attends a professional performance of a Shakespeare play (an experience objective). These objectives do not necessarily state that students will be changed in terms of their knowledge, skills, or attitudes, but simply say the students will do something. Objectives that do not specify what the students' behaviors, skills, or attitudes will be at the conclusion of a curriculum, but rather leave outcomes open-ended, are known as **nonpreordinate objectives.** These are in contrast to the more common **preordinate objectives,** which do give a specification of what successful learners can or will do.

Sources of Learning Objectives

Most learning objectives are revealed when the center or focus of a curriculum is analyzed in terms of general educational goals. If we have a broad goal of teaching students to understand the basic terms of literary analysis, and we have decided to center a specific curriculum unit on short stories, we probably will expect that students will learn about different types of short stories or will come to appreciate aspects such as plot, narrative, and character development. Similarly, if our general goal is for students to learn to drive a car safely and legally, and we are developing a unit on purchasing an automobile, we will want the student to learn how to compare vehicles in terms of safety, or to notice any unsafe characteristics of a used car they are considering. This illustrates the role that common sense plays in the development of learning objectives.

Besides commonsense embellishment of broad goals, another source of learning objectives for teachers is detailed statements of standards, such as those discussed beginning on page 9. In Illinois, for example, the Illinois Learning Standards are stated as twenty general goals, which are then described in more detail through benchmarks for each grade level. The benchmarks are then further defined through a set of detailed performance descriptors for each grade level. The performance descriptors *are* learning objectives, stated in terms of what the students will be able to do. Teachers in Illinois can easily look to the performance descriptors early in their curriculum planning and select a few performance descriptors as the primary learning objectives for their curriculum web. The same is true in most other states.

It is difficult to write learning objectives that do not begin to sound simply like laundry lists of skills. One way to avoid this is to vary the language used in explaining what students will be able to do. Rather than just using the word *understanding*, we can write objectives that talk about applying, calculating, employing, describing, diagramming, collecting, critiquing, and so on. These words also reflect behaviors that are easier to observe and to measure than understanding, and may reflect higher-order thinking skills. Table 3.5 lists many different words that can be used for objectives of the knowledge type, grouped according to the taxonomy of objectives developed by Bloom (1956), in which knowledge objectives are at the lowest level and evaluation objectives are at the highest level. Similar sets of words could be specified for the other types of objectives we listed above.

Another advantage of using a variety of action verbs such as those listed in Table 3.5 is that it may be easier to use the learning objectives to brainstorm relevant learning activities or assessment techniques.

TABLE 3.5   Words Commonly Found in "Knowledge" Learning Objectives

KNOWLEDGE	COMPREHENSION	APPLICATION	ANALYSIS	SYNTHESIS	EVALUATION
cite	associate	apply	analyze	arrange	appraise
count	classify	calculate	appraise	assemble	assess
define	compare	complete	contrast	collect	choose
draw	compute	demonstrate	criticize	compose	critique
identify	contrast	dramatize	debate	construct	determine
indicate	describe	employ	detect	create	estimate
list	differentiate	examine	diagram	design	evaluate
name	discuss	illustrate	differentiate	detect	judge
point	distinguish	interpret	distinguish	formulate	measure
read	explain	interpolate	experiment	generalize	rank
recite	estimate	locate	infer	integrate	rate
recognize	examine	operate	inspect	manage	recommend
relate	express	order	inventory	organize	revise
repeat	interpret	predict	question	plan	score
select	interpolate	practice	separate	prepare	select
state	locate	relate	summarize	produce	test
tabulate	predict	report		propose	
tell	report	restate			
trace	restate	review			
write	review	schedule			
	translate	sketch			
		solve			
		translate			
		use			
		utilize			

Example Learning Objectives

For a typical curriculum web designed to encompass a weeklong sequence of learning activities you probably should be able to state a minimum of six and a maximum of about twenty learning objectives. The level of specificity should depend on what is appropriate to the subject matter. The learning objectives for our three example curriculum webs vary in this way. The "Our United States" curriculum web is fairly narrowly focused on geography, and so the learning objectives are fairly specific. The "Who Am I?" curriculum web is very broad and aimed more at creating an opportunity for self-exploration and discovery, along with writing and oral presentation, than at achieving predefined outcomes. The "Building a Curriculum Web with Dreamweaver" curriculum web is defined very specifically in terms of technical skills associated with a particular piece of software. (You can see another example of learning objectives in the Teaching Guide of the IQ WebQuest on page 26.)

"Our United States" Learning Objectives.   On completing this curriculum web, students will be able to:

- Identify six different geographical regions in the United States
- Use state web sites and other online sources to find basic geographical information about the United States
- Generalize the relationships among geographical, economic, and recreational facts. Specifically, they will be able to describe the relationship between a state's geography and its economic and recreational activities
- Apply the concept of self-sufficiency in making decisions about necessary trade relations between regions
- Make predictions about the economic activities of different regions of the world based on geographic information, giving evidence from their own research, and making analogies to situations in the United States
- Appreciate the value of geographical understanding in the real world
- Exhibit effective collaboration skills while working in groups to complete complex tasks

"Who Am I?" Learning Objectives.   The primary goal of this module is to increase the student's self-understanding through conducting guided research into issues of personal identity on the World Wide Web. Our primary goal is to involve our students in a process of self-exploration. Specifically, the students will:

- Engage in thinking critically about themselves and their places in American society
- Investigate their own personalities, values, and goals
- Demonstrate confidence in using computer technology and the resources of the Internet
- Access information via the World Wide Web
- Commit to the **Acceptable Use Policy** and proper netiquette of the Web
- Analyze, synthesize, and evaluate sources of information related to self-identity
- Create web pages related to personal identity

"Building a Curriculum Web with Dreamweaver" Learning Objectives. On completing the lessons in this module, participants will be able to use Dreamweaver to:

- Copy an existing web site from a remote server
- Utilize the extensive help files to discover new procedures or learn new skills as needed during the development of a curriculum web
- Set up a new web site from scratch using the site layout view
- Create a well-organized web site consisting of interlinked HTML documents
- Publish partial or completed web sites to the server
- Connect to the web site from a different computer, and download, modify, and republish that same site
- Create a template and apply it to a set of pages within a web site
- Incorporate library items into a web site design
- Understand the "web-safe" color space and use it on a web site
- Use menus and other procedures to add text, images, and other content
- Use the Dreamweaver property inspector to modify a wide variety of web-page elements
- Use the site files view to copy, move, delete, and update pages on a local computer and remote server
- Create and edit tables to effectively display content of all sorts
- Define behaviors and use layers to include interactivity in web pages
- Create a navigation bar with rollover buttons and apply it to a web site
- Diagnose problems with layout and fix them using the HTML tag selector and code view
- Extend editing capabilities by downloading and managing new extensions

ACTIVITY 3D ■ Writing Your Learning Objectives

Use a piece of paper, word processor, or web-page editor to complete the following steps:

1. Read over the general goals and subject matter description you wrote previously.
2. Consider how the general goals can be furthered through the specific subject matter of your curriculum web.
3. Ask yourself how specific your learning objectives need to be, given your subject matter and audience.
4. For each learning objective domain listed in Table 3.4, consider whether your curriculum web will seek that type.
5. For each domain that is addressed by your curriculum web, write one or more learning objectives.
6. For each learning objective, include the behavior or skill that will be demonstrated, the subject matter or content area, (optionally) the conditions under which the demonstration will occur, and (optionally) the standard by which learning will be assessed.

7. Examine state or national standards relevant to the subject matter of your curriculum web to see if additional learning objectives can be stated.
8. If you accumulate more than twenty learning objectives, consider whether (a) your curriculum is too broad or (b) you can combine several subsidiary objectives into one broader one.
9. Continue this process until satisfied that you have completely stated your learning objectives for the curriculum web.
10. Revise as needed during further development of your curriculum web.

PREREQUISITES

Once a set of learning objectives is defined for your curriculum web, you need to determine what the starting point will be. What skills, knowledge, and attitudes can you expect your learners to come to the curriculum having already mastered? The more care that is devoted to this task the more effective the curriculum is likely to be. Although some review is a good idea in every curriculum web, it does not make much sense to ask students to spend a lot of time learning things they already know. On the other hand, if you expect your students to know or to be able to do more than they actually can, they will become frustrated and will be unlikely to achieve your desired outcomes.

To determine the prerequisites of your curriculum, think about both the *logical* precursors of what the students have to do in the curriculum as well as the *developmental* precursors. Logical precursors stem from the fact that some skills (such as writing a complete sentence) are necessary before other skills (such as writing a complete paragraph) are possible. Developmental precursors are those that usually occur biologically before a given skill can be mastered. For example, we would expect young children to be able to delay personal gratification before we would expect them to complete regular homework assignments.

We recommend that you describe the logical and developmental prerequisites in three categories: skill, knowledge, and attitude. The first two are self-explanatory. Attitude is also important, because often students with poor attitudes or contradictory beliefs may not participate fully in a given activity. Students who consider themselves to be poor math students, for example, are less likely to respond well to complex mathematical formulas or procedures. When considering attitude, think about issues of self-identity, beliefs, motivation, character, and willingness to take risks in order to learn.

When prerequisites are ignored, there arises the problem that every learning activity must start at the beginning. In school systems in which it becomes impossible to assume that every fourth-grade student has mastered the basics of third-grade math, for example, the fourth-grade curriculum becomes watered-down. The other benefit of being clear about prerequisites is that learners (and their teachers) can decide quickly whether they are ready for a particular curriculum web.

In addition, prerequisites help to determine the kinds of learning activities that can be reasonably expected of the learners. For example, suppose you are writing a curriculum web on the use of data collection in science. The kinds of activities you include will vary considerably depending on whether you expect your learners to come with a preexisting understanding of the metric system, or prior skills in the use of computerized spreadsheets, or an understanding of basic statistical concepts.

However, we also want to urge some caution in terms of what you think your learners have to know in order to participate in higher-order tasks. It is important to make sure that the challenges you present to students are appropriate given their prior experiences, but it is also possible to support students in doing tasks that initially seem over their heads. With the right scaffolds, or supports for learning, students can achieve considerably more than they could achieve on their own, without support (Hogan and Pressley 1988). Proper prerequisites are not the solution to every teaching problem because a lack of prerequisites often can be overcome through attention to supporting the students and to planning an appropriate sequence of activities. Therefore, in addition to simply listing the prerequisite skills, knowledge, and attitudes necessary for successful use of your curriculum web, you should also consider ways to compensate if the learners have not mastered one or more of the prerequisites.

Example Prerequisites

You can see one example of a list of prerequisites in the IQ WebQuest Teaching Guide on page 26. Here are three more:

"Our United States" Prerequisites.   Before using the "Our United States" curriculum web, students should be able to:

■ Read at least at a fifth-grade level
■ Use a web browser to move between web pages
■ Be able to copy and paste text from web pages to a word processor
■ Be able to work cooperatively in teams to accomplish shared goals. (Students who do not have experience with cooperative learning may need additional supervision or preparation.)

"Who Am I?" Prerequisites.   Before beginning this curriculum, students should:

■ Be able to write coherent sentences and paragraphs
■ Read at a sixth-grade level or above
■ Be able to use a web browser and search engines
■ Be curious about themselves and their futures

"Building a Curriculum Web with Dreamweaver" Prerequisites.   Participants should know:

■ How to use the Windows or Mac operating system to create directories, copy and move files, and access menus
■ What a curriculum web is and what the required components are
■ How to use a web browser and conduct simple searches

In addition, participants should:

- Be motivated to learn how to build curriculum webs
- Be fairly comfortable learning new and complex software applications

ACTIVITY 3E ■ Listing Your Expected Prerequisites

- Using a piece of paper, word processor, or web-page editor, write down the assumptions you can or will make about what your learners will know, what skills they will have, and what their attitudes are. Think about both logical and developmental prerequisites.
- It might be helpful to think about each of your learning objectives. To achieve each objective, what specific knowledge or skills are needed? Will your curriculum teach all of it or will the learners already know some of it? If so, what?
- In terms of attitude, how motivated do you expect your learners to be? What assumptions are you going to make about their self-concept as learners in that particular area? Will their attitudes toward the subject matter, or toward use of technology, be relevant? Are you going to expect the learners to self-regulate their learning or merely to follow directions?
- Generally, you should expect to list between five and ten prerequisites for a curriculum web.
- For each prerequisite, also ask yourself: what can be done to compensate if any participants do not have this prerequisite? List your suggestions at the bottom of the list of prerequisites.

AIMS

An **aim** is simply a concise statement that summarizes the general purpose of a curriculum web. For example, a statement of the aim of this book is:

> *This book will teach computer literate educators how to develop web-based curriculum modules to support teaching and learning.*

You will note that the aim statement describes both our target learners ("computer literate educators") and the general subject matter or content that those learners will learn ("how to develop web-based curriculum modules"). We have also provided a very short summary of why curriculum webs are important: they "support teaching and learning." This suggests a kind of "formula" for the writing of an aim statement: in one concise sentence, describe the purpose of your unit in terms of *who* will learn *what* (and sometimes *why*)—plus include any additional information that helps someone who is unfamiliar with the subject matter, learners, or instructional plan to understand the unit's purpose better. For example, in the aim statement for "Our United States," we want people to understand that the curriculum web is different from other curriculums that teach geography in that the learners go on "missions" to discover information from web sites.

The aim statement's primary role is to serve as a summary of the curriculum web's purpose. When your curriculum plan is repurposed as a teaching guide, the aim statement should be placed first. Also, it is a good idea to put the aim statement on the home page, or entry point, of your curriculum web. The aim can also be included in the HTML code so that your curriculum web will be located by others doing a search on that topic. (For more on doing this, see page 228.) Putting the aim statement up front will help anyone who locates it on the Web to know fairly quickly whether the curriculum web is relevant to them or to their students. The aim statement will serve this purpose best if it is short and complete.

Example Aims

You can find one example of an aim statement in the IQ WebQuest Teaching Guide on page 24. Three more follow here. Each of these examples meets our criteria for well-written aims: they identify the who and the what, and they seem worthwhile as educational purposes.

"Our United States" Aim.   The "Our United States" curriculum web aims to promote middle school students' understanding of U.S. geography and the relationships among physical, economic, and recreational facts by sending them on fact-finding missions to state web sites.

"Who Am I?" Aim.   The "Who Am I?" curriculum web helps high school freshmen to understand themselves, their groups, and their culture, and to express this self-understanding through creating a presentation and (optionally) a web site.

"Building a Curriculum Web with Dreamweaver" Aim.   This curriculum web is designed to help educators who are fairly comfortable using computers to learn enough about Dreamweaver to be able to use it to create attractive and useful curriculum webs.

ACTIVITY 3F ■ Writing Your Aim Statement

Using a piece of paper, word processor, or web-page editor:

1. Look at the aim statements of several curriculum webs listed at *curriculumwebs.com*. Which ones are clear and concise, enabling you to understand clearly what the curriculum web is about?
2. Write a 15- to 30-word statement that describes the general purpose of your curriculum web. Include any additional summary information to help people understand what makes the curriculum web unique or important.
3. Make sure your aim states *what* you wish to teach to *whom* and possibly *why*.

RATIONALES

A **rationale** is a paragraph or short essay that justifies the use of resources to meet the aim; that is, it discusses why a particular aim is worthwhile. Some aims are widely shared among educators and therefore do not need a lengthy rationale. Other aims, however, require justification, especially if administrators, parents, or students are initially skeptical about the wisdom of teaching a particular subject or skill to a group of students or as part of a given class.

Controversial aims tend to be those dealing with controversial realms of behavior, or with topics that are contested in public life, such as the teaching of evolution or creationism in science, the likely impact of global warming, or the criteria for a successful resolution of the Palestinian–Israeli conflict. If your aim involves looking at a previously ignored aspect of a given subject, or at an interdisciplinary topic that might threaten existing departmental boundaries, or if certain members of your community regard the topic with suspicion, your rationale will be an important part of your curriculum plan.

The rationale is designed to convince anyone who needs convincing that the aim is worthwhile. It is, therefore, targeted to meet potential criticism. But it should not be defensive. Instead, it should give a justification for teaching the given aim to a given set of learners. It should state reasons why the learners will benefit from learning the subject matter, talk some about the costs of teaching that subject matter, and show that these costs are reasonable and worthwhile. Because the rationale will appear in the teaching guide on the curriculum web, the learners can also read it and be convinced that achieving the learning outcomes is worth their time and effort.

Not all rationales need to use this cost-benefit kind of reasoning. Often, the justification for a curriculum is social, emotional, or cultural, or based on reasons having nothing to do with measurable benefits. Again, because you are not justifying the curriculum in general, but for a specific set of learners, the rationale should be convincing to the learners or their parents and other stakeholders.

Rationales often discuss gaps between the desired and actual states of students. Often, the thrust of a rationale is the report of a **needs assessment**—a formalized process that will determine how great a given need is and assess the consequences of not addressing that need. We do not discuss formal needs assessments in this book; however, we provide some useful resources at the end of this chapter.

Example Rationales

You can see one example rationale in the IQ WebQuest Teaching Guide on page 25. Here are three more:

"Our United States" Rationale.   Through this curriculum, students will explore the five unifying themes of geography promoted by the National Geographic Society (NGS).

Now more than ever, citizens of the United States can ill afford to ignore their own lack of geographical understanding. Americans' ignorance of their own country and of the world will have dire consequences for our nation's welfare and our interdependence with the people in other nations. Geographic education is vital to correct this ignorance and can give future generations the knowledge and understanding they need to manage the Earth's resources wisely.

Geographic education can satisfy our deep need to know about other people and places, it can teach us about the natural environment and the capacity of the Earth to support human life, and it can inform our individual perceptions of places. Geographic education requires knowing *where* things are located, but, more important, requires a system for inquiring *why* they are there and *where they should be*.

This unit is focused on U.S. geography. Many students in fourth through eighth grade lack basic understandings of both the scale and diversity of the United States. Many students do not understand that different regions of the country have different topographical, economic, and recreational features. The activities of "Our United States" are especially designed to show the interrelationship of the topographical features with economic and recreational activities commonly seen in different regions of the country.

"Who Am I?" Rationale.   Young people ages 14 to 17 are beginning to differentiate themselves from the crowd and make decisions about what kind of values, behaviors, and aspirations they are going to pursue as they move into adulthood. Because the high school environment is not always as nurturing as previous levels of schooling, students often find themselves bewildered or apprehensive about their self-identity, self-worth, sense of self-efficacy, and future goals. By exploring self-identity in a nonthreatening, reflective activity, students may feel more in control and less likely to drift with the crowd or pursue unhealthy activities.

By studying various web-based resources containing observations about teenagers and about their own ethnic groups, and then creating a presentation about themselves and the ways that they both share and don't share attributes of these groups, students may come to a better understanding of themselves. This curriculum web can also be expanded to include the publishing of student essays through a class web site or an individual web page for each student.

"Building a Curriculum Web with Dreamweaver" Rationale.   Dreamweaver simplifies the entire process of web design, from creating the initial structure to applying a consistent look and feel. The product has many more functions than other web-page editors such as Mozilla Composer. Although this additional functionality can be quite useful for teachers and other creators of web sites that are designed to support teaching and learning, it also requires the user to learn a lot more about the program. Therefore, we have built this curriculum web to support the somewhat steep learning curve experienced by new users of Dreamweaver. The web has the additional benefit of modeling some techniques that may be useful in other curriculum webs.

ACTIVITY 3G ■ **Writing Your Rationale**

Using a piece of paper, word processor, or web-page editor:

1. List any stakeholders who might need to be convinced that your aim is worth achieving. This should include the learners and, possibly, teachers, parents, community members, and school administrators.
2. Consider whether there are national, state, or local commissions that have constructed arguments for including certain topics in the school curriculum. If so, read those reports to get a sense of the reasoning behind their arguments. List the most compelling arguments that can be used to justify the aim of your curriculum web.
3. Think about why the learning objectives you have selected are important. Think in terms of the values they represent, the ways they open up possibilities for further learning, and their importance for helping the learner to achieve other goals having to do with career, family, or society.
4. If the subject matter has been ignored in your school's curriculum, think about what the reasons for this may be. Is the topic controversial to some members of your community? If so, why? What arguments can you make that the topic should now be covered, even if it is controversial?
5. Write a short essay summarizing your reasons for trying to achieve your aim and objectives. Write the essay for a general audience that includes students. If there are specific audiences that need convincing, address them in separate paragraphs.
6. Share your aim and rationale with another person who has not helped you to plan your curriculum web. Ask him or her if the rationale makes sense and if he or she can think of further reasons that you may have left out for spending time on the objectives of your curriculum web. If possible, share your rationale with someone who may be disposed not to agree that the subject matter should be taught in your school. Listen to them respond to the rationale, and use what they have said to make an even stronger argument.

Chapter Summary

This chapter:

- Describes a process for formulating the goals of a curriculum web
- Defines a set of elements that become the building blocks for a curriculum plan and a teaching guide
- Discusses the relationship between general educational goals and the specific objectives of a curriculum web

- Details the importance of understanding the needs and prior skills of your learners before you design your curriculum web
- Gives examples of each element of a curriculum plan and provides guidance for you to create your own

Questions For Reflection

In this chapter, we mentioned that schooling in the United States has had two sometimes conflicting goals: passing along the skills, knowledge, and attitudes of prior generations and fostering creativity and individuality. Think about your own school in terms of this dichotomy. Which goal is emphasized? In what ways is the other goal compromised or ignored?

1. Is it possible to imagine a school that serves both goals equally, without compromising one for the other? What would such a school look like? Would it be possible to build a school like that in your community? Why or why not?
2. Is it possible to achieve both types of goals with your curriculum web? Why or why not?

Your Next Step

Download Hands-On Lesson 3 for your specific software. This lesson teaches you additional web-page editing and design skills. Completing Lesson 3 will get you ready to begin building your curriculum web.

Once you have framed your purposes and drafted your curriculum aim, rationale, description of learners and subject matter, and learning objectives, it is time to start working on your draft teaching guide and learn some more about page design principles. That is the topic of Chapter Four.

For Further Learning

- See *curriculumwebs.com* for some links pertinent to the topics in this chapter.
- These books can help you to develop useful activities to do with the Web: Berger 1998; Gooden 1996; Grabe and Grabe 2000; Hackbarth 1997; Harris 1998; Jonassen 2000; Joseph 1999; Leu, Leu, and Coiro 2004; Serim and Koch 1996; Warlick 1998.
- The *National Educational Technology Standards for Students: Connecting Curriculum for Technology* (ISTE 2000a) provides a huge variety of activities that can be enhanced with the use of computer technologies, for all grade levels preK–12.

- These books are helpful for instructional planning in general: Ornstein and Hunkins 1998, Pratt 1994.
- See Siegler and Alibali 2005 for a comprehensive discussion of cognitive development from infancy through adolescence, and Huitt 1997 for some practical suggestions related to teaching learners at different stages of cognitive development.
- Needs assessments, helpful for identifying possible educational goals, are discussed in Tanner and Tanner 1985 and Pratt 1994.
- These books provide lots of useful information on how the Web can change teaching and learning: Abbey 2000, Aggarwal and Bento 2000, Khan 1997.

CHAPTER 4

- - - - - - - - - - - -

LAYING OUT AN EFFECTIVE WEB PAGE

Overview

This chapter discusses the process of building web pages from a generic standpoint, that is, without reference to any specific web-editing software. Besides providing the background you need to create an effective, attractive web page for the curriculum plan (or draft teaching guide) you worked on in Chapter Three, it covers the structure of HTML, page layout, color choices, fonts, links and other navigational elements, and how to make your pages accessible to a variety of learners.

WHAT IS HTML?

A computer stores a web page as a sequence of words and annotations. The words make up the informational content of the page, whereas the annotations control the visual presentation of the material (that is, the way the material looks on the page). These annotations are HTML **tags,** and usually come in pairs: a start tag and an end tag.

The HTML tag to start italicizing text is `<I>`, and the tag to end italicizing text is `</I>`. Any text between `<I>` and `</I>` tags will be displayed as italicized. This

```
This is <I>really</I> fun!
```

will be displayed by a web browser as

This is *really* fun!

Similarly, you can use the `<B>` tag to make text bold:

```
<B>This is <I>really</I> fun! </B>
```

This will be displayed by a web browser as

This is *really* fun!

Other tags specify the position of text on the page, colors of both background and text, the placement of graphics and other multimedia, and the inclusion of **hyperlinks,** which are points within the page that, when clicked, will take the user to another place on the Web.

HTML tags are written with a less-than sign (<) followed by the tag's name, possibly followed by additional tag information known as **attributes** and values, followed by a greater-than sign (>). (The less-than and greater-than symbols are usually located on your keyboard as the shifted comma and shifted period. HTML coders refer to these symbols as "brackets.")

Many HTML tags can be customized with various attributes and values. For example, the <BODY> tag indicates the section of the document that is displayed in the browser window. The body of the page can be modified in many ways. For example, you might want the text on the page to appear in red. One way to do that is to add the TEXT attribute to the tag, along with the value "RED":

```
<BODY TEXT="RED"> . . . . </BODY>
```

Additional attributes for the <BODY> tag include those that affect the color of links, color of the background, and whether there is a background image. See the HTML Reference at *curriculumwebs.com* for additional details about tags, attributes, and values.

Because these symbols, and all the letters inside of the brackets, can be typed using an ordinary computer keyboard, you can create HTML documents using any software that creates text documents. Windows computers usually come with an application called Notepad that works well; Macintosh users can use TextEdit and save as text only, or download an application called Plain Text Editor from the *apple.com* web site. You can create HTML pages in any word processor; however, you have to be sure to save the file in text format; otherwise the software will fill your file with various other codes that are **proprietary** to the particular word processor. These proprietary codes will cause web browsers to interpret the HTML incorrectly. (Many word processors now have the capacity to save any document in HTML format, which essentially turns them into HTML editors. They often do not work very well, and can result in some pretty ugly code, but this capability provides an easy way to create web pages for those more comfortable with a word processor than a web-page editor.)

One very attractive feature of the Web is that you can always view the HTML code that lies behind any web page. If you see a page that you like and that you would like to emulate, use your web browser to look at the HTML that creates that page. This HTML is often referred to as the **source code,** or simply the source of the page. In Mozilla, you can view the source of any page by clicking the View menu and choosing Page Source. In Internet Explorer, you click the View menu and choose Source. In Safari, you click the View menu and choose View Source. This tool is a great way to learn more about HTML and apply what you learn to the creation of your own pages.

As a beginning web designer, however, you do not need to create web pages using raw HTML code. Instead, you can choose to use a software tool to implement your web-page designs. These tools are known as web-page editors or **WYSIWYG** editors (What You See Is What You Get—pronounced *whizzi-wig*). Because these editors automatically produce the HTML for a web page, using one relieves you of needing to know a lot about the intricacies of HTML. Even professionals use these tools! However, to get the best out of the software tools, to understand the design of the web pages you admire, and to be able to "tweak" your page to make it look exactly as you planned, a good understanding of the underlying HTML is essential. Therefore, in this chapter and elsewhere we do discuss the HTML behind the design principles and elements we introduce. See our companion web site at *curriculumwebs.com* for a comprehensive guide to HTML tags.

CASCADING STYLE SHEETS (CSS)

Cascading style sheets (CSS) are an add-on to HTML that allow the web designer more control over the look of a web page. You can change the font, text size, line height, even the space between letters with these styles. You can set margins, outline blocks of text or surround them with color; you can even change how the web browser's cursor behaves. Just as with HTML, CSSs are easier to implement using a web-page editor, but we will show some simple implementations throughout this chapter. See *curriculumwebs.com* for comprehensive coverage of the CSS markup language.

CSS styles can be defined in the HTML code of a web page itself, between the <HEAD> and </HEAD> tags. Style definitions need to be enclosed by the <STYLE> tag, and can either redefine the look of an existing tag, or create a completely new style, as shown here:

```
<STYLE TYPE="text/css">
.purpleText {color: #330066;}
</STYLE>
```

Applying this style to text will result in—you guessed it—purple text. To apply, use the <SPAN> tag with the CLASS attribute:

```
<SPAN CLASS="purpleText">This text is purple!</SPAN>
```

CSS styles can also be defined in a separate document that is referred to by every page in your web site. This is a good way to ensure consistency of design among all the pages on your site. However, linked style sheets are beyond the scope of this book. To find out more about CSS, see *curriculumwebs.com* or check out For Further Learning at the end of this chapter.

A Note on Filenames

Whether you use a WYSIWYG web editor or create a page from raw HTML, you will have to name your **files** when you save them. There are some important things to keep in mind when naming your files:

- The filename **extension** cannot be omitted, as it tells the web browser how to interpret and display the file. HTML files must have the extension .htm or .html. Graphics files must have the extension .jpg, .jpeg, or .gif, depending on the file format.
- You can use either the extension .html or .htm for your HTML files, but it is best for you to be consistent in using one or the other throughout your site. If you have named a file activity.html and then try to link to it using the name activity.htm, the link will not work. The same principle applies to the graphics file extensions .jpeg and .jpg.

- Filenames should not have spaces in them. Use underscores or careful use of capital letters to make a filename readable if it is more than one word. Instead of `Teacher Info.html` for a filename, use `teacher_info.html` or `teacherInfo.html`.

- The case of filenames and filename extensions is important, too; the filename `activity.html` is not the same as `Activity.html`. Choose a standard (such as all lowercase) and stick to it; this reduces time spent in troubleshooting your site later.

- Some filenames have special significance for the Web. For example, `index.html` and `index.htm` and (sometimes) `default.html` and `default.htm` have special significance because they are treated by web servers as the primary page within any **directory.** If a web browser requests the URL *http://cuip.uchicago.edu/ CurriculumWebs/WhoAmI*, giving no filename, the web server looks for a file in the WhoAmI directory called `index.htm` or `index.html`, and if such a file is found, serves that page. If the web server does not find any of these special filenames, the server will deliver a listing of the contents of the directory. So by naming one file in each directory `index.htm`, the web designer achieves two purposes: (1) time may be saved because users do not have to enter a filename, and (2) this is a way of preventing the users from easily seeing a list of all the files within a directory.

- When you point your web browser to *curriculumwebs.com*, you are entering only a domain name. The web server that hosts the *curriculumwebs.com* web site will deliver a page called `index.htm`. For this reason, *http://curriculumwebs.com/ index.htm* is the same as *http://curriculumwebs.com*.

■ ■ ■ ■ ■

BACKING UP

As a rule of thumb, you should always keep at least two copies of each page in your web site. A good way to do this is to keep a working version and a backup version. At the end of each design session, you should make a copy of the pages you have changed, label it with the date, and keep that copy somewhere away from your work area. You do not want a hard-drive failure, a fire, or a burglary to wipe out all your hard work!

To learn more about the technical issues behind files, paths, formats, and so on, it would be helpful for you to read the Appendix (An Overview of Web Technologies) before you proceed with the rest of this chapter.

BASIC PAGE DESIGN PRINCIPLES

When designing the layout of a web page, it is best to keep in mind a couple of principles of good design:

- *Format for maximum readability.* Make sure that items are separated by enough white space that users' eyes can distinguish between unrelated items. Also, avoid brightly colored text on a dark background, as it is fatiguing to read.

- *Format for efficiency and consideration of download times.* The typical user will wait no more than 15 seconds for a web page to download before giving up and clicking away from your site. Keep the user with a 56k **modem** Internet connection in mind and avoid including items such as large graphics, animations, **JavaScript** or java **applets** simply because you can. Make sure that each addition to your web page improves the content of your web site and is worth the download time!

Designing a good page layout involves taking the following into consideration:

- Use of white space to separate design elements
- Use of color
- Font faces and size
- Use of horizontal rules or boxes to organize information
- Clear presentation and labeling of the navigation elements

For each of these topics, we will discuss design considerations and also how to implement your decisions using HTML and/or CSS.

USE OF WHITE SPACE ON THE PAGE

Vertical White Space

Good use of both vertical and horizontal **white space** will add to the readability of your web page. Vertical white space, which is the vertical space between visual elements such as graphics and text, or between blocks of text, conveys meaning to the reader. Magazines, for example, break paragraphs into groups with subheads, and books use successive paragraphs with breaks only at chapters or subchapters. In both these instances, the white space tells you where one section ends and another begins. On your web page, systematic use of white space can vastly improve the presentation of text for easier reading and better comprehension.

Paragraphs of text are not normally indented on a web page. In the early days of the Web there was no HTML tag to indicate a tab character, and no easy way to indent paragraphs. In order to indicate to the reader where one paragraph ends and the next begins, an extra line of white space is usually added. This visual clue greatly aids the reader in defining the organization of the text. Now it is fairly easy to indent paragraphs using CSS, but the style of putting white space between paragraphs has stuck; in fact, some print publications have followed suit.

You can insert vertical white space into your web page by using:

- The <P> tag. This is created by your web-page editor when you press the Return or Enter key. It places the succeeding text or graphic on a new line, with a blank line before it. It is intended to specify a new paragraph; however, it does not provide indentation of the first line of the new paragraph as most readers are used to.
- The <BR> tag. This is created by your web-page editor when you press the Return or Enter key with the Shift key depressed. It places the succeeding text or

graphic on a new line, with no white space before it. Multiple `<BR>` tags can be used to create large blocks of vertical white space.

- A one-**pixel** graphic. Many advanced designers feel limited by the inability to specify vertical white space that is less than one line of text in height. They will often insert a white or transparent GIF image that is one pixel in height and width. See Chapter Nine for more details on inserting graphics.

Indentation

If you want to break with web tradition and indent the first line of your paragraphs, there are two ways to do so:

- A nonbreaking space can be used to create the necessary white space. HTML ordinarily allows only one space between words or other design elements; a nonbreaking space can be repeated multiple times. Three to five of these spaces is enough to create a discernable indentation—but then you should be sure to use the `<BR>` tag and not the `<P>` tag between paragraphs. You can insert a nonbreaking space into your web page by using the HTML code ` `. This is an HTML character that indicates a single blank space (do not forget the semicolon!). Most web-page editors will include one of these nonbreaking spaces if you hold down the Option key (Mac) or Control key (PC) while using the space bar.
- Cascading style sheets can be used to redefine the `<P>` tag so that it indents. The following code will indent all the paragraphs on the page by 20 pixels:

```
<style type="text/css">
p {    text-indent: 20px;
</style>
```

Remember that CSS style definitions go in the head of an HTML document, between the `<HEAD>` and `</HEAD>` tags, before the `<BODY>` tag.

Horizontal White Space

Pages without horizontal white space are very hard to read. (See Figure 4.1.) Using invisible table cells and characters to create margins and indents can turn even the most badly written text into a readable page (of badly written text!).

Margins. One of the few ways in which web pages are like printed media, such as books, is in the presentation of text. Nothing beats margins in helping the reader have a pleasant reading experience. A margin separates the text from all the noise on the screen, making it easy for the reader's eye to pick up the next line as it moves down the page. The broader the margin, the more the text stands out. When the type goes all the way to the edge of the window, it is easier for the eye to go back to the current line or to skip ahead two lines than to land on the correct next line of text.

Line length is an issue related to margins. Long lines of text make it harder for the eye to get back to the left margin and pick up the next line. Ideally, blocks of text should have 10 to 12 words on a line for normal reading. (Longer lines are more difficult to read; the eye loses track of where the next line starts when it must track a long way back to the left.) On the Web, because you do not know the width of the reader's "page" (i.e., the width of their browser window), you, as the web designer, must do some creative implementation in order to create an easily readable page.

The best way to implement margins and to control line lengths is by using **tables** to specify the page layout. If the table is specified to have no visible border, the reader will not even realize that a table is being used; he or she will only see easily readable text and graphics.

Here is the HTML code for a simple table with left and right margins. The lines beginning with `<!--` are comments inserted just to communicate to you or another web designer). This code produces the table used in Figure 4.2:

```
<TABLE WIDTH="100%" BORDER="0">
    <TR>
        <!-- This table column establishes the left-hand
        margin containing only a non-breaking space -->
        <TD WIDTH="10%">   </TD>
        <!-- This table column holds the content of the
        page -->
        <TD WIDTH="*"> <!-- text goes here --> </TD>
        <!-- This table column establishes the right-hand
        margin -->
        <TD WIDTH="10%">   </TD>
    </TR>
</TABLE>
```

By specifying that the margins are a percentage of the window width rather than a defined number of pixels, you create bigger margins on wider pages, which helps to shorten the line length, and smaller margins on narrower pages, which helps to increase the line length.

On the other hand, you can use fixed-width table columns to control line length exactly. Column widths are specified in pixels, which as a general rule run 72 to the inch. In other words, a 72-pixel-wide table column will look 1 inch wide on most computer monitors.

Here is the HTML code for a simple table of fixed width, with 1-inch margins and a 320-pixel-wide (4½-inch) text area:

```
<TABLE WIDTH="464" BORDER="0">
    <TR>
        <!-- This table column establishes the left-hand
        margin -->
        <TD WIDTH="72">    </TD>
        <!-- This table column holds the content of the
        page -->
        <TD WIDTH="320"> <!-- text goes here --> </TD>
        <!-- This table column establishes the right-hand
        margin -->
```

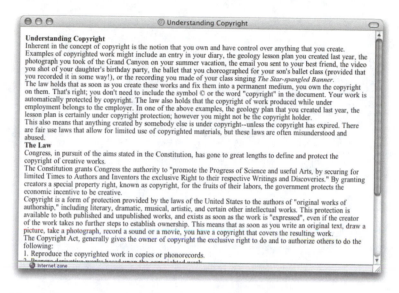

Figure 4.1   A web page with unformatted text.

```
<TD WIDTH="72">     </TD>
   </TR>
</TABLE>
```

Using a fixed-width table like this helps the user control the line length, keeping it within an easily readable 10 to 12 words per line. However, there are some drawbacks to this method. The size of the browser window—which the user, not the designer, controls—dramatically affects the readability of the page. If the browser window is resized so that it is narrower than the fixed-width table, the user will have to scroll sideways to read text, which makes the page almost unreadable.

You can see the difference in page readability the careful use of white space can make by comparing Figure 4.1 and Figure 4.2.

Creating Margins with CSS.   You can also use CSS to create fixed-size margins. Inserting the following code in the head of an HTML document will result in 50-pixel left and right margins, and 20 pixels of white space at the top and bottom of the page:

```
<style type="text/css">
body {
       margin-left: 50px;
       margin-top: 20px;
       margin-right: 50px;
       margin-bottom: 20px;
}
</style>
```

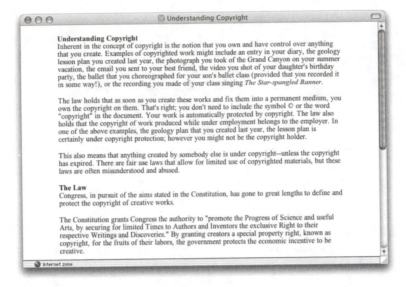

Figure 4.2   The same web page as Figure 4.1 formatted with vertical and horizontal white space.

ACTIVITY 4A ■ Laying Out Your Teaching Guide

Take the teaching guide elements that you developed in Activities 3A through 3G and insert them into a web page. Use vertical and horizontal white space to maximize the readability of the page. Hands-On Lesson 4 found at *curriculumwebs.com* shows you how to do this with your particular software. You'll jazz this page up a bit in the other activities in this chapter.

Layout of Text and Graphics

Any graphics you intend to use should be included in your page layout plan. Images often take up quite a bit of space and their visual heaviness can greatly affect the overall look of a page. Because of the importance of images, we've devoted most of Chapter Nine to them. Here we will only cover the bare bones of using images and talk mostly about how to put them into a page..

The <IMG> tag is used to insert an image into a web page. Within the <IMG> tag, you must specify which image file is to be displayed.

A copyright symbol and heading could be added to the web page shown in Figure 4.1 and Figure 4.2 with the following HTML:

```
<IMG SRC="CopyrightSymbol.gif">
<BR>
<B>Understanding Copyright</B>
```

UNDERSTANDING THE SRC ATTRIBUTE

The SRC attribute of the `<IMG>` tag specifies where the file that contains the graphic is to be found. If the file is in the same directory (or folder) as the HTML page, then the name of the page is sufficient (as in `<IMG SRC="CopyrightSymbol.gif">`). However, if the image is in another location, the *path* to the file must be specified (as in `<IMG SRC="images/CopyrightSymbol.gif">`). Notice that the file `Copyright-Symbol.gif` is not the same as `copyrightsymbol.gif`—case matters! See the Appendix (An Overview of Web Technologies) for more details on filenames and paths.

An image can be inserted on its own line, aligned with a single line of text, or have text wrapped around it. To put an image on the same line as the text, make sure there is no `<P>` or `<BR>` tag between them:

```
<IMG SRC="CopyrightSymbol.gif">
<B>Understanding Copyright</B>
```

To make text wrap around an image as in Figure 4.3, include the `ALIGN` attribute within the `<IMG>` tag:

```
<IMG SRC="CopyrightSymbol.gif" ALIGN="LEFT">
<B>Understanding Copyright</B>
```

You can add more white space around the image by including `HSPACE` and `VSPACE` within the `<IMG>` tag. See our HTML reference at *curriculumwebs.com* for more details.

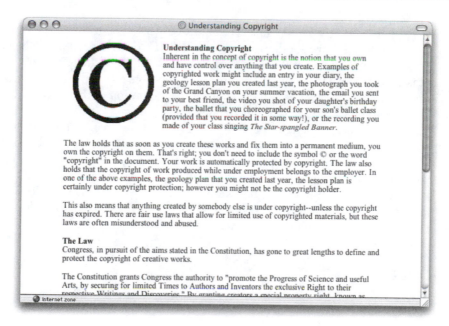

FIGURE 4.3   An image aligned left of a block of text.

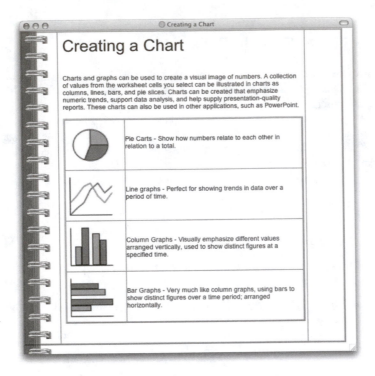

FIGURE 4.4   A web page that aligns text and graphics by means of nested tables.

A popular way to align images and text is by using tables and nested tables (tables within tables). Figure 4.4 shows a nested table. The outer table defines the page's margins and makes sure that the page content is to the right of the part of the background graphic that looks like a spiral binder. The inner table aligns the smaller graphics with the text that refers to them. In the actual implementation of this layout, the table borders would be set to 0 so as to be invisible.

Remember to take into account the trade-off between the use of graphics and slow download times! In the previous example, the picture of the copyright symbol adds no additional meaning to the content of the page, and serves only to make the page more visually exciting. The trade-off is probably worth it, in this case, as the graphic file is only 9K in size. If it were a large file, with a long download time, a web designer should think twice before including it. More details on the relationship between download times and graphics can be found in Chapter Nine.

USE OF COLOR

Color can improve or detract from the readability of your web site. Bright color schemes that might be appropriate for an introductory **splash page** will be inappropriate on a page on which users are expected to do any amount of reading. There are several color decisions to be made in the design of any web page:

- Background color or background image
- Color of text
- Color of link text

Background Color and Images

On pages where users are expected to stay and read for more than a few seconds, choose fairly plain background colors. It is fun to look at a bright blue page for about 30 seconds, but after that the eye gets tired of the color. In addition, a bright background draws attention away from the actual content of the web page. The default color for a web page is not white, as many designers believe, but gray. (This is because originally the Web was designed for physicists to share pictures and diagrams, which showed up best against a gray background. It was only later that the use of text became an important consideration on the Web.) Unless a background color or image is specified, many browsers will show a gray background. To avoid this, always set the background color—even if you are using white.

To set the background color, add an attribute to the `BODY` tag. `<BODY BGCOLOR="#FFFFFF">` will set the background color to white. See the sidebar on page 83 for an explanation of color codes.

Or you can use CSS to redefine the `<BODY>` tag. The following definition will set the background color to black:

```
body {background-color: #000000;}
```

As always, CSSs must be delineated with `style` tags (omitted here). See Hands-On Lesson 4 for instructions on setting the page attributes such as background colors in various web editors.

Background images are very popular on the Web. These are loaded in the body tag of the web page, and replace whatever background color has been defined for the page. Unless the background image is at least as large as the browser window, the browser will *tile* the image, repeating it over and over until it fills the browser window. This may or may not be what you want; be sure to test your background image in a very large browser window to ensure the result that you are after. One way to avoid tiling is to extend the right-hand side of your image out to more than 1,200 pixels. Usually, you'll choose a color that is already in the background of your image for this extension.

To set a background image, add the `Background` attribute to the `BODY` tag of the document's HTML. `<BODY BACKGROUND="backgroundfile.gif">` will specify that the GIF file called `backgroundfile.gif` will be tiled in the background of the page.

Again, you can use CSS to redefine the body tag: `body {background-image: url(backgroundfile.gif);}` in the head of the page.

Background images should be very subtle if text is to go on top of them! Text does not show up well against patterns. Figure 4.5 shows a web page created with two different backgrounds. The first has a clean and crisp look, with a large white space

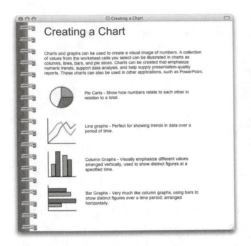
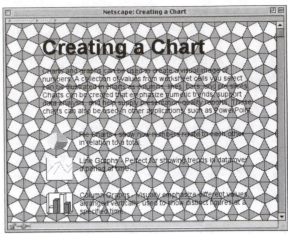

FIGURE 4.5   A web page created with two different backgrounds.

that shows up the text nicely. The background of the second is too busy and obscures the text, making it almost unreadable.

Table cells can each have their own background color or image. This can be useful in distinguishing columns or rows of a table, especially when the designer decides not to show the table borders. Choice of color should follow the same guidelines as for page background colors.

Text Color

The prime consideration in text color is readability. A text color that is too close to the background color will render the text unreadable. Many web pages with dark background colors use white text for high contrast. Be careful in choosing this option, since problems arise when a reader prints the page. The default printer setting for most web browsers is to *not* print the background of the page. This results in the user printing out white text on a white piece of paper (very difficult to read indeed!). The "fix" for this is to set the browser preferences to use black text on a white background before printing. Of course, this negates the effect the designer was probably after. Also, in some school settings the computers have software that prevents the user from changing the browser preferences, thus rendering the user unable to print a readable copy of the page at all. (One way to avoid this problem is to include PDF files of any documents that you intend the user to print. See page 195.)

Again, beware of bright colors. They are fatiguing to look at for any length of time.

To set the text color for an entire page, add an attribute to the BODY tag. <BODY TEXT="#FF0000"> will result in bright red text. If you do not specify a color, the text will default to black. In a web-page editor, the font color is usually set in the same dialog box as the background color and link colors.

To change the color of a block of text within the page, use the <FONT> tag. <FONT COLOR="#00FF00"> This text is green.</FONT> will result in a line of green text.

You can use CSS to set the text color for an entire page by redefining the <BODY> tag. In this example the background color is set to blue and the text color is set to white:

```
body {
        background-color: #0000FF;
        color: #FFFFFF;
}
```

Link Color

The default color for links on the Web is blue. You do not have to stick to this convention, however, since it is a settable attribute of the <BODY> tag, just as text color is. Or a CSS style can be used to redefine the <BODY> tag and specify the link color. Making link color different from the normal text color helps the user easily pick out the links. Many web browsers have their preferences set to also underline text links, further helping the users to distinguish links from other text, but the web designer cannot count on the user having that browser setting. Choose one color for the links throughout your web site and stick to it.

You can specify another text color for visited links. If the user has been to the page recently enough that the page is still in the disk **cache,** then the link will show up in this other color. This helps the user remember which links have been followed and which have not. The default color for visited links is a bluish purple.

■ ■ ■ ■ ■ ■

HOW TO SPECIFY COLOR CODES

Specifying the background and text colors for a web page can be fairly simple, a matter of choosing the color from a palette of choices. However, the resulting HTML might make you scratch your head. Here is a fairly technical explanation: Colors are specified in HTML with a six-digit hexadecimal (base 16) number, such as 9C3163 (a deep pink) or B5B5FF (a light blue). In base 16, the digits go from 0 to 9 (as in base 10) and then continue from A to F. This gives us the 16 digits we need to represent numbers in hexadecimal. (Think of FF in hexadecimal as being like 99 in base 10.) The first two digits of this six-digit number represent the amount of red in the color; the second two digits represent the amount of green; and the final two digits represent the amount of blue. For example, FF0000 would be a color with as much red as possible, and no green or blue. FF00FF is a color with red and blue but no green (i.e., purple). A few experiments soon show the novice designer what is going on. Contrary to intuition, black is 000000 (the absence of any color), while white is FFFFFF. When all the numbers are the same, such as 777777, the resulting color is a shade of gray.

These numeric representations of the color wheel are used primarily in the BODY tag, as in:

```
<BODY BGCOLOR="FFFFEE" TEXT="000000" LINK="940000"
VLINK="550000">
```

(continued)

CONTINUED

which will result in a web page with a very pale yellow background (FFFFEE), black text (000000), links of a bright maroon color (940000), and visited links of a darker maroon (550000).

Properly speaking, hexadecimal numbers should be preceded by a pound sign (#), but almost every browser will work properly without it.

Hexadecimal color representations are similarly used in specifying the background color for table cells or portions of text that are a different color than the rest of the web page.

A limited set of colors can also be referred to by name. Not all browsers support the same list of color names, but the standard colors are usually included in the list. The following tag will work in most browsers:

```
<BODY BGCOLOR="yellow" TEXT="black" LINK="maroon">
```

Use of Horizontal Lines or Boxes

Horizontal lines—also known as "rules"—can be used to separate sections of text within a web page. In dividing a web page into sections, be careful not to put too many different ideas on the same page! (See page 167 for a discussion of dividing up your information into appropriately sized chunks.) You can insert a horizontal line in HTML with the `<HR>` tag, or you can use a graphic. Graphics as horizontal dividers can reinforce the metaphor of a web site, as in Figure 4.6 taken from "Our United States," which reinforces the atlas metaphor of the curriculum web.

A box around a block of text is an effective means of drawing the eye to an important item. This is easily implemented by inserting a table with one row and one column and a visible border. If the inside of the box is shaded a different color, it is even more eye-catching. Or a CSS style can be defined in which text has a colored background and a border around it. (See page 200 for an example of how this is used as part of a rollover link.)

STYLING TEXT

Choosing a Font Face and Size

The font face and size that you choose can either strengthen or weaken the readability of text on your web page. There are two types of font faces: *serif* and *sans serif*. Serif typefaces have serifs, which are the little strokes at the ends of letters as shown below. The purpose of serifs is to make the text flow from one letter to the next, improving readability. Sans serif fonts lack these serifs and have a much "cleaner" look. Generally, serif fonts are used for passages of text, and sans serif fonts are used for headlines, but designers often don't follow this general rule.

Times is a serif font face. So is Palatino.

Arial is a sans serif font face. So is Helvetica.

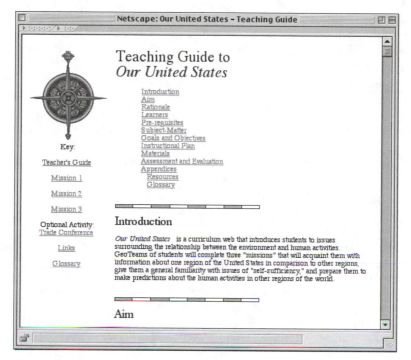

FIGURE 4.6   A graphic resembling the distance scale of a map, used repeatedly in the "Our United States" curriculum web.

One problem with choosing a font face when designing a web page is that not all computer systems have the same set of fonts installed. If you choose a font that is found only on Macintosh, then PC users are likely to be left with their system's default font. Designers can get around this with the use of the `<FONT>` tag. The tag `<FONT FACE="Arial, Helvetica, sansserif">` specifies that the browser should use the Arial font (a sans serif font) if it is available, Helvetica (also sans serif) if Arial is not available, and the default sans serif font if neither is available.

There are two font faces that have been developed especially for the Web, and are found on most up-to-date systems, including Macs and PCs. The sans serif font is called Verdana, and the serif font is called Georgia. To be safe, the best font specifications to use are:

`<FONT FACE="Verdana, Arial, Helvetica, sans-serif">` for sans serif fonts

`<FONT FACE="Georgia, Times New Roman, Times, serif">` for serif fonts

The fonts discussed above are all *variable-width* fonts, in which skinny letters like "i" take up less horizontal space than fat letters like "m". In *fixed-width* or *mono-spaced* fonts like `Courier`, each letter is the same width. These fonts are tiring to read and should be avoided in normal text; they are typically used for special purposes such as representing computer input or output. (The HTML code in this book is displayed in Courier.) In that case, the best font tag to use is `<FONT FACE="Courier New, Courier, mono">`.

Font size can be used to draw the eye of the user to headlines and special areas of the screen, and can also be used to convey meaning. For example, a larger font size is appropriate for younger viewers (think of the type in books for small children). On the flip side, a large font may seem "babyish" to teenage readers. Font size is usually specified in HTML as a relative size—relative to the user's default font size.

You can also use CSS to specify a fixed size, such as 12-point. You can even use CSS to dictate the space between lines of text, as in Figure 4.7. See the CSS guide on *curriculumwebs.com* for details.

There are a few pitfalls in the use of font faces that novice designers often fall into.

- AVOID SENTENCES IN UPPERCASE LETTERS BECAUSE THEY ARE DIFFICULT TO READ. People read not by looking at each letter in a word, but by recognizing entire groups of letters as complete words by the shape. Because all uppercase text has the same shape, the human eye has trouble picking out the words. It is fine for headlines, but not for more than a few words at a time.
- **Avoid overuse of bold or italic text.** These are used to draw the eye to *certain* words within a text block. If you want a whole text block to stand out, use another method of attracting the reader's attention, such as placing it inside a table with a visible border.

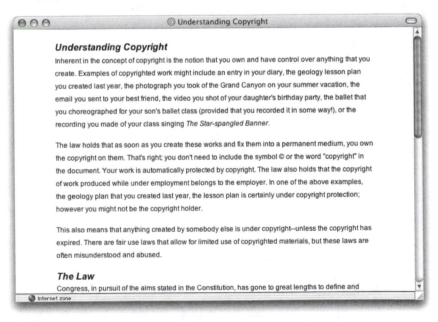

FIGURE 4.7 **The web page shown in Figure 4.1 and Figure 4.2, with font formatting added.**

Headings

Headings are typically rendered in heavier, larger letters than the text block that they introduce. They are also offset from the text block by some vertical white space. There are three primary methods of creating text headings for a web page:

- HTML provides six levels of headings, ranging from `<H1> . . . </H1>` through `<H6> . . . </H6>` tags (with `H1` providing the largest and `H6` the smallest heading). These tags provide the vertical white space for you, as they are put on their own line with white space before and after. The amount of this white space depends on the size of the heading. This works well, unless the white space is either too large or too small for your liking.
- Use the `<FONT>` tag to increase the size of text in a heading. This, combined with the `<B>` tag, which bolds the text, can create a heading more pleasing to the eye. In addition, the `<FONT>` tag can be used to specify a different font face and/or color for the heading, which further serves to draw the user's eye to it. You will need to offset this heading vertically from the text block by the use of a `<P>` or `<BR>` tag.
- Graphics that contain text are another popular method for creating headings. In that case, the vertical white space can be included in the graphic and can be made exactly as tall as you wish. In addition, you can use a different font face and color, and you don't have to worry about whether the font is available on the user's computer.

ACTIVITY 4B ■ **Formatting Your Teaching Guide**

Choose appropriate background, text colors, and font choices for your draft teaching guide. Implement your color choices on your web page. Use white space, text headings, or horizontal dividers to separate the elements of your guide. Specific instructions for how to do this in your particular software are contained in Hands-On Lesson 4 at *curriculumwebs.com.*

Hypertext

When surfing the Web you have surely encountered both pictures and text that you could click on to take you to another web page. Links are popularly implemented with buttons, which are graphics that usually have words included. Graphic links can be eye-catching, and consistent color schemes can make the navigation scheme easier to use. (See the next section for more about graphical links.) However, text links are more easily edited and updated when you expand or update your curriculum web, while redoing all your graphics can be a tedious task.

Hypertext is easily created within web-page editors. In HTML, the `<A>` tag is used to create hypertext by specifying exactly which file is to be opened when the user clicks on the text.

For example, the tag

```
<A HREF="activity1.html">Activity 1: Mapping</A>
```

will create a hyperlink of the text "Activity 1: Mapping" that will take the user to the file activity1.html.

Here is another example:

```
Click <A HREF="activity1.html"> here </A> to go to the
first activity.
```

The web page that is linked to by hypertext does not always have to appear in the same browser window as the original page; you can specify that a new browser window should be created. The TARGET attribute names the window or frame that is to display the web page that is linked to. If a window with that name is already open, the web page will be shown in that window; otherwise a new window will be created.

The examples above assume that activity1.html is in the same folder as the current document. If it is not, you'll have to include the path name in the link. For example,

- for files in "parent" folder (the folder that contains the folder that holds the current page), precede filename with ../
- for files in another subfolder of the parent, use ../anotherfolder/anotherfile.htm

See the Appendix (An Overview of Web Technologies) for more information about path names.

Named anchors are used to create links that lead the user to a new place within the same web page. To implement this, two <A> tags are needed: one for the link and one for the destination (known as a **named anchor**). In the following example, the text "See the prerequisites" is a link to an anchor named "prereqs" that is defined elsewhere in the page.

```
<A HREF="#prereqs">See the prerequisites</A>
```

and elsewhere in the web page is the link's destination:

```
<A NAME="prereqs">Prerequisites</A>
```

Notice that the attributes of the two <A> tags are different. The first represents a link *from* the text "See the prerequisites," while the second is a link *to* the word "Prerequisites." This is sometimes confusing for new web-page designers. Also, note that the named anchor is referenced in the first <A> tag with a number sign (#). The number sign indicates that this is a named anchor within the page, rather than a link to a different page.

One common use of this technique is to create a table of contents, or menu, at the top of a web page. (See Figure 4.6 for an example.) The <A> tags in the menu use the HREF attribute to point to named anchors that are defined (using the NAME attribute) at the appropriate points in the page.

Graphical Links

Buttons are **clickable** images that link to another web page. Their use is very popular on web pages, as they help define a consistent look and feel to web sites. To implement an image as a link, simply enclose an <IMG> tag within the <A> tag:

```
<A HREF="activity1.html"><IMG SRC="button1.gif"></A>
```

Other image topics, such as rollover buttons that visually change as the user points to them with the mouse pointer, are discussed in the Hands-On Lessons that are found at *curriculumwebs.com.*

Buttons create problems for users who browse the Web with a text-based browser or who have disabled graphics loading so that web pages load faster. Using the ALT attribute within the <IMG> tag for a button will help these users navigate your web site.

ACTIVITY 4C ■ Creating a Table of Contents

Use named anchors to create a table of contents at the top of your draft teaching guide web page. The specific techniques for doing this with your particular software are found in Hands-On Lesson 4 at *curriculumwebs.com.*

MAKING ACCESSIBLE PAGES

Normal use of a web site assumes that users have certain abilities or skills, including the ability to see, read, use a mouse or other pointing device and a graphical user interface, understand the language in which the site is written, and use a browser capable of interpreting the site's content. Some of these limitations can be overcome by supplying new hardware or software; however, often people have special needs that cannot be easily solved. These needs can, however, be met to some extent by designing web pages with these users in mind.

The Center for Applied Special Technology (CAST) helps to ensure that web sites are accessible by people with disabilities. CAST has developed a concept known as Universal Design for Learning (UDL), which suggests that the best way to develop web sites, curriculum, or assessments is to design for the widest possible base of users. UDL makes four basic assumptions about design: first, people with special needs are seen to be on a continuum of learner differences rather than constituting a separate category of user; second, teachers should continually adjust their activities for all learners, whether the learners have special needs or more common ones; third, that curriculum materials should be varied and should include digital and online resources and not just traditional textbooks; fourth, that the responsibility for adjustment lies with the curriculum developer and not the individual learner. As stated on CAST's web site:

> The central practical premise of UDL is that a curriculum should include alternatives to make it accessible and appropriate for individuals with different backgrounds, learning styles, abilities, and disabilities in widely varied learning contexts. The "universal" in universal design does not imply one optimal solution for everyone. Rather, it reflects an awareness of the unique nature of each learner and the need to accommodate differences, creating learning experiences that suit the learner and maximize his or her ability to progress. (*http://cast.org/udl*, last accessed October 2004)

UDL suggests that effective curriculums should include activities that challenge a wide variety of capacities, across the range of multiple intelligences. Digital and Web technologies have the potential to radically increase the range of learning activities and therefore are seen as allies in CAST's efforts.

CAST has developed some important tools to help open access to learning to as wide a population as possible. One example is CAST eReader, which is software used to provide text-to-speech conversion so that those with visual disabilities can access the Web or other digital documents. Another CAST-developed tool is "Bobby," a technology for checking web pages for accessibility. Bobby looks for many different types of design elements in web pages. Some examples include:

- For any nontext information (such as that conveyed by images, video, sound, or animation), include the text equivalent for this information.
- All images should have `ALT` text attributes, for example `<IMG SRC= wolfeel.jpg ALT="Picture of a wolf eel">`. (Doodads and other insignificant images should still have the `ALT` attribute, but set to null, or "" to indicate that no information is conveyed.)
- Be sure that the foreground (text) color contrasts well with the background color.
- Use headings in the hierarchy they were designed for, with `<H1>` as the highest and `<H6>` as the lowest level of heading, so that the headings form a logical outline of the content.
- Include a table of contents or easily accessible site map in your curriculum web.
- The navigation structure and tools should be consistent and easy to use.
- Any use of color to convey information (such as color-coded text) requires the use of another means to convey that same information.
- Each page should include a `META` description tag, for example: `<META DESCRIPTION="This web site provides supplemental information to support the book Curriculum Webs by Craig A. Cunningham and Marty Billingsley">`.
- Links should have descriptive TITLE attributes in anchor tags, for example: `<A HREF="http://curriculumwebs.com" title="Companion web site for Curriculum Webs">curriculumwebs.com<A>`.

Bobby is now maintained by Watchfire, a for-profit company that provides a free tool for checking individual web pages. Teachers who want to increase the accessibility of their curriculum webs are urged to find out more about Bobby—and to test their pages for compliance—by visiting *bobby.watchfire.com*.

Chapter Summary
. . . .

This chapter:

- Explains basic HTML tags and CSSs and how you can use them to build the pages in your curriculum web
- Catalogues and explains the elements of good design you should use when you create the pages in your curriculum web
- Discusses ways to make your web pages more accessible for learners with special needs

Questions For Reflection

Use *google.com* or another search engine to explore at least 20 web pages related to a topic of your choice. Pay attention to the page design. Make a list of things you see that you like, and things you see that you don't like, on each page you visit. Categorize the two lists of likes and dislikes. Do your categories relate to the design principles discussed in this chapter? Is so, how? Are there categories that do not appear in this chapter? Check this book's index to see if we cover them elsewhere.

Make a list of your own principles for good web-page design, including what you have read here and discovered as you looked at web pages. Feel free to share these with us at *curriculumwebs.com*.

Your Next Step

Download Hands-On Lesson 4, which shows you how to use your particular software to implement the techniques discussed in this chapter.

The next step in developing your curriculum web is to choose the learning activities you want your learners to do in order to meet the goals that you have developed. This very important step is the topic of Chapter Five.

For Further Learning

- See *curriculumwebs.com* for some links pertinent to the topics in this chapter.
- Musciano and Kennedy 2002 is a complete reference manual for HTML. Spainhour and Eckstein 2002 is an easy-to-use reference. You can also use our reference guide found at *curriculumwebs.com*.
- Siegel 1997 includes an excellent discussion of web-page layout and implementation.
- For more layout ideas, although in a commercial environment, see Sather et al. 1997 and Harris and Zee 2002.
- The best book on CSS is Meyer 2002. Another useful resource is Lie 2005. You can also find helpful tutorials at *wdvl.com*.

CHAPTER 5

CHOOSING LEARNING ACTIVITIES

Overview

This chapter focuses on selecting learning activities that will help learners to achieve learning objectives. It discusses the complexity of learning, the importance of individualizing or differentiating the curriculum to meet diverse learning needs, some reasons for—and approaches to—grouping learners, and some criteria you should use when selecting learning activities. It also provides several useful lists of ideas for learning activities and for the kinds of products that can result from learning activities.

THE COMPLEXITY OF LEARNING

We know that to learn anything, learners have to *do* something. This is because human beings are organic, and molecules have to actually move for the brain or body to change and grow. But the choice of activity is not always easy. Not only should activities lead to the desired outcomes, but they should also be engaging and meaningful in their own right. Also, the choice of activity will be influenced by the resources available, the particular needs of your audience, and by such situational factors as time and the number and type of computers.

Sometimes, deciding what the students should do is a straightforward process. Many learning objectives are met by *having students engage in the skill being taught*. For example, to learn how to use a hammer, the student probably has to use a hammer, bending a few nails (and hitting a few thumbs) in the process. Similarly, to learn how to solve word problems, a student probably has to solve some word problems, breaking a few pencil points along the way.

But, of course, learning is not always that simple. Even the most basic of tasks are best learned not simply by jumping in and doing the task itself, but by doing some other activity, often in preparation for learning to do the task, or perhaps as an ongoing complement to the task itself. It is not usually enough just to do what is being learned. In addition to swinging the hammer, for example, the learner must also first observe someone else hammering. The teacher may not only show the learner how to hammer but also how to hold the hammer, how to hold the nail, and how to stand. The instruction often includes comments about common mistakes, safety, or the importance of good tools. As the learner gains basic skills, the activities may be extended to include a variety of hammers, nails, or woods. If the learner desires to truly master hammering, he or she needs to participate in a wide range of hammering situations. Thus the apprentice becomes a journeyperson and eventually a master craftsperson. Similarly, for students to learn how to use a web browser or to search the Web, they need to use these tools first in simple tasks, and then in increasingly more complex tasks. This strategy of progressive difficulty ensures that students continue to grow through their participation.

Some skills, like reading or Web searching, are best learned when they are broken down into smaller steps that are easier to master. **Task analysis** is the process of dividing a task into the specific individual steps necessary for completing the task (Merrill 1987). This is an essential part of planning for the teaching of very complex procedures or techniques. But not every complex task is just a matter of mastering a sequence of more simple steps. Some tasks, such as painting a picture, composing a poem, understanding the causes of historical events, or producing an effective curriculum web, require both the perfection of individual skills and experience with larger integrative processes that can only be mastered through participation in the whole. In general, learning activities should move from the simpler to the more complex; sometimes, starting with a simplified version of the entire process provides the sense of the whole that motivates learners to push through more difficult tasks in anticipation of being able to put it all together. (This is why, in Chapter Two, we started teaching about curriculum webs by providing a sense of what a whole but simple one looks like.)

The organization of learning activities into an effective learning sequence is generally the responsibility of the curriculum developer or teacher. Because of the complexity of learning and of curriculum planning, we can provide no step-by-step recipe for curriculum developers to follow to identify the learning activity or sequence of activities that will best lead to any given learning objective. Rather, we can attempt to provide general principles that apply in a wide variety of situations as well as numerous examples. It will be up to the curriculum developer or teacher to decide how these principles and examples apply in any specific learning situation. An effective teacher or curriculum developer will continually reflect on his or her choices—and actually observe some learners using the curriculum web—in order to improve the sequencing and, where necessary, provide additional resources or supports along the way.

One very important issue to consider when planning for learning is whether to utilize a **direct instruction** or **inquiry-based learning** approach. Direct instruction involves presenting information or describing skills for students to absorb, often through repeated practice with more and more complex problems. Inquiry-based learning (also known as constructivist teaching) engages students in more open-ended activities as a way of generating their own learning. When learning is based on inquiry, students are not given information as an end in itself, but are guided in a process of asking questions and conducting investigations to figure things out for themselves. Unlike in most school assignments, where learning culminates in separate assessments, inquiry culminates in a real resolution of the problem or situation, meaning that assessment is often more authentic (Cunningham 2003).

Roblyer (2004) provides a useful guide to helping to decide whether direct or inquiry-based methods are more appropriate in a particular teaching and learning situation. Direct instruction is better when learners do not need additional motivation in order to learn something, when they have little experience in the topic and need to acquire basic understanding or skills, and when the subject matter is very well defined and organized. Inquiry-based learning is better when students do not necessarily understand how the skills or knowledge can be applied in real situations, when they have some prior experience with the subject matter, or when the subject matter is only vaguely defined or poorly organized. For many topics, a combination of direct instruction with inquiry-based learning may be the most appropriate.

No matter what the learning situation or instructional approach, there are certain issues of instructional planning that are likely to present a challenge to the curriculum developer. These include curriculum **differentiation** or individualization to account for diverse interests or learning styles, **grouping** learners to facilitate different kinds of learning activities, choosing activities from among those likely to lead to learning objectives, selecting resources to be provided for each activity, and **sequencing** of activities so that they build toward learning objectives. We will discuss each of these issues in turn. By the time you complete this chapter, you will be ready to work on the instructional plan for your curriculum web.

DIFFERENTIATING THE CURRICULUM

Curriculum differentiation refers to the process of structuring a curriculum to provide different learning experiences for each learner or group of learners. A curriculum that asks each learner to use the same resources to complete the same tasks in the same order and at the same time is *un*differentiated. A curriculum that is structured to allow each student to pursue his or her own path toward shared learning objectives is highly differentiated. (Differentiated curriculums that allow each learner to pursue his or her *own* learning objectives rather than shared ones are said to be highly "individualized.")

Schools tend to differentiate curriculum either by dividing students into groups according to previous academic performance (a process known as "tracking") or by allowing students to choose their own courses. Differentiation *within* courses is more difficult, because teachers are expected to guide the learning of many students at once, and traditional methods of whole-group instruction do not allow for much differentiation. In large classes using traditional media (such as textbooks, chalkboards, and worksheets), where the differences between students are not significant, it is not only easier for the teacher to have every student follow the same curriculum but often effective as well. The fact that some students may actually differ in their needs, interests, or learning styles is either ignored or treated as a problem for school administrators, rather than teachers, to solve.

With the availability of **computerized** learning environments and the Web, curriculum differentiation has become easier within classrooms (provided that computers are available). Curriculum webs can be designed to allow for multiple pathways for learning, resulting in more appropriate activities or resources for each learner. Students can be encouraged to reflect on their own needs and desires, and to choose relevant activities rather than feel as if their individuality has to be set aside. While complete differentiation may not be necessary in most school settings—given the extent to which students of similar age and prior experiences often share the same interests and needs—building in strategies to allow for student choice or to respond to student differences is likely to result in better engagement in learning and better outcomes even in classes that have been carefully selected to ensure similarities among students.

It may be tempting to treat the Web as if it were a giant learning arena, in which students are urged to look around, explore, and learn, without much direction or attention to the relationship between these explorations and desired learning outcomes. This would result in a completely open curriculum—one that is highly differentiated—but would mean that any sense of standards or shared learning objectives would be lost. The other extreme is to use the Web as if it were a traditional textbook, saying something like, "Okay, children, point your web browser to page *blah.blah.org* and start reading the passage. When you are done, click on the link at the bottom of the page and answer the questions." While this activity may foster desired outcomes in all of the students, it may also alienate them, and will certainly miss opportunities for healthy individualization, collaborative division of labor, or open-ended tasks that lead to creativity and serendipitous discoveries.

One strategy for differentiating the curriculum is to allow the learners to choose what is important or interesting, perhaps from a previously constructed list of possibilities. Another approach is to negotiate topics among teacher and students, with the teacher always seeking to help the learners grow in understanding and skill no matter what the subject. Teachers who use this approach may see themselves as facilitators of the student's own learning plan, rather than arbiters of the official curriculum. Teachers in such roles may develop curriculum webs specifically for the self-designed learning of a student or groups of students. This approach is sometimes referred to as "demand-driven" education. When student demands are the basis of curriculum, teaching becomes in part the intelligent provision of learning opportunities to students as the students ask for them (Bastiaens and Martens 2000). While such approaches may seem foolish to educators who believe that all students must master a common set of skills and knowledge, they seem much more appropriate in preschool and graduate school situations, and should be considered for some situations involving grade-school students as well. Indeed, building in student choices in some curriculum units is likely to build motivation that will spill over into those units that "just have to be done" by all students.

A happy medium between directing every move the students make in a classroom and allowing the students unlimited freedom in determining the direction of their learning is to construct curriculum webs that provide multiple pathways to learning, along with guidance to help the learner choose among the pathways. Sometimes the teacher will want to dictate which path a particular learner should take, based on a needs assessment or other predictor of how the student will respond to various challenges. This can be as simple as saying, "Okay, those of you who got B's or better on the quiz open *thispage.edu* and those of you who got less than a B open *thatpage.edu*, and follow the instructions you find," or it may be as complex as allowing students to work their way through a complicated hypertext web space at their own pace, perhaps producing products meeting shared criteria as they work.

Allowing students to work at their own pace raises the possibility, of course, that some students will finish very quickly. Then what? The graded structure of most contemporary schools is based on the idea that groups of children can learn more or less the same things in more or less the same amount of time. If teachers open up the possibility of students working through materials at their own rate, some students will outpace the group and even get to the "end" of a grade-level curriculum before the other students. One solution is for curriculum developers to build enrichment and remediation activities into their curriculum webs, knowing that only some students will need them but certain that for those students these activities may be the key to successfully reaching the learning objectives. Students can be asked to complete a preassessment activity and, based on the results, directed either to brush up on prior concepts or skills or skip through certain activities to get to those that are more appropriate. Enrichment activities need not be spelled out entirely, but can include only a suggestion or guiding question, with a list of resources that can serve as a starting point.

Another long-term strategy for differentiation is to start out with a curriculum web that is relatively undifferentiated, and then gradually add choices and multiple pathways as you see how different learners respond to the activities you have developed. Because it is easy to change or add to your curriculum web after it is initially constructed, you can add activities and pathways later, as it becomes clear that its effectiveness can be increased in that way. This approach relies on one of the great features of curriculum webs—as opposed to textbooks—as a primary means to deliver curriculum to students: they are very easy to modify as the teacher or curriculum developer gains new insights into the audience, new resources, or alternative approaches.

A valuable tool for planning your curriculum is to construct a visual representation of the path that learners will take through the curriculum web. This representation can be quite simple, or can involve elaborate detail, depending on how complicated your curriculum web's learning activities or differentiation strategies become. We have constructed a set of sample diagrams that can inspire you as you create your own.

The least differentiated curriculum will be one that provides for one learning path for all learners, without any means to determine whether this one path is appropriate. Such a curriculum could be represented visually with a diagram like that shown in Figure 5.1. Every learner would enter at the same point, and complete the activities, or challenges, in the same order. A slightly differentiated learning path is shown in Figure 5.2. In this curriculum, learners will follow different paths depending on how they perform in a preassessment activity.

FIGURE 5.1   An undifferentiated learning path.

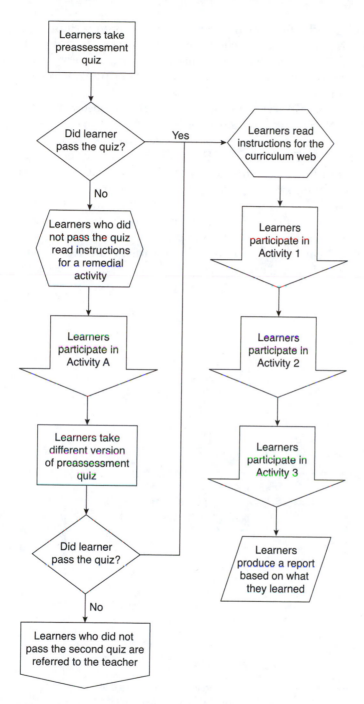

FIGURE 5.2   A learning path with two paths based on the results of a preassessment.

The learning path of a more differentiated curriculum is shown in Figure 5.3. This curriculum expects learners to chart their path based on the information generated during the initial set of activities. The final assessment may vary depending on the topics selected, but will assess whether the same shared learning objectives have been met for each student.

There is one more aspect of curriculum differentiation that deserves mention. The choice of alternative pathways need not be determined by the results of a prior assessment of the learner's needs in terms of knowledge or skill, but could be a result of other characteristics. The "Who Am I?" curriculum web, for example, envisions a similar learning path for all students, but includes differentiation in several respects. Because the focus of the curriculum's subject matter is the learner, the learning activities vary according to differential characteristics of the student. One activity varies based on whether the learner is male or female. This is because many issues and resources relevant to girls would not be interesting or useful to boys, and vice versa. The "Who Am I?" curriculum web also allows learners to select resources at each stage based on their ethnic and cultural background and on their career interests.

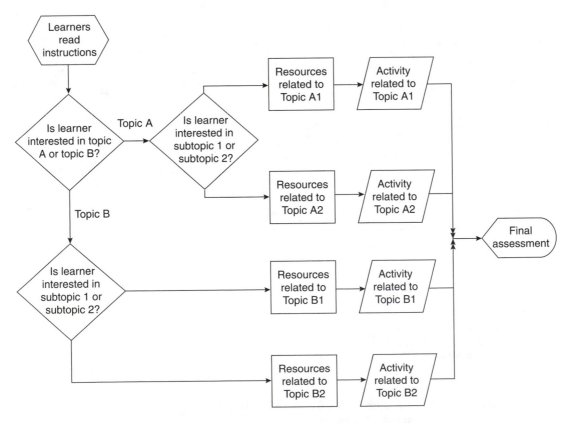

FIGURE 5.3   A complicated learning path in a differentiated curriculum.

ACTIVITY 5A ■ **Considering Curriculum Differentiation** _____

Reflect on the learner description you wrote for Activity 3B. Are there differences within the group of learners that might suggest that differentiating your curriculum web is a good idea? What about their interests, prior experiences, or learning styles might be better served by allowing for learner choice? Be careful if your conclusion is that no differentiation is necessary. It is rare that a group of learners will be homogenous enough to warrant an undifferentiated learning path.

GROUPING LEARNERS

Grouping refers to the process of structuring curriculums so that learners work together. It is important to consider grouping strategies early during the development of your curriculum plan. It is not easy, nor often effective, to add grouping onto an activity that was designed for individuals. Grouping affects the range of activities that are possible, the ways in which preassessment activities can be used to structure participation, and the products that will result from learning activities.

There are essentially three options for grouping learners. The first is no grouping at all: having each of your learners work independently. The second is small groups of students that work together and produce shared products. The third is to structure the activity so that the entire class works together. You can mix and match these options, so that learners are sometimes working independently and at other times working together.

An important consideration is how to place your learners into groups. Learners can be grouped by ability, so that all the fast learners or better-prepared learners work together, and all the slower or less well-prepared learners work together. This allows each group to find its own pace. Or learners can be grouped by interest, for example, by having all the learners who want to write a play based on Lincoln's assassination work together while all the learners who want to write a play based on the Confederacy's surrender at Appommatox can work on that. Another way to group learners is to create mixed ability groups, so that each group has strong readers as well as slower readers, or those who are skillful at using the computer along with neophytes. This grouping strategy is often called **cooperative learning.** Many teachers find that this is the best strategy for ensuring that all the groups reach the learning objectives, and also for fostering a sense of community in the classroom. The key to having learners work together is to create a sense of interdependence so that the success of the group in reaching its goal is seen to be identical with the success of each of the members: they "sink or swim together."

Grouping can involve some competition, for example, having each group of students trying to be the first to find a solution to a problem. Competition often results in high levels of engagement by the more competitive students in the class, but also results in the disengagement of students who either dislike competitive pressures or do not have the skills or knowledge to be able to compete on certain kinds of tasks. It is also possible to combine competition with cooperation, for example by having the groups compete to see which one works together most effectively. Many students are familiar with competition, whether through participation in games, sports, or such academic competitions such as spelling bees. Cooperation is more alien to some, and these students will need explicit instructions in how to cooperate with one another. Cooperation involves actively listening to others, contributing to group discussions and decision making, praising team members for their efforts, restating the ideas of others or summarizing the results of group discussions, taking turns, resolving conflicts, showing leadership as well as "followship," and offering helpful criticism at appropriate points in the process. These are important skills for students to learn, and despite being often ignored by schools they are highly valued within the knowledge economy that many twenty-first-century students will enter when they leave school (CEO Forum 2001).

An effective strategy to increase cooperation within groups is to assign each individual learner a role within a larger team. If a student's role within a group is to plan searching strategies, for example, there would be no reason for that student to try to compete against other members of the group. Additional roles might be the convener of the group, the recorder (who takes notes during group meetings or during search activities), the archivist (who keeps and organizes documents for the group), and the reporter (who makes regular reports to the entire class or to the teacher). Assigning roles within groups still leaves the possibility that the group as a whole may try to compete against other groups, but such competition may be a healthy inducement to successful cooperation within the group. It is not necessary for the teacher to be the one who assigns the roles within the group, and in fact it may be a healthy and educational part of the group process for the group to figure out how to structure its activities. The teacher could then stand by, ready to assign roles if things are not going well within a particular group.

Some advocates of cooperative learning believe that it is important to hold individuals accountable for their contributions to the group. (See, for example, Slavin 1994.) This prevents the problem of a few students carrying the burden of responsibility for a larger group. One way to structure individual accountability is to assess learners on their contributions to the group product, or to ask each learner to produce a by-product of the larger group effort. Group members can be asked to rate each other's contributions to the group, or to reflect on their own contributions. It may be helpful to structure this sort of reflection by having a periodic assignment for the group to assess progress or suggest improvements in group functioning. (See Table 6.2, page 124, for a list of criteria for evaluating participation in cooperative learning groups.)

ACTIVITY 5B ■ Planning For Cooperative Learning

Although you have yet to select the learning activities that your learners will do in your curriculum web, you should now spend some time thinking about whether your learners can be effectively placed into heterogeneous or homogenous groups for the purpose of cooperative learning. Consider the social and cognitive benefits of incorporating teamwork into your learning activities, and the synergy that can result from people finding ways to build off each other's strengths. Consider as well the relative roles that cooperation and competition should play in your curriculum web. Write a short rationale for why grouping (or no grouping) is likely to be the most effective strategy in the case of your learners and your curriculum web.

SELECTING LEARNING ACTIVITIES

Almost any activity can lead to learning. Some are traditionally employed in schools, such as reading, answering questions, writing, solving paper-and-pencil problems, listening to lectures, taking notes, working in small groups, completing projects, studying for tests, and participating in educational games. All of these traditional schooling activities can benefit from extension to the Web.

Learning can also happen during activities that do not typically take place in classrooms. Lots of **extracurricular** activities are educational, such as participating in musical or dance rehearsals and performances, building or making things in a shop, editing a newspaper, or producing radio or TV shows. The fact that many people are actually more engaged in such extracurricular activities than they are in their schoolwork has caused some educational leaders to urge teachers to adopt some nontraditional techniques and roles in the regular curriculum, such as "teacher as coach; student as worker" (Sizer 1992). Extracurricular activities generally have real products or performances that motivate the participant. (See Cunningham and Joseph 2004 for an approach to increasing student engagement in curriculum webs through the use of hands-on projects and performance assessments.)

Other activities are more likely to take place outside of school, including going to a restaurant, walking in a park, participating in a political protest or fundraising walk, and traveling. These activities can also be educational, and the Web makes it possible to bring at least some aspects of these experiences into the classroom. To the extent that this eliminates some of the traditional isolation of school life from life outside of school, the Web has the potential to increase both the relevance and the effectiveness of schooling as an educational institution. However, care must be taken to ensure that you bring into the school that which is educational, and leave the merely entertaining or diverting out.

Criteria for the Reflective Selection of Activities

Given the wide variety of possible learning activities, how does the teacher or curriculum developer decide which activities will best help students to meet learning objectives? Unfortunately, we cannot provide detailed guidance on each case. However, we can present some criteria that provide a starting point for guidance. Of course, specific factors in your given teaching and learning situation should be given priority, and will shape the way these general criteria are applied in each case. As always, reflection that takes account of the real situation faced by learners (and by teachers) is necessary in order to apply general principles to specific decisions.

- *Plan authentic activities.* Authentic learning activities are activities pursued for their own sake, or those that resemble activities engaged in life outside of school. (See Dewey 1985 [1916].) We say an activity is authentic if a person outside of school might pursue it. For example, if we want our students to learn addition, we could either have them do a worksheet containing multiple addition problems (an activity that isn't very much like things we do in real life), or we could run a school store or conduct an inventory of classroom materials (an activity that is certainly authentic and may in fact result in more learning of addition). Similarly, if we want students to understand the process of writing history, it would be good to have them engage in the activities that historians engage in, like interviewing people or analyzing original documents. Authentic activities also generally involve some audience or consumer other than the teacher or the learners, are open-ended in terms of how much time they will take to complete, and often require collaboration among students or with outside experts. Authentic learning activities also often involve problem solving that is more complicated or messy than the typical kinds of problems found in textbooks. Table 5.1 lists additional qualities of authentic problems that may be conducive to learning.

- *Promote self-directed learners.* Self-directed learners manage their own learning by making smart choices about their use of time, subject matter of inquiry, or even criteria of successful learning. Allowing students to make decisions about specific topics or products that are of interest to them, or involving them in determining learning or assessment criteria, fosters self-directed learning skills. You can also encourage students to self-direct their own learning within your curriculum webs by providing access to a wide variety of resources related to any given subject matter or skill, by presenting clear and complete instructions for each activity so that learners are not as dependent on the teacher to tell them what to do at each stage, by letting learners see assessment rubrics and criteria for success before beginning any activity, and by including examples of how a given challenge has been solved by others.

- *Go beyond one subject area.* Real life is not broken down into easily defined chunks of language arts or science. Rather, most real-world situations involve multiple topics or avenues of inquiry. Running a school store, for example, will involve activities related to mathematics, language arts, human relations, and computer use. Similarly, making recommendations to a town planning board about what to do with some empty industrial buildings will bring up subject matter related to

TABLE 5.1   Qualities of Authentic Problems

- It is not always immediately apparent that authentic problems exist in any situation; they have to be recognized and defined before they can be solved. This can be made part of the learning activity.

- Authentic problems rarely come bundled with all the information that is needed to solve them; they require problem solvers to figure out what information is needed and how to find it.

- Authentic problems are defined by and within a particular context, and their solutions are often not applicable beyond the particular situation.

- Authentic problems may have many different possible solutions, or none at all (not every problem is solvable).

- Authentic problems often require interdisciplinary groups of people in order to find a solution.

Source: Adapted from Siegel and Kirkley 1997.

the environment, local history, geography, and budgeting. It is always a good idea to encourage the exploration of cross-disciplinary questions and issues, even when the primary purpose of a curriculum web is to increase knowledge or skills within a defined subject area.

- *Use multiple approaches.* Students differ in terms of what kinds of activity will work best for them. This is because each student has a unique profile of intelligences that determines their learning style or mode (Gardner 1983). Lazear (1991) lists seven intelligences: body/kinesthetic, interpersonal, intrapersonal, logical/mathematical, musical/rhythmic, verbal/linguistic, and visual/spatial. Each intelligence is addressed through different types of activities. If you plan a diverse range of activities that address all types of intelligence, each student will have a greater likelihood of learning. For example, in addition to writing a term paper, it might be helpful to have students prepare an oral presentation, create an artistic representation (such as an original song or painting), or to create a web site about a topic.

- *Go beyond retelling.* The best learning activities go beyond mere retelling of facts (also known as "regurgitation") to include such higher-order activities as compilation, solving a mystery, designing a product or plan, building consensus, persuading, seeking self-knowledge, or making judgments according to predefined or newly created criteria (Dodge 1999). Learners are much more likely to understand what they learn if they actually use the information in a context that has meaning, rather than to merely transfer information from one location (such as a textbook or web site) to another (such as a worksheet). Understanding is much more resilient than memorization. Similarly, if learners are actually interested in what they are learning, and if they have used it in an authentic context, they will be more likely to be able to recall it when it is needed later.

- *Keep it simple.* As a general rule, simpler curriculum designs and web pages are easier for both teachers and students to use. Complex designs may be called for in some circumstances, but when complexity results from lack of planning or foresight, both learners and teachers can get confused and distracted from the aims of the curriculum. Once again, the solution to the problem of overly complex web sites or learning activities is planning, along with careful reflection on what actually happens when learners use the curriculum web. (Having one or more learners work through a curriculum web while it is still under construction can help the developer to spot aspects of the curriculum design that may be too complex or confusing.)

- *Borrow activity ideas from others.* Judi Harris's 1998 book, *Virtual Architecture: Designing and Directing Curriculum-Based Telecomputing*, provides a useful overview of the kinds of activities that are supported by the Web and other forms of telecommunications. She describes a series of what she calls "activity structures" that provide general frameworks for organizing learning across a wide variety of subject areas and learners. Among the activity structures she describes are: interpersonal exchanges such as e-mail pen pals and electronic or virtual appearances by experts or people familiar with historical events (or people pretending to be so); information collection activities such as information exchanges, database creation, and electronic publishing; online field trips; collaborative problem-solving activities such as information searches, treasure hunts, parallel problem solving, and sequential creations; and simulations. Each of these structures can be used to support a wide variety of learning objectives as they share some of the special qualities that distinguish the Web from other media.

■ *Touch imagination.* Learning does not happen only as a result of intellectual activity. If students are given the opportunity to become emotionally involved in wonder, creativity, self-expression, and re-creation, they may be more likely to put energy into a learning activity or to expose themselves to the possibility of failure (Eisner 1985.) Looking for the mystery or excitement in the subject matter can also help get the teacher or curriculum developer more engaged, and therefore willing to put additional effort into making an activity engaging for his or her students. One simple strategy for touching imagination is to figure out how to involve students in the appreciation or creation of art (music, painting, sculpture, creative writing, drama, dance) as part of any curriculum web. Aesthetic experiences often bring nonlinguistic, nonrational, emotional, or sensual aspects of learning topics to the fore, making it easier to care about them and therefore to learn. Such strategies also help to serve multiple intelligences.

■ *Build to promote intentionality.* The key factor in effective higher-order learning activities is that the learners possess *intentionality*; that is, their activities should be conducted with a clear purpose, and any information they access should be necessary to achieve the learner's goals (Jonassen 2000, 177). For example, it is much better to have students use the Web to conduct fact-finding research when those facts are going to be used in a project or presentation, than just to complete a worksheet for the teacher. Having students plan strategies for their own work, rather than simply providing them with a procedure up front, will result in more ownership of the work and better learning results.

■ *Engage the learner.* Make sure that the activities and subject matter are truly interesting to the learner, and that the challenges are appropriate given the learner's current skills, knowledge, and attitudes. Table 5.2 lists indicators of whether a learning activity is likely to engage the learner. Note that engagement means more than just enthusiasm. You can use the various indicators of **engaged learning** to critique your learning activities and modify them to make them more effective, especially for students who are not usually interested in traditional school activities. You'll notice that some indicators listed on the table echo principles we've mentioned before, such as authentic tasks and effective grouping. It is also important to reflect on the entire learning situation, in terms of whether it supports engagement in multiple ways.

■ *Build on controversy.* Consider building curriculum units around controversial or sensitive issues that traditionally are ignored in schools, including issues around changing gender roles, sexual morality, the positive and negative effects of capitalism, the government's role in reducing (and encouraging) crime, the changing nature of civil liberties, or censorship. The Web offers a superb environment for accessing and comparing different views on these topics. By building on controversy, you will be more likely to catch the students' attention, and to help them

TABLE 5.2   Indicators of Engaged Learning

Vision of Learning: Learners are involved in decision making; learners have big picture of subject matter; learners develop a repertoire of thinking/learning strategies; and learners find purpose and meaning in participation in the curriculum.

Tasks: Subject matter and activities pertain to the real world; activities are difficult but not totally frustrating; curriculum integrates or spans disciplines.

Assessment: Involves a performance or demonstration of newly acquired knowledge or skills; assessment activities have meaning for the learner. (See Chapter Six for more on assessment.)

Instructional model: Teacher or program empowers students to action; instruction is oriented to constructing meaning rather than having students regurgitate knowledge or facts.

Learning context: Activities are collaborative; activities bring multiple perspectives that contribute to shared understanding for all; activities go beyond brainstorming to actual construction of solutions or models.

Grouping: Learners work in small groups of different abilities; groups are organized around and for different instructional purposes.

Student Roles: Learners explore new ideas and tools; they are encouraged to teach others; learners develop products of real use to themselves or to others.

Source: Adapted from Jones et al. 1994.

to feel that their work is relevant to the real world. What's more, controversial topics include an element of ideological or cultural conflict—a reality in our global society—that increasingly requires the involvement of experienced and sensitive citizens.

■ *Use characteristics of the Web,* including hypertext, **multimedia,** communication tools, and **interactivity.** Some of these features are new to educators, who may need special assistance in changing their habits to recognize new possibilities. For example, learners can now publish the results of their research on the Web and build in ways to encourage and respond to feedback from outsiders. Such external feedback traditionally has not been part of school-based learning. However, it is certainly a regular aspect of real-world research, where peer review and comment are valuable correctives to bias or methodological errors. Similarly, the availability of online videos for learning opens new opportunities for just-in-time learning (in which learners access videos as they need them in order to complete certain tasks or projects). Teachers and curriculum developers need to be reminded of such possibilities and to practice incorporating them into lessons and curriculum units.

■ *Build activities around current events* or issues that come up in the lives of your learners or the larger community. Current events relate to many topics that appear in the school curriculum, including geography, history, science, literature, and the arts, and can be used to show the relevance of mathematical procedures and concepts. Centering learning activities on current events also increases learners' awareness of their world and prepares them for real-world problem solving. The Web offers numerous resources for responding to current events, from newspaper and network news web sites, to government and foundation sites containing reports and other data, to foreign news sources that can increase learners' awareness of multiple perspectives on the news. One interesting activity is to have students read about a recent event as it is portrayed by several different news or cultural organizations, and attempt to understand the reasons for the different perspectives. Including editorial cartoons as well as video and audio broadcasts—all increasingly available on the Web—adds a multimedia dimension to this activity and is likely to increase the interest of some learners.

- *Use non-Web materials, events, and locations.* Do not use the Web for everything. Learners should spend some time working cooperatively offline or with print materials, with real objects or at significant locations. Indeed, even as the Web exponentially increases the resources available to teachers and learners, it may take attention away from hands-on, real-world experiences that will supplement traditional school materials more than the Web ever will. We suggest including at least one non-Web activity in every curriculum web, just to remind yourself and your learners that, although the world may appear to be increasingly "online," in fact very little of it actually is.

- *Facilitate spontaneity and discovery* by finding the proper balance between teacher control and student freedom. Because your learners are likely to live in a vastly different world than the one in which you grew up, you cannot possibly plan for every learning need that they will experience. Although it is very difficult to plan for serendipitous experiences, it is certainly possible to give students choices that may increase their interest and engagement. If you plan for open-ended inquiry by letting students make choices within a set of educationally sound boundaries, you will increase the likelihood that unexpected ideas or resources will emerge that will lead to memorable and significant learning.

Suggested Learning Activities for the Web

To help you imagine a wide variety of learning activities for the development of your curriculum web, we offer in Table 5.3 a list of suggestions for web-based learning activities that go beyond the traditional activities of school. The table also includes some traditional activities that hold the promise of remaining valuable learning experiences if they are shifted to the Web. In each case, students will probably need to visit a variety of web sites in order to complete the activity. We have suggested some starting points for each of these activities on *curriculumwebs.com*.

Some of the activities we have listed in Table 5.3 may seem too advanced for some students in K–12 schools. Certainly some may be beyond your particular group of learners. However, we urge you to think in terms of what they might be capable of doing if given the chance and the proper **scaffolding.** We think even students in elementary schools will benefit from some of these open-ended or highly challenging activities, provided that teachers have prepared their way by supplying appropriate links to resources and general guidance and supports.

TABLE 5.3   Potentially Engaging Web-Based Activities for Teaching and Learning

- Write a biography of a famous living person, using the Web as a resource.
- Compile a list of lists of seven related things (seven seas, etc.), using the Web as a resource.
- Compile a list of all the names for colors (red, burnt sienna, etc.) that students can find on the Web.
- Research the development of park land in your community, state, or nation. Create a chronology of major events, with specific attention to controversies that have emerged about the parks.
- Use the Web to find out the process for making cheese. Create a web site that shows the differences among different kinds of cheeses.
- Make a list of the 100 most common place names on Earth. Categorize the names according to whether they are named after geographical features, people, or indigenous names.
- List the 50 most important inventions of the twentieth century. Rank them in terms of their importance.
- Describe the Sun relative to all the other stars of the Milky Way, in terms acceptable to professional astronomers.
- Collect as much evidence as you can that shows that global warming results from burning hydrocarbon fuels.
- Compare the Bible to another major religious text or social document, in terms of the moral rules it contains.
- Use the Web to find as many historical maps of the United States (or another country) as you can. Use image-editing software to create an animated GIF or Flash movie that shows the historical development of the country using the maps. (See Chapter Nine for more about the technologies involved.)
- Research a country that you know little about. Create a web site or presentation that describes the country to your classmates or to the students in another grade in your school, or plan the itinerary of a trip there.
- Find out how many languages there are in the world, and what percentage of the Earth's population speaks each language.
- Compare the major causes of death in the United States, Sweden, Russia, China, India, Angola, and Nigeria.
- Chart the world's governments in terms of whether they are democracies, oligarchies, totalitarian dictatorships, or other forms of government.
- Estimate the total mass of all the life forms on Earth. Compare this to the mass of the Earth. Estimate the total mass of all the life forms that have ever lived on Earth.
- Construct a time line showing the development of major forms of entertainment and sport.
- Read the constitutions of at least 10 different countries. Select the best ideas from each and construct an ideal constitution for a country you would like to live in.
- Choose a recreational activity or hobby that you either enjoy or wish to enjoy. Create a web site containing useful information for other people who want to engage in the activity in your community.
- Visit the web sites of 60 major world museums. List the six you would most like to visit. Explain why.
- For each century period since the year 3000 B.C., select the person who was most influential on the daily lives of the people in the world. Create a web site that provides a justification for your selections.
- Explain the relationship between the political philosophies and scientific explorations of Thomas Jefferson, Benjamin Franklin, and Marie Curie (or another group of three multidisciplinary thinkers).

(continued)

TABLE 5.3   Continued

- Look at the web sites of the governments of 40 different countries. Construct a definition of *propaganda* and find examples of propaganda on each web site. Make a list of the countries most likely to use propaganda on their web sites. Is there a relationship between this likelihood and the form of government?

- Make a chart showing in rank order the proportion of public park land to total area in the 50 states in the United States. Explain what you find.

- Write a paper on the changes that have occurred in your state constitution since the state was founded. What changes would you undo if it were up to you? Why?

- Graph the world's population since 3000 B.C. Make an estimate of what the population will be in 100 years, 500 years, 1,000 years, and 3,000 years. Justify your estimates and list the assumptions you have made.

- Research the causes of diabetes (or another disease that has reached epidemic proportions worldwide in recent years). Write a report on how individuals, communities, nations, and the world could work together to reduce the disease's impact.

- Choose a favorite folk tale. (If you don't have a favorite, read some examples and choose one.) Research the folk tale in terms of its standard "tale type," historical roots, similarities to tales found in other cultures, and moral or ethical implications. Create a presentation or web site about your folk tale.

- Create a "family history" web site, complete with genealogy, transcripts of interviews with family members, pictures, and maps.

- Create a web site describing the trends in fashion that are influencing the way the students at your school dress.

- As a class project, construct a web site that teaches the world about your community.

- Come up with a product that can substantially improve the quality of life for a large portion of the world's population. Then develop a web site for the company that will market the product.

- Create a web site in memory of the terrorist attack that occurred on September 11, 2001. Include information about victims and repercussions for daily life.

- Study the history of terrorism and create a list of suggestions for the United Nations that might reduce its occurrence.

- Make a list of the reasons that nations go to war. For each reason, list two or three examples. Conduct a web-based survey of the students in your school as to whether the reasons are legitimate. Create a web site based on the results.

Project-based Learning

Project-based learning (also known as PBL) is an umbrella term for long-term, interdisciplinary, student-centered learning activities that involve authentic tasks and often result in a real-world product. The students have a goal—completing the project or product—that is separate from the grade they will receive, fostering more motivation, more attention to detail, and more pleasure and pride in the result.

The project or product itself should have a purpose beyond the learning. Table 5.4 lists a wide variety of products that can motivate learning activities. You can use this list to brainstorm activities that will help your learners to meet your learning objectives. Each project, product, and performance listed in Table 5.4 can be the object of single learning activity, or can be the end result of a sequence of such learning activities. In this latter case, building the product or preparing the performance becomes the final or

TABLE 5.4   Potential Products of Learning Activities

Web page or web site	Newspaper	Play or drama
Database	Literary magazine	Presentation
PowerPoint slide show	Documentary	Tutorial
Video	Lesson plan	Curriculum web
Audio tape	List	Rank-ordered list
Brochure	Solution to a problem	Recommendation
Poster	Position paper	Academic article
Time line	Career plan	Service learning plan
Exhibition	Portfolio	Vertical file
Scrapbook	Book review	Interview
Book of short stories	Constitution or Bill of Rights	How-to manual
Travel journal or log	Travel plan	Narration
Mural	Survey or report of results	Debate
Comparison	Outline	Concept map
Hypothesis	Prediction	Artistic performance
Song	Editorial	Collage
Reflective essay	Checklist	List of suppliers
List of ingredients	Pie chart	Graph
Diary	Imaginary diary	Business plan
Architectural plan or drawing	Map	Agenda
Procedure	Model	Animation
Bulletin board	Draft legislation	Proposal
Menu	Guest list	FAQ (frequently asked questions) file
Résumé	Response to an essential question	TV commercial

culminating activity of the curriculum, helping to "tie together the varied experiences provided throughout the unit. This facilitates integration and aids the student in organizing his own understanding, attitude, and behavior" (Tyler 1949, 102).

Many of the products listed in Table 5.4 intrinsically have, or at least suggest, an audience. Any curriculum web in which the audience of the learner's work is not the teacher should pay explicit attention to helping the learner to consider the implications of audience for the tone, complexity, and purposes of the product. Such considerations are likely to increase the learner's own understanding of the topics.

Projects created as the culminating activity of a curriculum web can be used to help determine whether learning objectives have been met. Including a rubric or criteria for assessment in the curriculum web can increase student ownership of their learning and can result in much better products as well. See Chapter Six for more about using culminating products for assessment.

ACTIVITY 5C ■ Brainstorming Activities

Write a list of 10 to 20 activities that learners could do that might lead them toward the learning objectives you wrote in Activity 3D. Consider having your learners complete projects, create products, or make presentations. Consider the criteria for selecting learning activities that we have listed in this chapter.

Rank each activity or sequence of activities according to the following criteria:

- How closely does it align with your general educational goals and specific learning objectives, or with any required standardized assessments?
- How engaging is the activity likely to be for your particular learners?

The activities that rank high in both criteria are likely candidates for your curriculum web. You can certainly select more than one learning activity. Are there natural groupings of affinities between the activities near the top of your list, so that the activities could be done in sequence or according to student choice?

Sequencing Learning Activities

Curriculum, as we have defined it, is a plan for a sustained process of teaching and learning. Curriculums differ from lesson plans in that lesson plans generally include only one or at most a few activities, whereas curriculums can include a longer sequence of activities usually taking place over a longer period of time. Organizing these multiple activities so that they build toward complex learning objectives is the focus of this section. There are several common considerations that go into planning how activities within a curriculum will be organized, or how a curriculum unit will fit into the larger curriculum of a class, program, or school (Ornstein and Hunkins 1998). These include scope, articulation, alignment, balance, sequence, and continuity.

Scope refers to the combination of a curriculum unit's breadth (or width) and its depth. Curriculum webs can be very broad (for example, guiding students toward a general understanding of the history of the United States), or very narrow (for example, helping students to understand the causes underlying a particular historical event such as the September 11, 2001, terrorist attack). Decisions about level of detail, variety of subject matter, how much you want the learners to practice what they are learning, and the inclusion of enrichment or review activities all affect the curriculum web's scope. It is important when building your first curriculum web to have a somewhat limited scope. You don't want to get yourself in over your head by planning something that simply cannot be completed in the time you or the students have available. We suggest planning for no more than one or two week's work of activities (assuming a typical class period each day) for your first curriculum web, organized closely around a particular topic, process, or aspect of your learners. You have already considered scope in Chapter Three on identifying goals.

Articulation refers to the ways that different parts of a curriculum interrelate. Vertical articulation concerns the relationship of a given activity or unit to those that come before or after, that is, articulation over time. An example would be the ways that the high school U.S. history course relates to earlier units in middle school. Teachers would benefit from knowing more about the previous educational experiences of their students, simply to avoid the common problem of students thinking that they have learned everything there is to know about the topic in prior grades. Vertical articulation also refers to how experiences early in the school year relate to those that come later. Horizontal articulation concerns the relationship of a unit to other activities taking place at the same time, for example, in another class or subject area. It is important for coherent student learning that the various topics articulate in some way. Grade-level teams of teachers are one means of ensuring horizontal articulation. Schools that combine curriculum webs into a school web as described in Chapter One can make such links explicit (and clickable!).

One aspect of articulation is **continuity,** or the ways that learning activities relate to the concepts and skills introduced in earlier activities. The spiral curriculum, developed initially by Jerome Bruner, represents a metaphor for learning that emphasizes the importance of continuity. Learners do not master an activity the first time they do it. They need to do it over and over. As they master the basics of a new skill, they need to do increasingly difficult activities that provide practice in more nuanced aspects of the skill. Textbook publishers understand this very well, which is why every textbook series used in elementary schools is built on the spiral metaphor. Each year, while some new material is introduced, the bulk of the book reviews skills and concepts introduced in earlier years, usually at a somewhat higher level of difficulty. (One criticism of elementary school curriculum in the United States is that often the "spiral" comes more to resemble a vicious circle in which students forget everything from year to year and have to learn it all over again. The vicious circle is also the result when teachers and curriculum developers pay too little attention to prerequisites. See Schmidt and McKnight 1998.)

Alignment represents the way the curriculum and instruction relate to assessments, especially to standardized tests. Some educational leaders believe that the only curriculum worth teaching is curriculum that is very closely aligned to standardized tests, whereas other leaders believe the intrinsic meaning of any given curriculum is more important than whether it leads to higher test scores. The issue of testing has come to dominate discourse about educational policy in the United States, with the passage and gradual enactment of No Child Left Behind legislation. This legislation, and the ways it has been implemented in the various states, has meant that alignment has become a burning issue for schools and teachers. We believe the best approach to improving alignment is for teachers and test makers to pay close attention to detailed standards that reflect a shared understanding of what should be learned in schools, while schools find ways to empower teachers to develop creative approaches to helping diverse learners reach the standards.

Another issue that has had perhaps less attention recently, but which is perhaps even more important than alignment, is curriculum **balance:** the need to address all aspects of students, including their intellectual, physical, social, emotional, and spiritual dimensions. Standardized tests rarely assess most of these, yet students' social, physical, emotional, and even spiritual needs may be equally or more important to students, parents, and the community. Addressing these needs may be difficult when dealing with large numbers of students or diverse groups. Diversity of social, emotional, physical, or spiritual needs is one reason that some critics have suggested that schools should focus primarily on intellectual development. However, this advice is difficult in situations where other needs interfere with the students' capacity to pay attention to academic concerns. Balance also refers to trying to not overemphasize one or another type of learning activity, for example, writing, reading, memorizing, Web surfing, or preparing for a specific performance or assessment activity. We believe that individual curriculum webs (in addition to the school curriculum as a whole) also should have balance, in both senses of the term.

Sequence refers to how activities build (or do not build) on one another. Effective sequencing takes into account the developmental aspects of learning and also the intrinsic or logical structure of the subject matter. In general, curriculum should progress from the simpler to the more complex, from the concrete to the more abstract, and from the local to the more remote. The influences of subject matter structures are more difficult to generalize. In the "Our United States" curriculum web, for example, students learn how geography relates to economic activities before they attempt to predict one from the other. In "Building a Curriculum Web with Dreamweaver," students learn how to control the elements of page layout before they apply this knowledge to the design of a consistent page format, or template. Discovering the intrinsic or logical sequence of concepts within a curriculum relies largely on experience, having been a learner or a teacher. Someone developing a curriculum web in an unfamiliar area may want to refer to a respected text or web site to get a sense of how others address the issue of sequencing for that particular subject matter.

There are a few different patterns for the sequencing of learning activities. The simplest sequence of activities is a linear one in which activities follow one another in a predetermined order. Figure 5.1 on page 96 shows a very simple linear sequence of activities. Additional types of sequencing are hierarchical and hypertextual.

Hierarchical sequencing moves learners from pages with more general information or instructions to more specific pages. This sequence provides for a variety of pathways, often leaving decisions about sequence to the learner. See Figure 5.4 for a diagram of a hierarchical sequence for a curriculum web about the causes of the Civil War. An example of a hierarchical sequence for learning activities would be a curriculum web that helps people learn how to build curriculum webs, in which an overview of the whole process is supplied on an entry page, with links to more detailed pages about each phase or specific step in the process. This book's table of contents is another example of a hierarchical sequence. While the book carries a linear sequence in the physical ordering of its chapters and pages, the reader can easily use the table of contents to jump to topics of particular interest.

Hypertextual sequencing is a form of sequencing that invites the learner to find his or her own pathway through a curriculum web. An example of hypertextual sequencing is found in Wikipedia, the free encyclopedia at *wikipedia.org* that is built by its users using a unique technology known as a **wiki** that allows any user to add and edit content. Wikipedia includes numerous links among the pages, some leading to more general articles and others leading to more specifics and details. In addition, the site provides an internal search engine and other navigation tools to allow the learner to jump from topic to topic as his or her interests, or whims, dictate. This is not a complete curriculum web in the sense we have been using the term, but a learner can visit and use its links, search engine, and navigation tools to browse through the articles in whatever order makes the most sense to the user. (We are impressed with the possibilities that wikis offer in terms of collaborative learning, particularly as projects that are built by a learning community over a long period of time. More information about wikis can be found on page 216 and in Cunningham and Leuf 2001.)

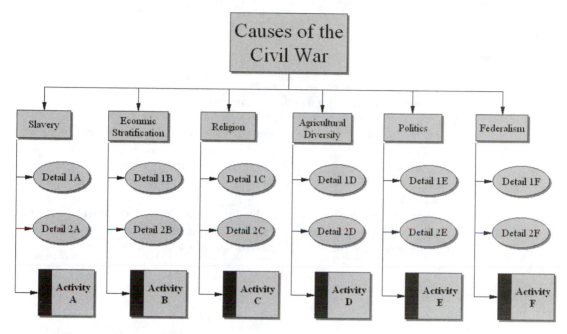

FIGURE 5.4   A hierarchical learning sequence.

Another example of a hypertextual sequence of learning is the index of this book. Learners do not have to read the book linearly, or even chapter by chapter, but can use the index to find what is most of interest to them. We expect that many readers will use the book in this fashion while they are working through the Hands-On Lessons or constructing their own curriculum webs after they have read the book for the first time. Site indexes with links can be included in any curriculum web. This is especially useful for sites full of information or a variety of procedures, or those that are used as a reference tool.

ACTIVITY 5D ■ Thinking About The Sequence of Learning Activities

- Consider the list of learning activities you brainstormed in Activity 5C.
- Among the activities near the top of your ranked list, are there a few that are your favorites in terms of likelihood for meeting your curriculum web's goals and engaging your learners?
- How do the criteria discussed in the previous section—such as scope, articulation, alignment, balance, sequence, and continuity—help you to decide among the activities or suggest a group of them that will work well together?
- What thoughts do you have about sequencing the activities that appeal the most to you? Are there particular reasons that a linear, hierarchical, or hypertextual approach may work best?
- Construct a draft diagram of the possible learning sequence for your curriculum web.

Chapter Summary

This chapter:

- Discusses the complexity of learning
- Describes options for differentiating the curriculum
- Provides some strategies for creating learning groups
- Identifies a set of criteria you should use when selecting learning experiences for your students
- Catalogues an extensive list of potentially engaging Web-based activities for teaching and learning and gives examples of products that can result from learning activities
- Discusses some general issues involved in curriculum development—including scope, articulation, continuity, alignment, balance, and sequence—that might impact the effectiveness of your curriculum web

Questions For Reflection

Traditional curriculums tended to have a linear sequence that predetermined the appropriate order of learning activities. It is easy to imagine curriculum web topics that would also benefit from this traditional sequencing. However, the Web is not really a linear medium. It lends itself to learning pathways in which learning experiences are sequenced in hierarchical or hypertextual ways.

What would be the benefits of structuring a learning pathway for your curriculum that allows for student choice rather than dictating a predetermined sequence of activities? Consider the relative advantages of hierarchical and hypertextual structures. Are there particular topics or foci that would be especially well-suited to these latter forms?

Your Next Step

Download Hands-On Lesson 5, which helps you to learn about some more advanced page-editing features of your particular software.

In Chapter Six, you will finalize your instructional plan and choose assessment activities, in preparation for gathering resources and building your web site in subsequent chapters.

For Further Learning

- See *curriculumwebs.com* for some links pertinent to the topics in this chapter.
- Curriculum organization is discussed in practical terms that can be utilized by teachers by Pratt 1994, Harris 1998, and Eisner 1985.

- *Curriculumwebs.com* provides useful online resources for the activities listed in Table 5.3.
- Useful ideas for creating cooperative learning groups are given by Sharan 1999 and Slavin 1994.
- The general use of the Internet for learning (beyond the World Wide Web) is discussed by Crotchett 1997, Serim and Koch 1996, Leshin 1998, Skomars 1998, Bruce 2003, and Leu, Leu and Coiro 2004.
- Some good examples of web sites useful for young learners are listed by Glavac 1998, Leebow 1999, and Joseph 1999.
- See ISTE 2000a for many examples of learning activities that integrate the use of technology with various subject matter.
- An excellent source of ideas for involving children in the design of web sites is Lachs 2000.

CHAPTER 6

PLANNING INSTRUCTION AND ASSESSMENT

Overview

> This chapter helps you to finalize your curriculum plan and prepare you for designing a curriculum web that will effectively lead learners to the learning objectives. It discusses the instructional aspects of building a curriculum web, how to support learners as they use the web, and alternative ways to assess the learning that results.

PLANNING INSTRUCTION

During the early and mid-twentieth century, some curriculum theorists made a firm distinction between curriculum and instruction, as if they were completely separate activities. Many embraced the view that curriculum is the content of teaching, while instruction is the method. The curriculum developer selects and organizes the content; the teacher decides how to teach that content. This view was never without its critics. John Dewey, for example, maintained throughout his writings that there is no way to separate content and method. For him, education was a process of reorganizing experience so that the experience becomes available as a resource for controlling future experiences (Dewey 1985 [1916]). Curriculum development and instruction are phases in that reorganization of experience, and for them to be relevant and meaningful in the lives of learners, both need to connect with the learner and with the learner's experience in an organic or holistic relationship. (See Tanner and Tanner 1985.)

Even our definition of curriculum as a plan for sustained teaching and learning may be taken to imply that implementation of that plan is someone else's responsibility. According to this view, the curriculum developer writes the curriculum plan, and the teacher instructs or implements that plan. This distinction makes sense when curriculum development and instruction are removed from one another in time and space (as they are, for example, in the production of printed textbooks). However, when teachers build curriculum webs for their learners—and especially when the teachers continue to reflectively improve curriculum webs over time—the distinction between curriculum planning and curriculum implementation breaks down, becoming useful only as a **heuristic** device for understanding the processes involved so they can be effectively learned.

When teachers instruct with a traditional curriculum, they provide all kinds of subtle or implicit assistance to their students to help them learn. Teachers ask leading questions at the beginning of new lessons to help students to relate new subject matter to what they have learned before. Teachers sometimes explicitly describe the learning objectives of a lesson up front in terms that the students can understand. They ask and respond to questions during the class, which helps them to determine if students are "getting it" along the way. They pay attention to students' facial expressions and body language. Whereas teachers using curriculum webs in the classroom will still be able to offer assistance to their learners in person, the developers of curriculum webs need to build as many of these kinds of instructional supports as possible into the web site itself, considering issues of instruction as part and parcel of curriculum planning. The ideal curriculum web will have—already built into it—all of the supports that learners need as they learn with the web. Thus, successful development of curriculum webs requires the developer to be able, to some extent, to "get inside the head" of the learners to be able to predict exactly what the learners will need at each stage in the learning. Indeed, curriculum web developers need to anticipate their learners' needs even more than traditional classroom teachers do.

Examples of Instructional Supports

Bastiaens and Martens (2000) provide a useful overview of how web-based learning activities can be made more instructive. They list a variety of what they call "embedded support devices." These devices support learning and may also help the teacher manage the classroom or assess learning activities—often involved in instruction. Among the many types of embedded support devices, the following are especially relevant to curriculum webs:

- Introductory pages providing overviews or contexts for the curriculum web's subject matter
- Alternative forms of navigation such as drop-down menus and site-specific search engines
- Site indexes or site maps, with links to relevant sections of the curriculum web
- Glossaries or definitions of important terms when they are introduced (perhaps popping up when the user clicks on the terms)
- Review pages describing what the student should have learned at that point in the learning
- Visual organizers such as concept maps in advance of or following more detailed textual descriptions of important information
- Animations or videos supplementing textual information or step-by-step procedures
- Summaries of concepts and procedures at strategic points
- Examples showing possible ways of completing an activity or demonstrating a new concept or procedure
- Opportunities for further exploration of topics when learners want or need them

- Links to external web sites that provide further information or examples
- Estimates of how much work or time an activity should take or strategies for being more time-efficient
- Teaching guides (which may be as useful to self-regulated learners as they are to teachers)
- Lists of additional ways for teachers or learners to get further information or guidance from the curriculum developer if necessary (including e-mail links)
- Questions for reflection or discussion
- Embedded assessments, including self-assessments and rubrics (see page 126)

Scaffolding Learning

John Dewey wrote more than a century ago of the need for teachers to pay "serious attention to what the child *now* needs and is capable of in the way of a rich, valuable, and expanded life" (1976 [1899], 37). Empathizing with the learner's point of view and understanding his or her likely needs will help the curriculum web to appeal to the learner and meet those needs. Nathan Shedroff writes about the same idea in his *Experience Design* where he describes a new field of study called "interaction design," which "specifically focuses on the interactivity between an experience and its audience" (2001, 134). Given that the audience may be diverse in terms of prior experiences, attitudes, and needs—and thus will respond differently to a curriculum web or other experience—interaction design is a complicated endeavor.

Teachers among all professionals are probably the people best situated to understand the ways that learners approach learning activities, and will rely on their personal and professional experience and on continued reflection to help them decide what kinds of instruction and supports are helpful at each stage. The concept of scaffolding is relevant here. Scaffolding is providing assistance for some aspects of the learning activity so that students can focus on other aspects (Grabe and Grabe 2000, 43). For example, younger learners will benefit when the curriculum developer has supplied a short list of relevant links to further information, rather than simply suggesting that the learners conduct a search of the Web. For another example, it may be useful to provide brief summaries of external web sites to help learners decide which available resources will help them the most. For another, you might want to provide access to an online calculator when students need to compute something as part of their learning activities.

Curriculum developers who understand the learner will be able to scaffold challenging activities to maximize learning for all learners. Another useful concept for considering the instructional supports that learners will need is the **zone of proximal development,** which defines the difference between what students can do on their own, and what they can accomplish with support. The best learning activities will be those that are within the zone of proximal development—that is, those that the learners cannot accomplish on their own but can successfully complete with the assistance of the instructional supports and other scaffolding offered in the curriculum web.

ACTIVITY 6A ■ Writing a Plan for Scaffolding Learning

Go back and reread the "Learner Description" you wrote in Activity 3B and the list of activities you brainstormed in Activity 5C. Consider the kinds of learning scaffolds learners may need at the following points:

- When they come to the entry point of the curriculum web for the first time
- When they are beginning to participate in each of the learning activities
- During learning activities
- When they have completed each learning activity
- When they are finished with the learning activities

At each stage, consider the specific supports that you can build into your curriculum web to scaffold learning in your learners' zones of proximal development. Consider at least those instructional supports listed on page 117.

EMBEDDING ASSESSMENT

Traditionally, assessment has also been considered a separate activity from instruction. On this view, instruction takes place first, and then student learning is assessed, usually through an activity designed to find out what students have learned and not necessarily to help them learn, such as formal quizzes, exams, and recitations.

This traditional view has recently come under criticism. Contemporary curriculum theorists argue that assessment is an integral part of learning. (See, for example, Wiggins and McTighe 2000.) Rather that delaying assessment until after learning is finished, this view suggests that learning activities themselves should result in products that demonstrate the desired skills or knowledge. Or, we can ask learners to participate in presentations, demonstrations, or dramatizations; to solve real problems; to design or conduct experiments; to prepare for and participate in debates or fieldwork; or to create portfolios (Ornstein and Hunkins 1998, 339), and assess learning through an evaluation of these products. When the creation of a project or product, or the preparation for a performance is the primary learning activity in curriculum, and when grades are based on whether the product or performance meets specified criteria, assessment is said to be **embedded** in the learning.

Products and performances will be more effective as embedded assessments if they:

- Relate specifically to what was learned during the curriculum
- Have inherent meaning for the student
- Require complex thinking rather than simple regurgitation or self-expression
- Embody standards
- Focus on learning objectives and minimize the effect of skills and knowledge not being assessed

- Are evaluated by multiple observers including the learner him or herself
- Are tied to explicit rubrics or criteria for assessment preferably available to learners in advance (Elliott 1995)

When the products or performances are the kinds of things and events that take place in—or resemble those that take place in—the real world, assessments are said to be **authentic.** The least authentic assessments are those that have no real parallel in the real world, for example, multiple choice exams and pop quizzes. Term papers can be somewhat more authentic, depending upon the particular assignment and context. It may be quite authentic in history class, for example, to ask students to analyze some primary source documents and make some conclusions in a formal paper. More authentic forms of assessment include: having learners make a presentation to a group of community members about a proposed solution to a parking problem; creating a budget for landscaping the front yard of the school; or writing interview question for a class web site on the ethnic and cultural makeup of the community. Artificial assessments such as standardized tests may be important for success in academic environments (especially recently). In the real world of work and community life, however, such skills as resourcefulness, interpersonal skills, information literacy, systems thinking, and how to troubleshoot technologies, and such personal dispositions as responsibility, self-esteem, sociability, self-management, and integrity are crucial. (See U.S. Department of Labor 1991 and CEO Forum 2001.)

Performance Criteria

The first step in designing an embedded or authentic assessment is to define the criteria that will be used to ascertain whether a given project, product, or performance is adequate in light of the curriculum's learning objectives. To do this, you look at the product or performance in relation to each of the goals and objectives you defined during the first phase of curriculum development. For each goal or objective, you state as precisely as you can what evidence of achieving that learning objective is likely to be seen in a successful product or performance. If your learning activities do not include products or performances that constitute embedded assessment, then you need to consider what evidence you will collect *following* the learning activities to determine whether the learning objectives have been met. This involves creating traditional assessments, for example, tests or quizzes.

Performance criteria are not usually difficult to write. For example, one of the learning objectives of "Our United States" is: "Students will be able to use state web sites and other online sources to find basic geographical information about the United States." The product of Mission 1 is for the students to produce a report describing their state or region's geography and economic and recreational activities. This particular learning objective has been met if the report contains basic geographic information about the state or region, and if this information was found on a state web site. Thus a suitable performance criterion could be "Students will include information in their reports that comes from state web sites and from other sites." If the students are asked to include citations in their report, and if those citations show that state web sites were used, then the students have met the learning objective.

The curriculum developer or teacher may want to define several stages or levels of meeting the learning objective. It may be sufficient for the students to include the state's or region's major geographic features, its area in square miles, and some information about the typical climate. To use traditional assessment terminology, this might be considered "passing." But the teacher may want to encourage the students to go into more detail. An exemplary level of meeting the learning objective might be for a student to also include information about the state's or region's river system, annual rainfall, population density, and underlying geological formations. This level may be considered "A" level, or excellent.

For another example, consider this learning objective from "Building a Curriculum Web with Dreamweaver": "Participants will be able to use Dreamweaver to create a template and apply it to a set of pages within a web site." For this objective, it may be sufficient if the participant creates a web site of at least five pages (containing nothing more than placeholder information), creates a template, and applies it to the five pages. This may be considered "passing." A higher level of achievement might involve some of the other learning objectives for the curriculum web. One of these is to "Create a navigation bar with rollover buttons and apply it to a web site." If we combine these two learning objectives, we can state a somewhat higher level of meeting the learning objectives in the performance criterion: "Participants will create a web site of at least five linked pages, and build a template with a navigation bar for those pages, and apply the template to the page." Still higher levels of accomplishment could be easily defined by incorporating additional learning objectives or criteria or by being more demanding as to the size or content of the curriculum web.

As you look at your learning objectives in light of the projects, products, or performances you have built into your learning activities, you will get a sense of the kinds of performance criteria that make sense in light of your learners, the curriculum's prerequisites, and how demanding or challenging the subject matter and learning activities are. It might be possible to encompass all of your learning objectives in one performance criterion; more likely, however, you will define a number of criteria, each defined in terms of levels or stages of accomplishment. By the time you finish with all your learning objectives, you will be ready to wrap them all into an assessment rubric. That is the topic of the next section.

To return for a moment to the situation where you have not built products or performances into your learning activities, writing a test question is similar to writing a performance criterion. For example, if your learning objective is for students to be able to use the periodic table to make predictions about an element's physical or chemical properties and vice versa, you might write a question like: "Element Z is a malleable and ductile metal with a melting point of approximately 960 degrees Celsius and very high thermal and electrical conductivity. What is your best guess as to this element's atomic number? Explain your reasoning." You may consider it good enough for the students to guess that the atomic number is somewhere between 26 and 30, 44 and 48, or 76 and 80. Or you may expect students to pinpoint the correct answer more closely. You need to consider what kind of explanation you are looking for, and define what will satisfy you, again, that the learning objective has been met. (Teachers usually communicate such expectations only implicitly. However, writing the performance criteria down and discussing these criteria with students in advance of the assessment helps them to prepare and gives them more involvement in shaping their own learning.)

ACTIVITY 6B ■ Writing Performance Criteria for Learning Objectives

Performance criteria state what evidence the product or performance must contain to indicate that the learner has achieved a learning objective. For each of the learning objectives you listed in Activity 3D, and each of the products or performances you have built into your learning activities, write a performance criterion. Think about whether individual performance criteria can be combined, and about what levels or stages of accomplishment might be evident.

If you do not have products or performances in your curriculum web but rather are planning to assess learning through a more traditional form of assessment, write test or quiz questions to assess each objective, and for each question, write a performance criterion that you can use to determine if the answer is adequate or excellent.

Using a combination of embedded assessments and more traditional assessments may be the most appropriate choice for more complex curriculum webs involving a large variety of objectives and activities.

Rubrics

To learn the most from a performance or from creating a product, learners need an opportunity to reflect on their performance. Teachers can facilitate this reflection by providing detailed criteria in advance of the learning activity, or by having the learners create their own criteria. By using rubrics, which spell out performance or assessment criteria in detail, the learners can take increasing responsibility for managing their own learning.

Rubrics are a means of communicating expectations to learners in advance of the learning. They state in an organized way the kinds of observable evidence—whether in the form of a product or a performance, or the process that was used to reach the product or performance—that will count toward showing that the student has successfully completed the learning experience. They state, in other words, the performance criteria that will be applied by those responsible for assessing learning. In addition, rubrics define two or more levels of success, such as Unsatisfactory and Satisfactory; or Unacceptable, Emergent, Developing, and Mastery; or Novice, Intermediate, and Expert. These categories imply a pathway of development from beginner to expert, and give learners clues as to what they need to work on in order to increase their facility or understanding. This increases the likelihood that the learners can self-regulate their own learning, by making decisions about what to focus on and what to skim through in order to reach the learning objectives efficiently and effectively.

In WIT, we provide a rubric specifically designed to help evaluate the teaching guides included in participants' curriculum webs. This rubric is reproduced in Table 6.1. (To save space, we've removed the final column, labeled "Comments," from the rubric.) This rubric is used for both self-assessment and peer evaluation of teaching guides. (See

TABLE 6.1   Rubric for Evaluating the Elements of a Teaching Guide

ELEMENT	NOVICE	INTERMEDIATE	EXPERT
Aim	Missing or incomplete	Present but not stated clearly, or does not adequately describe the primary aim of the curriculum web.	Completed, concise and clearly stated aim
Rationale	Missing or incomplete	Present but not stated clearly. Possibly convincing to neutral audiences.	Completed, concise and clearly stated. Likely to be convincing to skeptical audiences.
Learner Description	Missing or incomplete	Present but not stated clearly. Does not include information that might be used to modify use of the curriculum web for other audiences.	Completed, concise and clearly stated. Should differentiate between "basic" and "advanced" participants. Includes ways the module might be altered to suit other participants.
Prerequisites	Missing or incomplete	Present but not clearly stated, or not stated in a way that can be used to conduct a preassessment.	Completed, concise and clearly stated. Includes mention of other modules in WIT where appropriate.
Subject Matter Description	Missing or incomplete	Present but not clearly stated, or stated in vague or general terms.	Completed, concise and clearly stated. Includes outline or concept map of the subject matter.
Learning Objectives	Missing or incomplete	Present but not stated clearly, or given only in general.	Completed, concise and clearly stated goals and objectives presented as a list of the knowledge, skills, and attitudes that learners are expected to achieve.
Instructional Plan	Missing or incomplete	Present but not clearly stated, or not likely to be useful to a teacher who did not participate in the development of the curriculum web.	Complete, concise and clearly stated. Includes information that might be useful to teachers in figuring out how to use the curriculum web. Should include estimate of how long the module will take to complete, and suggestions for how to break it up into parts if it will take more than 50 minutes.
List of Materials and Equipment	Missing or incomplete	Present but not clearly stated, or leaves out substantial actual requirements for use of the curriculum web.	Complete, concise and clearly stated, including computer requirements, and any handouts or noncomputerized materials.
Plan for Assessment	Missing or incomplete	Present but not stated clearly. Does not include performance objectives or rubrics.	Completed, concise and clearly stated. Includes a list of performance assessments or a rubric for assessing products or performances. When the curriculum web does not include

(continued)

TABLE 6.1   Continued

ELEMENT	NOVICE	INTERMEDIATE	EXPERT
			products or performances, includes exam questions and performance criteria for assessing answers to the questions.
Plan for Evaluation	Missing or incomplete	Includes plans for getting feedback from participants.	Includes plans for getting feedback from learners in addition to a plan for collecting assessment data or other feedback from teachers.

Chapter Eleven for more on curriculum web evaluation.) The rubric, like all rubrics, helps the learners to be critical of their own work or the work of others without being personal about it. The person doing the assessment or evaluation can simply say that he or she is applying the rubric.

More complicated performances or products will require more complicated rubrics. Table 6.2 is a rubric that can be used for assessing a learner's contribution to a cooperative learning group. Another approach to assessing the same contributions is shown in Table 6.3. The latter one includes some helpful verbal evidence of each behavior. One option is to have every member of a cooperative learning group assess every member, including themselves, to come up with an average score. Assessments of other types of activities will require different categories. If students give oral

TABLE 6.2   Rubric for Assessing Participation in a Cooperative Learning Group

CATEGORY	BEGINNING	DEVELOPING	FOCUSED	EXCELLENT
		Contribution to Group		
Punctuality	Doesn't hand in assignments	Hands in many assignments late	Hands in most assignments on time	Hands in all assignments on time
Research Information	Does not collect	Contributes little information	Contributes information that mainly relates	Contributes a great deal of relevant information
Shares Information	Keeps information to self and doesn't share with group	Shares some information with the group	Shares important information with the group	Communicates and shares all information with the group
Cooperates with Team Members	Never cooperates	Seldom cooperates	Usually cooperates	Always cooperates

TABLE 6.2   Continued

Cooperation within Group				
Listens to Group Members	Always talks and never allows others to speak	Talks much of the time and rarely allows others to speak	Talks too much at times but usually is a good listener	Balances listening and speaking well
Makes Fair Decisions	Always wants things their way	Often sides with friends and doesn't consider all viewpoints	Usually considers all viewpoints	Total team player
Responsibility to Group Members				
Fulfills Duties	Does not perform any duties	Performs very little in way of duties	Performs nearly all duties	Performs all duties
Shares Responsibility	Always relies on others to do work	Rarely does work— needs constant reminding	Usually does the work—seldom needs reminding	Always does assigned work without being reminded

TABLE 6.3   Another Approach to a Rubric for Assessing Cooperative Learning

NAME: _____

Key: 1 = never 2 = seldom 3 = often 4 = always		1	2	3	4
LOOKS LIKE . . .	**SOUNDS LIKE . . .**				

Encourages others
- smiling
- maintaining eye contact
- signaling thumbs up
- giving a pat on the back
- nodding approval
- giving a "high five"

- Awesome!
- Good job!
- That's excellent!
- Super!
- I like your idea.
- What you've said is great!

Listens attentively
- looking at the speaker
- leaning forward
- concentrating on what is being said
- smiling, nodding approvingly
- using open body language

- Could you tell me more about that?
- only talking when necessary
- avoiding interrupting
- staying on topic

(continued)

TABLE 6.3   Continued

Disagrees in an agreeable way ■ minimizing gestures ■ maintaining eye contact	With a calm, controlled voice: ■ That's a possibility. Would you consider . . . ? ■ I understand your opinion. However, would you . . . ? ■ Yes, I see that. What about looking at it from the point of view that . . . ? ■ I guess we agree to disagree . . .
Summarizes for understanding ■ having eye contact with all group members ■ assuming open body posture	■ So, these are the main points of our discussion . . . ■ Our major ideas seem to be . . . ■ Is what I've said clear? I can repeat if you want me to . . . ■ This is what our main ideas are. Does anyone want to add something?
Criticizes ideas, not person ■ smiling, nodding appropriately as you listen ■ concentrating on statements by other person ■ using open body language ■ looking at the speaker but also at others	■ I don't agree with that idea; would you listen to mine? ■ That is one viewpoint. But what about this idea? ■ Yes, I see that, but would you consider . . . ?

Source: Adapted from *http://www.sasked.gov.sk.ca/docs/health/health1-5/asses.pdf.*

presentations, as they do in the "Who Am I?" curriculum, the rubric will include categories pertaining to organization, research, presentation, and audio or visual aids.

Self-Assessments

Self-assessments are tools that enable students to check their own learning either before they begin working on a curriculum web or to make sure they are ready for a final assessment activity. Self-assessments conducted before the learning activity—known as pre-assessments—can serve multiple purposes. They can (1) indicate that a student has not mastered the prerequisites of the curriculum web, leading to a decision to provide activities to help the student meet the prerequisites before continuing with the curriculum web; (2) indicate that a student has already mastered the learning objectives of the curriculum web, and should probably spend his or her time on something more challenging; (3) help to create a baseline of prior knowledge in order to measure the learning

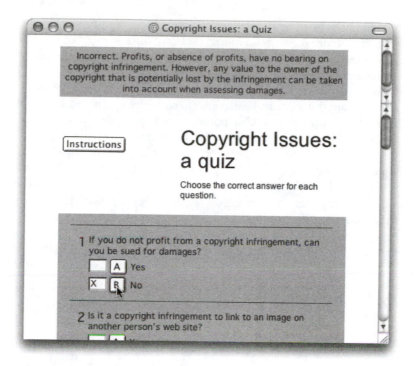

FIGURE 6.1   A sample online quiz in which the user chooses the wrong answer. Feedback is immediately supplied at the top of the window.

that is actually fostered by the curriculum web; or (4) help to organize the students' thinking in advance of the curriculum web, drawing their attention to past learning and bringing it to the forefront of their minds.

Self-assessments can be placed online, providing immediate feedback to the learner or the teacher as to the learner's current understanding or skills. The Web makes it easy to create self-assessments that can be taken at appropriate points in a learning experience. These can range from a single multiple-choice question with the different answers linked to different pages ("Do a feather and an anvil fall at the same rate in a vacuum?" Yes/No), to an e-mail form sent to the instructor containing a checklist of topics the learner believes he or she has mastered, to a multi-question test with automatic scoring such as the one shown in Figure 6.1. While sophisticated online tests may be beyond the technical capabilities of most developers of curriculum webs, a number of web sites provide tools for facilitating their construction. See *curriculumwebs.com* for some examples.

Online Assessments

In addition to including embedded assessments as an integral part of learning activities, curriculum webs can also include more traditional types of assessments. Referred to as **online assessment,** Web-based quizzes and tests often grab the students' attention and have the added bonus of being graded automatically if in a multiple-choice or short-answer format. Figure 6.1 shows a multiple-choice quiz given at the end of a lesson on copyright issues. Feedback is given on both incorrect and correct answers, and the running score is automatically computed (see Figure 6.2).

Online quizzes are often implemented using JavaScript—but you don't have to know much or anything about Javascript; there are programs and web sites that will produce the JavaScript for you. One popular site is *quia.com*, which makes online quiz creation easy, and offers a 30-day free trial. There are also commercially available software packages that can provide schools or universities with many web-based resources, including online assessments. Two of the more popular of these packages are WebCT and Blackboard. Many higher education institutions have contracts with the companies that produce these packages, allowing all faculty access to the tools. More information about these programs is available on *curriculumwebs.com*. However, you do not need to have access to such elaborate packages in order to create engaging and effective online assessments. There are less expensive (even free) tools that can help you with this task. Hot Potatoes, for example, is an easy-to-use suite of programs that is free for use by educators in state-funded institutions. See *halfbakedsoftware.com*.

The HTML for the form shown in Figure 6.1 is too long and complex to review here. There is also no need, as the reader is not expected to be able to reproduce it.

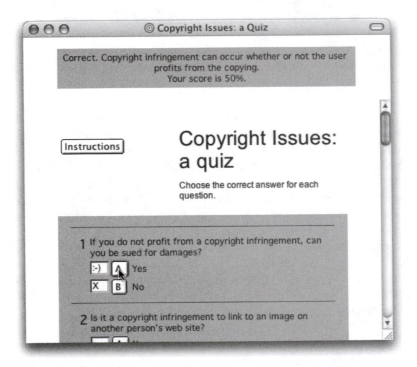

FIGURE 6.2   When the user clicks on the correct answer in the online quiz, feedback is provided and the running score is automatically computed.

INSTRUCTIONAL PLANS

The instructional plan is the heart of the curriculum plan and teaching guide. It serves a function similar to a traditional lesson plan or the teacher's edition of a textbook. The instructional plan should contain everything a teacher will need to successfully utilize your curriculum web with a group of students. It should show how various learning activities in your curriculum web relate to each other chronologically and thematically, and should help teachers and learners to make easy transitions between activities.

Your instructional plan should include:

- Things the teacher may need to do to prepare the students, classroom, or computers in advance of use of the curriculum web
- Suggestions for introducing learners to the curriculum web through classroom discussion or other activities designed to connect the subject matter of the curriculum web to the learners' prior experiences
- Step-by-step instructions for any non-web-based activities or teacher-delivered information necessary to facilitate learning with the curriculum web
- Discussion of how the learners should be grouped for the learning activities
- Ideas for how to organize student time during use of the curriculum web
- Ideas for extending the curriculum web into other activities or providing enrichment or further support for learners who might benefit

Also important in planning is the development of a learning plan. This plan is not an explicit part of the teaching guide but is certainly implied and embodied by the curriculum web itself.

Example Instructional Plans

One example of an instructional plan is found in the IQ WebQuest Teaching Guide found on page 27. We've included two additional instructional plans here and a third one at *curriculumwebs.com*.

"Our United States" Instructional Plan   This module is built on the principles of cooperative learning groups. To read more about cooperative learning, see the following web sites: *(Note: these are omitted from the book version but may be accessed on the companion web site.)*

- Divide your class into four to six groups of 3 to 7 students. Each group becomes a "GeoTeam" that will work on the "Missions" together.
- Discuss issues of division of labor within each GeoTeam. A possible set of assignments could include:

  Team Coordinator: responsible for assigning tasks, conducting meetings, and managing the task of putting final report together
  Recorder: responsible for taking notes during team meetings

Archivist: responsible for maintaining a folder that contains notes, printed information, and lists of resources

Geographic specialist: responsible for understanding and summarizing the region's geographic (physical and environmental) features

Raw materials specialist: responsible for understanding and summarizing the region's raw material situation (both those available within the region and those needed from elsewhere)

Economic specialist: responsible for understanding and summarizing the region's economic activities

Recreational specialist: responsible for understanding and summarizing the region's major recreational activities

(It may be necessary to combine jobs if the groups are small.)

- Assign one U.S. region to each GeoTeam. The regions and the states they contain are listed in a table on the curriculum web site.

The instructions for each Mission in this curriculum can be found on the student pages. We suggest you read through these pages now. In general, the sequence will be:

- GeoTeams work on Mission 1, collecting information about their region. Then each group presents an oral report to the class incorporating the information listed on the student page. Since the URLs of the state web pages may have changed since the curriculum web was prepared, be ready to suggest to the students that they use a search engine such as Yahoo to find the pages. Many states have multiple web sites, and Yahoo is a good place to look for them.
- Then the GeoTeams work on Mission 2, working on the question of to what extent the region is self-sufficient.
- The Trade Conference activity is optional, depending on the time you have available. Appoint or elect one representative from each GeoTeam to work on a Conference Planning Committee to determine rules and procedures. We have purposely left this activity open-ended to encourage the students to design their procedures for the conference.
- Mission 3 involves applying lessons learned so far to make predictions about "Mystery Regions." If you want to know the identity of the mystery regions, please send e-mail to the developer of this curriculum web stating that you are a teacher utilizing the "Our United States" curriculum web in one of your classes.
- The final project for the class could take the form of a web site describing each region and laying out a plan for trade based on the results of the Trade Conference.

"Building a Curriculum Web with Dreamweaver" Instructional Plan.   This module is intended to support the development of a complete curriculum web. The separate lessons of this module are designed to be used in sequence, but may be spread out over a series of days or even weeks.

For each lesson within this module, it is suggested that the mentors demonstrate the techniques described in the module using a projector to show the participants what they are doing, and then have the participants do the activities while mentors circulate and offer help. When everyone has successfully completed the task or activity, then the mentors demonstrate the next set of techniques.

Alternatively, the curriculum web can be used to support learning at the learners' own pace. This requires the learners to read through each lesson on his or her own, and complete the activities involved in the lesson. The mentor can be available to answer specific questions or to provide further suggestions geared to each learner's level and progress through the material.

ACTIVITY 6C ■ Writing Your Instructional Plan

It is now time to write a plan for how your curriculum web will be used in the classroom. It will become part of the teaching guide with the aim of helping teachers to use the curriculum web in their classrooms.

The following questions can help you to create a useful instructional plan:

- Is the instructional plan sufficiently detailed so that a new teacher could implement the module?
- Are additional resources related to the subject matter or learning activities included?
- Are methods built in for linking new knowledge/skills to prior experiences of students?
- Does the plan include an estimate of how much time the curriculum web will take to complete?
- Are suggestions included for breaking up this time if learning activities will take longer than a typical school period?
- Is the grouping of learners discussed in the plan?
- Are links provided in the instructional plan to all relevant web pages, worksheets, rubrics, resources, or external web sites?
- Are strategies included for extending the learning activities to provide enrichment for interested learners?

LISTS OF MATERIALS AND EQUIPMENT

Another section of your teaching guide should list necessary materials and equipment. This is probably the easiest part of the teaching guide to create. You should include:

- A list of the pages of the curriculum web and a description of their function. This could be in the form of a site map or site index
- A list of any worksheets or PDF files that need to be printed and made available to the learners

- A description of the computer hardware and software that will be necessary for students to participate in the curriculum web
- Any print resources, objects, or other materials and supplies necessary to complete the learning activities

Example Lists of Materials and Equipment

One example of a list of materials can be found in the IQ WebQuest Teaching Guide on page 26. We have included the "Our United States" and "Building a Curriculum Web with Dreamweaver" lists of materials and equipment here. Look for the "Who Am I?" list of materials at *curriculumwebs.com*.

"Our United States" List of Materials and Equipment.   The following web pages:

FILENAME	PURPOSE
Index.html	Entry page
Teacherguide.html	Teaching guide
Mission1.html	Provides instructions for learning activity 1, and an image map of the United States linked to official state web site
Mission2.html	Provides instructions for learning activity 2
Tradeconference.html	Provides instructions for the trade conference, an optional activity
Resourcecard.html	A sample of the kind of resource card the participants in the trade conference will produce prior to trading
Mission3.html	Provides instructions for learning activity 3
Region1.html Region2.html Region3.html Region4.html Region5.html Region6.html	Include listings of the available raw materials, major geographical features, climate, transportation issues, and educational level related to each of the six regions: Region 1: Steppesylvania Region 2: Archipelago Region 3: Urbania Region 4: Forest River Region 5: Glacierview Region 6: The Cactus Hills
Regionprediction.html	A worksheet to guide students to making their prediction as part of learning activity 3 about where their region is in the world
Tradeprediction.html	A worksheet to guide students to making their predictions about the kinds of trade that their region will engage in

Links.html	List of links relevant to geographical information about the United States
Glossary.html	List of vocabulary words introduced in the instructions or likely to be encountered while completing the learning activities
Research2.html	A description of the five basic skills
Assessment.html	A rubric for assessing the product of Mission 1

The following printed materials:

- A copy of the region prediction worksheet for each group
- A copy of the trade prediction worksheet for each group
- A copy of the assessment rubric for each group
- Optional: an atlas of the United States

The following computer hardware and software:

- For each group, a computer with access to the Internet, along with a web browser and word processing program
- Access to a printer for the whole class

If only one computer is available for the entire class, these activities will have to be combined with other activities not requiring the computer. Then groups can be cycled through the computer along with outside activities.

"Building a Curriculum Web with Dreamweaver" List of Materials

- An Internet-linked computer lab with one computer per participant (or one to be shared by pairs of participants)
- An instructor station with projector
- Dreamweaver installed on each computer
- One CD containing Dreamweaver for each participant in order to install the software on a home computer (PC or Mac)

ACTIVITY 6D ■ WRITING YOUR LIST OF MATERIALS

Write a list of the materials and equipment that are necessary to use your curriculum web. Include such items as hardware, software, books and other printed materials, tools, paper supplies, worksheets, and web pages. As with the other elements of your curriculum plan, the list of materials is only a draft at this stage; you will want to revise it before you publish it as the teaching guide for your completed curriculum web.

PLANS FOR ASSESSMENT

The plan for assessment should say how the teacher or learner will know whether learning objectives have been met, based on defined performance criteria or exam questions that you have written. If your learning activities involve products or performances (see page 108), you may wish to provide rubrics. If you have included an online quiz or worksheets, these should be described and links provided to the appropriate pages. If there are no embedded assessments, you may want to supply some quiz or exam questions or other suggestions for traditional assessments.

Example Plans for Assessment

One example of a plan for assessment can be found in the IQ WebQuest Teaching Guide on page 27. We have provided only one additional plan for assessment here. Assessment plans for "Our United States" and "Who Am I?," including rubrics for evaluating the products of their learning activities, are available at *curriculumwebs.com*.

"Building a Curriculum Web with Dreamweaver" Plan for Assessment.   Each session will include a "session goal." Activities are included in each session to determine whether the participant has achieved the session goal. Generally, participants will e-mail a URL to the instructor when they have completed each session's activity. Participants who do not achieve the session goal will be encouraged to work on the goals on their own or to seek the help of the instructor or other participants. Participants who have not yet met the "session goal" of any previous sessions will be asked to schedule a time to receive additional help.

ACTIVITY 6E ■ WRITING YOUR PLAN FOR ASSESSMENT

Using the performance criteria or exam questions you defined in Activity 6B, describe how learning will be assessed with your curriculum web. If necessary, create drafts of any rubrics, quizzes, or tests. (These will, of course, likely be revised as you develop your curriculum web further.)

Chapter Summary

This chapter:

- Discusses ways in which web-based learning can be supported
- Introduces several important concepts about assessment
- Provides an overview of self-assessment and alternative assessment through products and performances

- Includes an example of a rubric used to evaluate the product of a learning activity (the creation of a teaching guide in a class on developing curriculum webs) and two examples of rubrics used to evaluate a learner's participation in a cooperative learning group
- Guides you through writing an instructional plan, list of materials and equipment, and a plan for assessment

Questions For Reflection

Think about a time when you learned a very difficult skill or mastered a complex body of knowledge. Think about the instructional supports, materials, performance criteria, and self-assessments that helped you to master the learning objectives. Can any of these supports be helpful to your learners as they progress through your curriculum web?

Your Next Step

Download Hands-On Lesson 6, which guides you to the completion of your draft teaching guide and introduces some specialized procedures that you may choose to use when implementing your instruction and assessment plans.

Now that you have completed your draft teaching guide, you are ready to begin to gather web-based resources and materials that are relevant to your curriculum web. That is the topic of Chapter Seven.

For Further Learning

- See *curriculumwebs.com* for some links pertinent to the topics in this chapter.
- For more about scaffolding activities so they are appropriate for your particular learners, see Lachs 2000, especially chapter 5, "Audience."
- General information about assessment is given by Pratt 1994, Madaus and Kellaghan 1992, and Eisner 1985.
- Web-based assessment techniques and tools are discussed by Cucchiarelli et al. 2000.
- Performance assessment and rubrics are discussed by Wiggins and McTighe 2000, and Arter and McTighe 2000.

A valuable resource for the creation of rubrics is *rubistar.4teachers.org*, which provides a huge number of examples of rubrics, and also helps teachers to create rubrics from predesigned templates or from scratch.

CHAPTER 7

GATHERING WEB-BASED RESOURCES

Overview

This chapter discusses searching, organizing, evaluating, and utilizing existing web resources. Included is an overview of the kinds of materials you will find on the Web, procedures for bookmarking relevant web pages, discussions of search engines and directories, criteria for evaluating resources in terms of their educational appropriateness, and issues of copyright that define ethical behavior for the developers of curriculum webs.

WHY USE EXISTING RESOURCES?

Teachers and learners can find not only ready-made lesson plans and curriculum webs online, but also a whole host of other "raw materials for the mind" (Warlick 1998) that can be used as the basis for new lessons and units: scholarly information, reference materials, chronologies, archives of images, video and audio, maps, art of all kinds, product information, how-to's, advice, and much more. Table 7.1 lists some of the variety of resources you can find on the Web. If you visit *curriculumwebs.com* you can explore examples of each kind of resource listed here.

Preexisting resources on the Web are especially useful for the teacher or curriculum builder, who can access background information about the subject matter being studied or get ideas about real-world problems that may engage the learner. If, for example, a teacher is building a curriculum web on the history of African American migration from the South to the North in the twentieth century, he or she will want to spend some time researching the topic. Such research can be conducted in a traditional library or using the Internet. Information gained from this research can be summarized on a web site, or links to the information can be given to students to guide their own inquiry. Teachers and curriculum developers can also use this information to increase their own understanding of the subject matter, either to improve their capacity to teach effectively or simply because they wish to learn more.

Existing web resources can make the teacher's job as curriculum builder much easier, and also can make the students' task of learning much more engaging and effective. Students are more likely to be interested in creating a graph of population growth in

TABLE 7.1   Types of Resources Available on the Web

Portals
- Search engines
- Directories
- Clearinghouses
- Specialized indexes

Existing lesson plans, WebQuests, and curriculum webs

Data and information
- Government documents
- University documents
- Product information
- Historical data
- News media
- How-to information, manuals
- Maps
- Sites created by hobbyists and fans

Resources for building web sites
- Images
- Backgrounds
- Graphical elements (such as bullets and buttons)
- Sounds
- Animations
- Videos

People/communications
- Friends and acquaintances
- Experts
- Online discussions
- Listservs
- Web discussion forums and chat rooms
- Usenet newsgroups

Chicago during the last 200 years if the data they are using is real data found on the web servers of the U.S. Census Bureau than if they were given the data on a sheet of paper. Students will also be more likely to be able to retain the skills they learn in school if they learn how to find and access data in a real-world form. Similarly, if the students are working on a real-world problem—one that affects them or their families and community directly—they are more likely to find the problem engaging. Rarely is a teacher going to find real-world data about a real-world local problem in a traditional educational textbook, but such data can be found on the Web provided the teacher knows where to look.

Some learning situations call for students to look for relevant information on their own. You may give them some directions, such as: "Conduct a web search for population information on Chicago from 1800 to 2000." Or, perhaps more helpfully: "Use *google.com* to find population information on Chicago from 1800 to 2000. You might want to use search terms such as 'Chicago, population, demographics, historical, census.'" But in some cases a learning objective will be more efficiently met when the teacher finds the resource and weaves it into the curriculum web directly. For example: "Follow this link [link here] to U.S. Census information for Chicago from 1800 to 2000. Use this information to create a graph of population growth in Chicago during that period."

The curriculum developer will also want to consider using raw data in order to build more interesting problems: "Look at the following graph showing the population of Chicago from 1800 to 2000. Notice that there are several inflection points [link to definition of "inflection point" here] in the graph. Use the following links to find historical information that could help you form hypotheses about the causes of these inflection points." The choice of how to use existing raw materials will be determined by the decisions you have made about the purposes of your curriculum unit, the preexisting capabilities of your students, the specific learning objectives, and the learning activities that are likely to lead those students to the desired goals.

Your school's librarian is probably the best place to start when you are considering the use of existing materials. He or she can help you to brainstorm about possible sources of relevant information, will often be willing to do some of the searching for you, and may be specially trained in techniques for integrating technology into your teaching. He or she will also help you to remember that some resources on the Web are protected by copyright law. Teachers should model good practices with their students and avoid even the appearance that they are "stealing" materials that do not belong to them. Copyright issues are dealt with below, beginning on page 153.

ACTIVITY 7A ■ Creating a List of Potential Resources

The strategies described in this chapter can help you to find a needle in the haystack of the Web. But knowing how to conduct an effective search is useless if you have no clear idea of what you are looking for. Your goal in searching for resources will be to find materials that contain information, tutorials, images, data, or opinions that can serve as the content or raw materials for learning activities.

For each of the activities you selected in Activity 5C on page 109, list the kinds of web-based and non-web-based materials that might prove helpful. Use Table 7.1 to help you think of different types. Talk to a librarian to help you extend this list. You will search for some of these resources as you read further in this chapter.

BOOKMARKING FAVORITES

When you search the Web to find resources for a curriculum web, you will find materials that are useful. What do you do when you find them? One approach is to "harvest" the materials when you first encounter them on the Web (Warlick 1998). In this approach, you will read through the pages as you find them, locate the information you want, and then copy that information or notes about that information into a word processor or web-page editor. (Keep in mind that many materials may be copyrighted. To avoid copyright infringement, it might be better to note the URL and other information and then take notes and rewrite in your own words.) Mining or harvesting a web page as soon as you find it is a good idea if you are only looking for a specific piece of information. Once you find what you want, grab it (by copying it to **clipboard** or saving it to a folder on your computer), put or paste it someplace useful in your developing curriculum web, and move on to the next task. (If you do this, be sure to also copy citation information including the page title, authors, date accessed, and URL or web address so you can provide credit to the source.)

HOW TO COPY INFORMATION FROM THE WEB

Web browsers include tools that can help you harvest materials from the Web. For example, you can copy text for pasting immediately into another web page, and you can save images for later inclusion in your curriculum web. (Be sure you have permission before you copy anything from someone else's web site. It is not only unethical but often illegal to copy something you find on the Web. See our discussion of copyright, beginning on page 153.)

To copy text, simply highlight it by clicking and holding the mouse button at the top of the text, and then dragging to the bottom of the text. Once the text is highlighted, you can copy it to the clipboard, an area of the computer's memory that is available for temporary storage of text or images. On a Windows-based machine, the easiest way to copy a selection to the clipboard is by right-clicking on the selection, and choosing "Copy" from the pop-up menu, or simply hold down the Control key and press the "C" key. On a Mac, you can use the Edit menu and select "Copy," or click the selection and hold down the mouse button until the pop-up menu appears; then select "Copy," or hold down the Control key as you click the selection and select "Copy."

Now that the text has been copied to the clipboard, you can switch to your word processor or web-page editor and paste it where you want it. To do that, click with the mouse on the spot where you want to insert the copied text. On a Windows-based machine, right click and choose "Paste" from the pop-up menu or hold down the Control key and press the "V" key. On a Mac, use the Edit menu and select "Paste," or hold down the mouse button and choose "Paste" from the pop-up menu, or hold down the Control key as you click the mouse button and choose "Paste" from the pop-up menu.

You'll notice that when you paste multiple lines of text that have been copied from a web browser, there often will be numerous line breaks in the pasted text. You need to go through and delete the extra line breaks; otherwise the text will look messy when it is eventually viewed on your own web site. If you paste the text into Microsoft Word, you can see the line breaks by turning on paragraph marks. You can do this by clicking the button on the standard tool bar that looks like this: ¶. This will show both paragraph marks and spaces, making it easier to clean up the text.

Copying information from a table is more difficult, because usually the table itself isn't copied along with the text in the table. It might be easier for you to simply save the entire page onto your computer and then edit it in your web-editing software. To save the entire page, use the File menu and choose "Save As . . ." (On a Mac, be sure to save the page as "Source" and not as "Text.") Internet Explorer now includes an option to save a web page, including all of its graphics, into one "web archive" file, with an "*.mht" extension. This will be convenient if you want to view the entire page later while offline or to copy the page (and included graphics) to another disk or location.

(continued)

CONTINUED

To copy an image for later use in your curriculum web, either right-click the image (on a Windows PC) or click the image and hold the button down (on a Mac) or Control-click the image (on a Mac). Then choose "Save image as . . ." (or "Save picture as . . ." or "Download Image to Disk") from the pop-up menu. Choose a folder to save the image into, and give the image a filename that will make sense to you. (Consider whether the original name, such as "ygf003a.jpg," is going to make any sense later!) Do not change the file type from the type suggested by your computer. You cannot save JPEG images as GIFs or vice versa. (See Chapter Nine for more information about images and file types.) Again, keep in mind that much of what you find on the Web may be protected by copyright law.

Creating a List of Bookmarks or Favorites

Harvesting materials as you find them may result in quicker short-term development of a lesson or unit; however, it may be more useful in the long run to bookmark these materials as you find them so you can return to them later or build these links into your curriculum web. Then you will not have to repeat web searches you have made previously when it comes time to build your web pages. Indeed, it is possible to use your list of bookmarks or favorites as the basis for a web page, as you will learn in Hands-On Lesson 7, following this chapter.

Creating a personal list of URLs—called bookmarks or favorites—is easy. Tools are integrated into web browsers for saving them and, perhaps more important, for organizing them for later use. Teachers building curriculum webs should learn how to edit their personal bookmarks or favorites file. Effective use of a bookmark or favorites file means more than just automatically clicking "Add to Favorites" every time you find an interesting page. File your bookmarks or favorites into folders as you make them.

To create folders in Mozilla, click the "Bookmarks" button and then choose "Edit Bookmarks." This presents you with a window in which your bookmarks and folders are arranged in a hierarchical order. (It is a good idea to delete many of the bookmarks that come with Mozilla since these will just clutter up your bookmarks file, especially if you never use these preset bookmarks.) You can create a new folder, say "Curriculum Webs," by using the File menu and choosing "New Folder." You can set the new folder as the default folder for new bookmarks by using the View menu and choosing "Set as new bookmark folder."

Internet Explorer has similar procedures, but refers to bookmarks as "favorites." To create folders for your favorites in Internet Explorer, use the Favorites menu and choose "Organize Favorites." The screen that appears includes options for creating new folders, renaming folders, deleting folders, and moving a selected favorite into a folder. You should play with this utility until it becomes second nature. (Other browsers such as Opera and Safari have similar procedures. Consult your browser's Help menu.)

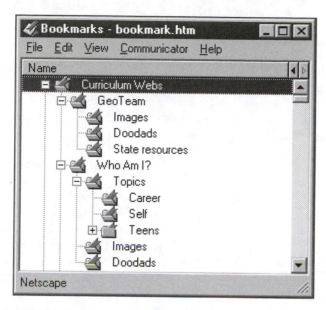

FIGURE 7.1   A starting bookmark or favorites folder structure for developing the "Our United States" and "Who Am I?" curriculum webs.

As you conduct your searches you should also think about the overall look and feel of your curriculum web. If you find sites that are good-looking or have graphical elements that you think might look good in your own curriculum web, touch on similar topics, or use interesting approaches, bookmark those sites into "images" or "models" folders. (You can create subfolders of bookmarks within other bookmark folders.)

As you write the elements of your plan, create bookmarks that will become **nodes** of your curriculum web. The arrangement of your bookmarks and folders may change as you think more about your aims. Your subject matter description and your bookmark folders will probably look similar in some respects. If you were creating the "Our United States" and "Who Am I?" curriculum webs, you might create an initial bookmark folder structure that looks like that shown in Figure 7.1.

ACTIVITY 7B ■ Designing a Bookmark or Favorites Folder Structure

Design a bookmark or favorites folder structure that will work to support you as you gather materials for your curriculum web. If you are still trying to determine which of several activities to pursue, based on the availability of resources, then create separate folders for each activity. Include subfolders related to subtopics within the curriculum web and/or images and other resources. Create this structure in your personal bookmark or favorites file on your computer and use it to store the locations of promising sites as you conduct your search for relevant resources. You will use this set of bookmarks in Hands-On Lesson 7 after you finish this chapter.

SEARCHING THE WEB

This is a topic that seems at first glance to be quite simple: to find web pages dealing, say, with the history of baseball, you go to a search engine, type in "history of baseball," and then look at the resulting pages to find what you are looking for. Right?

Well, sometimes. Searching the Internet is in some ways very simple, and it is becoming simpler all the time with the development of new kinds of search engines and directories. Some things are very easy to find on the Internet, for example, a list of the birthstones for different months or a chronology of the presidents of the United States. Any coherent set of facts that are commonly used in schools or daily life will show up near the top of any list of results in any search engine.

Harder to find are more complex facts or concepts, such as the temperature of the ocean at one mile deep or an explanation of the relationship between inflation and money supply. Also, it is difficult to find web pages that correlate different realms of information, for example, the relationship between population growth and economic prosperity. Searching the Web is complicated enough that entire books have been devoted to the topic (for example, Ackermann and Hartman 2002; Hill 1997). This is a skill that can only be mastered with time and with practice. You cannot memorize searching techniques in the same way that you can memorize a set of multiplication facts.

Teachers who are teaching web-searching skills can model appropriate decision making and thinking. For example, when the teacher is showing the students how to conduct a search, he or she should say things like: "Now I am going to open a new window so I can do a new search without losing this old one," or "I am trying to figure out why I am getting so many hits on this search, so I am looking to see if there are any common topics in the pages I am finding that are not relevant to our needs. If so, perhaps I should try to exclude them from the search." This kind of explication helps students to develop their own thinking and decision making.

Directories and Search Engines

There are many different online tools that can be used to locate suitable materials on the Internet. These tools can be categorized as directories, clearinghouses, search engines, and multiengine search tools. Also worth knowing about is the important job of searching within what is known as the "invisible Web." Each of these topics is discussed in turn.

Directories.   Directories (also known as subject trees) provide categorized listings of web sites, usually arranged in a hierarchy of topics and subtopics. The most famous example of this is the Yahoo web site, at *yahoo.com*. Yahoo allegedly stands for "Yet Another Hierarchical Officious Oracle" and it originally provided only lists of sites according to categories. Web sites are listed after being reviewed for content and suitability. Sites are listed in one or more categories, and are reached by browsing or "drilling down" into the directory. Drilling down is the process of choosing a top-level category, then choosing a second-level category, and so on until one finds what one needs. For example, on Yahoo, when first entering the site, one sees a list of categories including: Business and Economy, Computers and Internet, News and Media, Education, Entertainment, Government, Health, Arts and Humanities, Recreation and Sports, Reference, Regional, Science, Social Science, and Society and Culture. By looking at the categories used on Yahoo or other directories, one can see a sort of concept map of the World Wide Web, showing the kinds of resources one is likely to find. The categories are a great way to find out more about your particular topic. Other directories use different categories. One of the most interesting directories is *dmoz.org*, which is the web site of the Open Directory Project, a huge collaborative effort of volunteers around the globe to create and maintain a comprehensive directory that is not (unlike some of the commercial directories) subject to any for-profit pressures to list particular sites first or in inappropriate categories. The categories on DMOZ are edited by people who have some expertise in the topic, and for that reason may be somewhat more thorough (or idiosyncratic!) than Yahoo or other directories. The particular brilliance of DMOZ is that the editors are truly motivated by a passion for their work, seeing it as a way to provide community service while also furthering their own expertise.

Top-level DMOZ categories include Arts, Business, Computers, Games, Health, Home, Kids and Teens, News, Recreation, Reference, Regional, Science, Shopping, Society, Sports, and World. Let's say we want to find a historical map of ancient Greece around the time of Plato. Going to *dmoz.org*, you can see that "maps" is a subcategory of Reference. Clicking on Reference, then Maps, then Historical, one finds links to forty or more web sites with historical maps. There is also, on each page, a description of the particular category which helps you know whether you are in the right place. The description of the Reference|Maps|Historical category is "This category is for online viewable collections of historical maps. This category includes both antique maps and modern maps showing historical boundaries," which seems like exactly what we want. (The description also provides alternative categories for specialized collections of historical maps such those found on restricted sites or collectibles.) Remember that each link in the category has been manually added to the list by an editor, and each is briefly described (again, by the editor), so it is possible to look at the list and quickly find sites that might contain the kind of map you need.

When you find a directory page that is relevant to your specific interests or to your developing curriculum web, it is a good idea to bookmark that page to avoid having to click so many times next time you visit. For example, Yahoo has a specific listing on teenagers, found under Society and Culture > Culture and Groups, that would be especially useful for someone developing the "Who Am I?" curriculum web.

Directories list only a tiny fraction of all web pages, and generally include only the established web sites of organizations likely to remain in business for a long time. Some directories only include sites that are reliable as determined by subject matter specialists, or only those meeting certain criteria for quality. Note that it is also possible to search—as well as browse—most directories, including Yahoo and DMOZ. The search will look in the directory's categories, listings, and descriptions of listed web sites to find the term you are looking for. Some directories will also allow you to use their search engine to search an index of the entire Web, thus crossing into the category of search engine.

See our companion web site at *curriculumwebs.com* for a listing of additional directories.

ACTIVITY 7C ■ Using Directories to look for Relevant Sites

Use the "drill down" method to browse *dmoz.org* and *yahoo.com* for web sites relevant to the subject matter of your curriculum web. If you find any relevant categories or sites, add them to your bookmark or favorites list. Can you see any differences in the kinds of resources listed in these two directories?

Clearinghouses.   A **clearinghouse** is a type of directory that is created around a specialized topic or interest. For example, *k12connection.org* and *thegateway.com* list a huge variety of educational sites. Clearinghouses often provide in-depth reviews and have the advantage that any listed resources are directly relevant to the focus of the clearinghouse. The federal government has funded a number of clearinghouses, for topics in education, health, finances, small businesses, and the environment. To find relevant clearinghouses, use *google.com* or another search engine to search for "clearinghouse" and search terms relevant to your topic.

ACTIVITY 7D ■ Looking for a Relevant Clearinghouse

Use *google.com* to search for clearinghouses with contents relevant to the subject matter of your curriculum web. If you find any such clearinghouses, add them to your bookmarks. Visit the clearinghouses and browse them for more relevant resources. Add these to your bookmarks as well.

Search Engines.   A **search engine** generally includes a lot more web pages than any directory, because rather than reviewing the web site manually and assigning it to a category, search engines employ "web crawlers" or "spiders" that automatically move through the World Wide Web, finding new links and pages, and then automatically indexing these pages. Thus, when you use a search engine, you are not searching the Web itself, or any man-made directory or subject listing of the Web, but rather you are searching an index of the Web that has been created by computer.

Search engines generally return far more hits than searches of directories or clearinghouses, including many web pages that are "fly-by-night" (that is, they disappear very quickly after being created) or that are created by individuals who may or may not want to disseminate accurate information. In some cases, having so much debris in your net may be distracting and annoying. For example, when searching for the Smithsonian Institution, you are likely to receive hits of innumerable web sites that merely mention the Smithsonian Institution, in addition to all the Smithsonian's pages. For this reason, it may be better to use a directory to find established institutional web sites. Directories, of course, are also better if what you want is a relatively short list of reliable sources for particular kinds of information or resources.

But there are circumstances in which a directory will not return what you want. For example, say you are trying to find out what college Bill Gates dropped out of. (Using a directory, you might find pages devoted to Bill Gates, and by searching within these pages, you might find the answer you seek, but this might be very time-consuming.) A search engine is your best bet here; by entering the proper search terms into the search engine, you can probably find the answer in just a few seconds. (Go ahead and try that now!)

Search engines often return thousands or even millions of "hits," or relevant sites, on a given search term. A search in October 2004 on the phrase "Britney Spears" returned over 4 million hits! Of course, many of those web sites aren't really about Britney Spears. Rather, web sites about other things have added this very popular phrase to their site descriptions so that their sites show up in more searches. (See page 228 for a discussion of how this is done.) Such numbers can be overwhelming, although most search engines are pretty good at sorting their hits according to relevance. The sites near the top of a list of hits are more likely to be relevant to the search terms—or perhaps had paid money for their position!—than sites further down the list. See "search terms," below, for more about choosing good terms. Some search engines also score their hits with numbers that may not seem to make much sense. You can find out what these scores mean by visiting each site's help section. The Google search engine revolutionized searching by developing an algorithm for sorting the relevance of hits that places sites that are visited more often (hence, that are chosen as relevant by more users) near the top of the list. Google also automatically includes some variants on search terms, such as plurals, without the user having to specify these variants. According to *searchenginewatch.com*, as of October 2004 Google was used for about 15 percent of all searches, followed by Yahoo with 10 percent and MSN search (*search.msn.com*) with about 7 percent. (MSN's rating is higher than it might otherwise be because Microsoft's Internet Explorer will search it automatically if a search engine is not specified. All you have to do is type a series of search terms into the Address bar.) *Alltheweb.com* is another search engine that is particularly good for finding images.

See *curriculumwebs.com* for an updated list of search engines and other resources.

ACTIVITY 7E ■ Using a Search Engine to find Relevant Topics

Use *google.com* and *search.msn.com* to search the Web for sites relevant to the subject matter of your curriculum web. If you find any sites that are relevant, add them to your bookmark or favorites list. Do you notice any significant difference between the results returned by these two search engines?

Multiengine Search Tools.   A multiengine search tool—also known as a metacrawler or metasearch engine—utilizes a number of search engines in parallel. After you submit your search, the multiengine tool sends a properly formatted search request to other search engines, and then lists the hits either by search engine employed or by integrating their results into a single listing. The search method employed is known as a metasearch. Three popular multisearch engine search tools are *dogpile.com, vivisimo.com,* and *hotbot.com*. Vivisimo is interesting because it clusters hits according to conceptual groupings found within the search results. Thus, a search for "historical maps ancient Greece" returned clusters such as "historical maps," "culture," "ancient Greek world," "social studies," and "Athens." This is valuable because it helps the user to better understand the various ways that relevant resources might be classified or found.

Another metasearch tool that clusters results is *kartoo.com*. Kartoo uses a visual display to show how search results relate to one another, and highlights conceptual links among the pages. When you click on one of the concepts, a new search is performed that adds that concept to the original search. So when we searched for "ancient Greece maps," one of the conceptual links found was "history." When we clicked on the word "history," a new search was performed using the phrase "ancient Greece maps history." The display is interactive. When you point to one of the listed web sites, the display changes to show a description of that site, and the site is highlighted on the visual map. We think this tool is very useful and look forward to further developments in using visualizations for displaying the relationships among types of information.

ACTIVITY 7F ■ Using a Multiengine Search Tool

Use *dogpile.com* and *kartoo.com* to search for web sites relevant to the subject matter of your curriculum web. If you find relevant sites, add these to your bookmark list. Can you see the value of this kind of tool over a single search engine?

The Invisible Web

Search engines and directories provide access to many web sites; however, there is a lot of information on the Web that is not indexed by these tools. Search engines find web sites to index by using web robots or spiders to crawl the Web, following links from one web page to another. However, much information is located in databases that require users to complete search forms to access the information, and spiders skip or ignore these search forms when crawling the Web. In addition, many pages you find on the Web do not actually exist until you request them. Increasingly, sophisticated web sites generate their pages dynamically ("on the fly") rather than in advance. Dynamically generated pages cannot be found using a search engine; only static pages are listed. Search engines also often exclude web pages that contain a "?" in the URL; these pages are generated by scripts that can confuse spiders. Because entries in directories are compiled by humans, they provide better access to the information stored deep in the Web, but there are not enough people to index all of the information available via the Web, so even directories do not provide access to a lot of this hidden information, and can never list dynamically generated pages.

The information in the hidden Web is typically of very high quality and is invaluable to any researcher, so how does one find these resources if not by use of search engines or directories? One way is to include the word "database" in a search, along with search terms relevant to your topic. Another is to search *invisible-web.net*, a directory that lists such resources. SingingFish (at *singingfish.com*) is a specialized search engine that lists **streaming** resources (audio and video) that also might not be included in more traditional search engines.

ACTIVITY 7G ■ Searching the Invisible Web

Use *google.com* to search for databases relevant to the topic of your curriculum web. Simply add "database" to your search string. Also visit *invisible-net.net* and browse for relevant resources. (Instead of drilling down, as with Yahoo or DMOZ, you select subcategories from drop-down menus.) Add any relevant sites to your bookmarks.

Search Terms

The name for what you type into a search engine's search field is *search string*. Search strings are made up of search terms* and qualifiers (discussed in the next section).

The most important skill you will need for conducting effective searches is the determination of what term or terms to include in a search. The best term is one that will be found *only* within web pages that are relevant to your search topic. For example, if you want to find out about the biography of Maimonides, then "Maimonides" is a nearly perfect search term for finding what you want, because that term isn't likely to appear on pages not relevant to the famous Judaic philosopher. On the other hand, if you want to learn more about John Smith, early explorer of Virginia, including "John Smith" in your list of terms probably will not do as much good as would the word "Jamestown" together with "Virginia." Generally, the more unusual a word is the better search term it makes.

The only way to know for sure which term or terms to use in a search is to try a number of alternatives. This can be time-consuming because searches may return useless hits. One way to maximize productivity when searching is to conduct more than one search at a time. Your browser will allow you to have more than one window open at a time. You can have several browser windows open with the same search engine in each, and conduct slightly different searches in each window. For example, if you were trying to find out more about the Chicago fire of 1871, you might try one search with the search string "Chicago Fire 1871," another with "The Great Chicago Fire," and a third with "Chicago disasters." By comparing the results of these searches, you can try several refinements of the one that returned the best results. To open a new browser window, simply use File|New|Window in your browser. To switch between the windows, you can use Alt-Tab. If you hold down the Alt key (the Command Key on a Mac) and press Tab repeatedly, you will be able to choose among any of your open windows. This is a great way to conduct multiple searches simultaneously and save lots of time. Once a search engine returns its results, you can more easily evaluate multiple pages for relevance or for specific information by opening them into a new window. Simply right-click the link with a PC or hold down the mouse button on a Mac and choose "Open in New Window." You can do this with several of the listed sites, and not waste a lot of time

---

*Search terms are sometimes referred to as *keywords*. Librarians distinguish the two. Keywords are assigned to items in a database by human intervention, and can often be searched using what is known as a keyword search. Search terms, however, are used to search an entire web page, rather than just the keywords that may have been assigned to a web page by a cataloger or database developer.

waiting for an individual page to open. Also, this technique keeps your search available in its own window, so you will spend a lot less time clicking on the Back button.

One way to avoid too many hits for multiterm searches is to create phrases by enclosing the words in quotation marks. For example, you are much more likely to get pages relevant to the Museum of Science and Industry by enclosing the name in quotation marks. (If you do not, you will get pages containing the words *museum, science,* and *industry.*) Unless they are enclosed in quotation marks, little words like "of" and "and" are generally ignored by search engines, because they are very likely to be contained in nearly every web page.

Search terms are usually not case-sensitive; that is, "Chicago" and "chicago" will return the same results. However, some exceptions apply, and you should look at the Help pages of various search engines to find out how they treat upper- and lowercase. Some search engines, for example, treat terms as case-sensitive if the terms are placed in quotation marks. Others only look at the case of terms in "advanced" mode.

You might get better results in a search by approaching a topic from a completely different direction. For example, suppose you are looking for web resources related to the history of labor unrest in the United States. You could use the word "strike," but that will cause many unrelated pages to come up. You could also use the phrase "labor unrest," but that is not a very common phrase even in pages that touch on this topic. Your best bet might be to try specific terms related to the history of labor unrest, for example "Pullman strike" or "Haymarket Square" or "Eugene Debs." Again, the only way to know what will work best is to experiment and refine your search based on the results.

Qualifiers.   The results returned by search engines in response to a given search are generally based on an underlying logic, although this logic may not be immediately clear. For example, when you include a long list of search terms, some engines will return as hits all pages that include one or more of the terms. Thus, the longer your list of terms, the more results you are likely to get. In other words, the search engine is looking for all the pages that have term 1 *or* term 2 *or* term 3. (You do not have to type "or" between the terms, because this is implied.) Fortunately, search engines order their hits by placing those web pages that contain most or all of the terms first, then those containing just a few of the terms, and finally those containing just one. So the long list will usually have the most relevant hits near the top. (Google bucks this trend by assuming an *and* between multiple terms.)

One consequence of the implied "or" in long lists of terms is that the more terms you include, the more hits you will get. In a search for "'Philadelphia School District' museums," the search engine returned all the pages containing either the phrase "Philadelphia School District" or the term "museums." Many pages did not contain both. By eliminating the word "museums" from the search string, the search engine returned fewer pages (that is, only pages containing the phrase "Philadelphia School District.") This is counterintuitive. You would think that the more terms you included the more precise would be the search.

If you want to make a search more precise by adding search terms, you will need to use the "and" qualifier. For example, the search "'Philadelphia School District' *and* museums" is more discriminating than "Philadelphia School District" by itself. The search engine will only include those web pages containing *both* the phrase "Philadelphia School District" *and* the term "museums." Most search engines allow you to use the plus sign "+" to represent the "and," as in "'Philadelphia School District' + museums." Some search engines do not allow the "and" qualifier (they simply ignore it as a small common word); others expect you to conduct an "advanced" search in order to include this qualifier.

It is often helpful to exclude web pages that include certain words. For example, when searching for "Chicago Fire" some pages will be returned that apply not to the infamous Chicago fire of 1871 but to the modern-day soccer team, the Chicago Fire. One way to avoid this is to add to your search string something like "not soccer." Thus, "'Chicago Fire' not soccer" is a very precise way of accessing web pages specifically dealing with the fire and not the Fire. Most search engines let you use a minus sign "−" to represent the "not," as in "Chicago Fire −soccer."

It is also important to realize that some search engines will not return hits for "museums" when conducting a search using the term "museum." Different search engines deal differently with the issue of stems or root words. For example, suppose you wanted to find web pages dealing with volcanoes, but in addition you also wanted to find pages dealing with volcanic rock. You could just include all three of the following terms: volcano, volcanoes, volcanic. Another approach (depending on the search engine) is to use volcan*. The asterisk implies that the ending of the word could be any sequence of characters. Similarly, some search engines allow the use of a question mark to indicate one missing character. So "Indian?" would return pages containing Indian and Indians and Indiana, but not Indianapolis.

In some search engines, such as *alltheweb.com*, complex combinations of qualifiers can be grouped together with parentheses. For example, if you wanted to find web sites comparing the number of people who died in the Chicago fire of 1871 and in the San Francisco earthquake of 1905, you might construct a very complex search string that looks like this:

> ((Chicago AND fire AND 1871) NOT soccer) AND ("San Francisco" AND earthquake AND 1905) AND (deaths OR fatalities OR dead OR casualties)

We do not suggest you try to start your searches with such a string, but be prepared to construct one if the circumstances call for it.

ACTIVITY 7H ■ Creating a Precise Search String

Using search terms and qualifiers, construct a search string that will locate very precisely one of the resources that you are looking to add to your curriculum web. If you need help constructing a good search string, ask your librarian for assistance. Test the string in the advanced search mode of *alltheweb.com*, using the Boolean search mode. If you find any relevant sites, add them to your list of bookmarks or favorites.

EVALUATING WEB-BASED RESOURCES

Once you have located a resource that is related to topics or issues relevant to your curriculum web, it is necessary to evaluate the resource in terms of its value. You may find that some resources are best used to help *you* design a good curriculum web, rather than to be used by your learners as part of their learning activities. In either case, you will want to make some determination of how reliable the site is, in terms of the quality of the information given there. Brunner and Tally (1999) discuss Five Critical Questions that they say must be addressed in determining whether a given resource is worth using or relying on. (See also Kapoun 1998.) These questions are:

1. How was it constructed?
2. What values underlie it?
3. What are the conventions used?
4. Who is the intended audience?
5. Who owns it and who benefits from it?

Careful application of these questions by developers of curriculum webs (and by students who utilize the Web for learning) can help avoid embarrassment, unintended consequences, and student exposure to incorrect or biased information. Students need to be explicitly trained to ask these questions again and again as they access information, whether on the Web or elsewhere (Healy 1998, 252). Raising these questions can help determine a web site's accuracy, objectivity, and authority.

Among the additional issues you will want to consider as you evaluate resources that you have found on the Web are:

- *Purpose.* Some materials are clearly designed for instruction. They include helpful introductions, attempt to relate their material to a larger context of subject matter, and provide explicit support for helping the reader to understand new concepts or to promote further learning. If the target audience for the author is compatible with your learners, some materials will not require a lot of separate introduction or supports from your curriculum web. However, many materials with potential educational value were created without any educational intent. For example, parodies or satires can be educational because they point out the hidden biases or perspectives of what they parody. Government agencies often provide data, reports, and manuals online that were intended for a sophisticated population of users. Such sites or data can, however, become useful resources for a curriculum web when the curriculum developer adds introductory or support materials. You can construct a web page that explains the context or structure of the materials, with a link to the materials themselves and perhaps to additional support materials such as background reading, definitions of important words, maps, illustrations, or summaries. Depending on the copyright status of the material, you can even build your own **frameset** that allows your support materials and the information to be displayed on the learner's screen at the same time. (See Chapter Eight for more on the use of frames. This chapter discusses some of the copyright issues that may be involved.)

- *Bias.* Some materials are clearly produced by people with a personal or professional interest in putting forward a particular opinion or point of view. Still other sites are clearly meant as hoaxes, either for the purpose of humor or more nefarious reasons. (See Piper 2000 for links to some of these.) Such materials are not necessarily off-limits for use in curriculum webs, particularly if the curriculum is seeking to teach the learners something about an issue that is controversial or subject to debate. Materials with clear or implicit bias should be introduced in such a way that the learner is not likely to mistake the page as an objective or neutral account, and followed up by activities that help the learners to place the material into a larger context. It is important for the curriculum developer to ask, while considering the use of such materials, whether the producer of the material has any particular stake in promulgating a given perspective, and whether it is possible or desirable to expose students to the material as it is presented on the site. (An interesting but somewhat tangential question is what readers actually *look for* when they assess the credibility of the information on a web site. Some researchers at the Stanford University Persuasive Technology Lab have been working on this question. Interestingly, they have found that readers are more likely to rely on the overall visual attractiveness of a site rather than more rigorous and relevant criteria such as who created the site or for what purpose. See Fogg et al. 2002.)

- *Credibility.* Does the information on the site have any basis other than that it is stated there? Are there links to sources for additional information? Follow these links and scan the sources for additional data or evidence of an objective outlook. Is there a bibliography? If so, are the sources listed of a scholarly nature? Sites that are truly well researched tend to have a lot of information about the sources of their information. If data or information has been copied from somewhere else, is it complete and unaltered? Are a variety of viewpoints presented, or just one? Is the site listed on a directory such as the Librarian's Index to the Internet (*lii.org*) or DMOZ? What is said about the site on these directories? (You can always do a search to find who is linking to a particular site, using instructions provided on page 228. Who links to it? Are those sites reliable, or is a pattern of bias found in all the sites that are interlinked?)

- *Currency.* How current or timely is the information presented? Does this site have a lot of dead links? Does it appear to have been updated recently? Links on the Web often break with the passage of time. Sites at which a substantial number of the links are "dead" will frustrate your students rather than engage them. Also, if the author(s) of the material aren't regularly updating the site, they may be missing more recent, crucial information about the topic, especially if it is a topic affected by the rapid rate of technological change.

- *Who wrote it?* Does the site clearly show who the author is, and provide information that can help you to know whether the author knows much about the topic? If the author is an academic, what can you find out about the college or university that he or she works at? Is the author's résumé or *curriculum vitae* available so you can see if he or she has had other publications or conference presentations dealing with the topic? If you can't find anything about the author on the site, use Google or another search engine to find out more. Also, ask yourself why the author might not want to be well known by the readers. Sometimes you can find out more about the author by truncating the URL of the site—that is, by cutting off the filename and/or one or more directory names at the end of the URL. For example, on one of this book's author's personal web sites there is an article that describes web pages that criticize the philosophy and educational methods of the philosopher John Dewey. The URL is *craigcunningham.com/dewey/part3.htm*. By cutting this URL back to *craigcunningham.com/dewey* you can find other articles about Dewey created by the same author, and by cutting it back again to *craigcunningham.com*, you can find out that the author is a college professor and access additional information about him and his work. (Note that simply because a web site has a .com at the end of it, you cannot assume that it does not therefore contain academic resources.)

- *Readability.* Consider your learners' reading ability. The print materials and web pages you select must make sense to your learners. If you know your students' reading level or grade, you can use a readability index to know whether a particular piece of reading will be easy or hard for them. You can use Microsoft Word to generate a readability index. (Check the Help window in Word for more information.) In addition, there are several web sites that allow you to check the readability of a passage of reading. Check *curriculumwebs.com* for some links to these tools.

- *What about advertising?* Web sites that contain advertising create special problems of evaluation. Ads are distracting to students and can lead them to pursue links that are not related to the instructional activities you have designed for them. Also, the purpose of advertising is often either to build brand loyalty or to conduct market research. Consider whether you wish to build brand loyalty among your students. Does it compromise your educational function as a teacher? If your students click on ads that ask for information (buying habits, etc.), they may be compromising their privacy or at least doing things that do not contribute to their learning. But remember that many web sites "advertise" a particular point of view or approach without necessarily including content that is traditionally described as advertising. Many governmental web sites, for example, push a particular point of view rather than offering a balanced perspective. The presence of advertising *per se* cannot be taken as an absolute reason for not including a particular web site. The producers of the information may simply need to support their work financially. This point is demonstrated by Kathy Schrock's Guide for Educators, which includes much valuable information (including information about how to evaluate web sites that have advertising, at *school.discovery.com/schrockguide/eval.html*), but her site itself contains advertising for the Discovery Channel and others.

In addition to evaluating the reliability or other qualities of specific information or images found on the Web, teachers also need to evaluate the presentation of that material in terms of how useful the web site will be to the students who access it. The American Library Association has developed an "Evaluate A Web Site" checklist, which we have expanded for the use of participants in the Web Institute for Teachers. You can find the expanded version on *curriculumwebs.com*. Generally, the kinds of things to consider when evaluating a web site for usefulness are the same questions that you need to teach your students, because they will need to be careful and critical consumers of information and resources on the Web.

COPYRIGHT ISSUES

When you use preexisting materials that have been created by someone else you need to consider whether such use is legal and ethical. The primary legal issue is whether a use of a given resource is allowed within U.S. copyright law. The law gives educators certain privileges not extended to the general public; these privileges are known as the "Fair Use Doctrine" and provide certain exemptions to copyright restrictions. However, since the copyright law was last given a major revision in 1976, long before the development of the World Wide Web, there are some gray areas in which the law's application to new media is not entirely clear. Below, we explain the law and provide some general guidance so you can know whether a given use is likely to be legal or illegal.

Before we go into the legal issues surrounding use of materials on the Web in more detail, we want to stress that it is also important to consider the ethical issues raised in such use. Because teachers are, by their nature, serving as examples to their students, they should be careful to serve as good examples that students would do well to emulate. An important principle to follow is: "always give credit where credit is due." Even if a web site gives explicit permission for you to use something you find on that site, or even if the resources are explicitly in the **public domain,** it is always good practice to give notice of where you found it and to give thanks to those who made it available to you. Such notice can be as simple as including the word "Source" with a link to the page where you found the material, or an explicit acknowledgement statement at the bottom of each page: "The designers of this curriculum web gratefully acknowledge the XYZ organization for making these images available on its web site at *xyzurl.org.*"

(Please note, as we discuss in more detail below, that *citing the source of copyrighted material does not make the use of such material legal.* You may also need to receive explicit permission for such use.)

■ ■ ■ ■ ■ ▬▬▬▬▬▬▬▬▬▬▬▬▬▬▬▬▬▬▬▬▬▬▬▬▬▬▬▬▬▬▬▬▬▬▬

CITATIONS

If you want to follow accepted citation procedures, you can include a citation in proper MLA or APA style.

MLA Style for citing web-based sources

MLA style of citation (named after the Modern Language Association) is normally used in humanities texts. The order of information includes the author (if known) or the owner of the page, the title of the page in quotations, the title of the larger work of which it is a part (if there is one, in italics), the date of last revision (if known; if not, use N.d. for not dated), the larger web site of which the page is a part, the date last accessed, and the URL). Note that each of these elements, except the last two, are separated by periods. A sample citation in MLA style is as follows:

```
Amon, Connie. "Information Literacy." 2003. Web Institute for
    Teachers. Oct 2004 <http://
    webinstituteforteachers.org/~camon/infoliteracy/
    infolithome.htm>.
```

(continued)

CONTINUED

APA Style for citing web-based sources

APA style of citation (named after the American Psychological Association) is normally used in scientific texts. The recommended format is as follows: the author (if known) or the owner of the page, the date of last revision in parentheses (if known; if not, use N.d.), the title of the page, the date last accessed, the title of the larger work (if known), and the URL. A sample citation in APA style is as follows:

```
Amon, C. (2003). Information literacy. Retrieved Oct, 2004,
    from Web Institute for Teachers Web site:
    http://webinstituteforteachers.
    org/~camon/infoliteracy/infolithome.htm.
```

Note that these formats are still somewhat in flux, and if you want to ensure that your formatting is correct (as when submitting an article for publication), you should consult with the latest edition of the *MLA Handbook* or the *Publication Manual of the American Psychological Association*. Links to current versions and additional citation resources (including David Warlick's very useful online citation generator) are provided on *curriculumwebs.com*.

The Basics of Copyright

Inherent in the concept of copyright is the notion that you own and have control over anything that you create. Examples of copyrighted work might include an entry in your diary, the geology lesson plan you created last year, or the recording you made of your class singing *The Star-Spangled Banner*.

The law holds that as soon as you create these works and fix them into a permanent medium, you own the copyright on them. You do not need to include the symbol © or the word "copyright" in the document. Your work is automatically protected by copyright. (At one time a copyright holder was required to give notice of a copyright; however, the Berne Convention, signed by the United States in 1989, established that all works saved in a permanent medium are copyrighted even if no notice is given.) The law also holds that the copyright of work produced while under employment might belong to the employer (depending on the employment contract).

This also means that anything created by somebody else is under copyright—unless the copyright has expired. There are Fair Use laws that allow for limited use of copyrighted materials, but these laws are often misunderstood and abused. We discuss Fair Use laws below.

The Copyright Law

Congress, in pursuit of the aims stated in the Constitution, has gone to great lengths to define and protect the copyright of creative works.

The U.S. Constitution grants Congress the authority to "promote the Progress of Science and useful Arts, by securing for limited Times to Authors and Inventors the exclusive Right to their respective Writings and Discoveries." By granting creators a special property right, known as copyright, for the fruits of their labors, the government protects the economic incentive to be creative.

Copyright is a form of protection provided by the laws of the United States to the authors of "original works of authorship," including literary, dramatic, musical, artistic, and certain other intellectual works. This protection is available to both published and unpublished works, and exists as soon as the work is "expressed," even if the creator of the work takes no further steps to establish ownership. This means that as soon as you write an original text, draw a picture, take a photograph, record a sound, or shoot a movie, you have a copyright that covers the resulting work.

The Copyright Act generally gives the owner of copyright the exclusive right to do and to authorize others to do the following:

- Reproduce the copyrighted work in copies or phonorecords
- Prepare derivative works based on the copyrighted work
- Distribute copies or phonorecords of the copyrighted work to the public by sale or other transfer of ownership, or by rental, lease, or lending
- Perform the copyrighted work publicly, in the case of literary, musical, dramatic, and choreographic works, pantomimes, and motion pictures and other audiovisual works
- Display the copyrighted work publicly, in the case of literary, musical, dramatic, and choreographic works, pantomimes, and pictorial, graphic, or sculptural works, including the individual images of a motion picture or other audiovisual work

It is illegal for anyone to violate any of the rights provided to the owner of copyright. These rights, however, are not unlimited in scope. In particular, the doctrine of Fair Use allows for limited reproduction of copyrighted materials, as described below.

Creating a Copyright

Any time you fix an original expression in a fixed medium, you have a copyright on that work. But what is meant by an original expression? And what is a fixed medium?

Expression. A fact or idea cannot be covered by copyright, but the unique description of an idea can be. An author cannot claim ownership of the idea of a boat filled with animals and a huge rain that flooded the Earth, but if he or she writes a story about Noah's Ark it becomes his other property, protected by copyright.

Original. The work must originate from the author who created it and not someone else; it must be the product of the creator's own creative labor. Copying the work of someone else is not an original enough expression on which to justify asserting a copyright on the finished product, and it violates the original creator's copyright.

Fixed Medium. The work must be captured in some permanent medium in order to carry a copyright. A speech that is given and never recorded is not covered by copyright, but if it is written down (even in note form from which the speech is read), saved on a teleprompter screen, or recorded by a TV camera, then the speech is copyrighted. Recent court decisions have determined that a computer's memory or hard disk is a fixed medium; this means that web pages, e-mail, chat room conversations, and similar Internet communications are covered by copyright.

The creator of a work does not have to take any further steps to protect the copyright of his work. As we mentioned previously, a copyright symbol is not required, nor is any declaration of copyright.

Penalties for Copyright Violation

The owner of a copyright can sue the violator for damages (usually computed by looking at the actual harm incurred as a result of the infringement, although in some cases there are statutorily imposed minimums). Copyright violation is also a federal crime, which means that violating a copyright could make the infringing party subject to fines, jail sentences, or both.

In a suit for copyright infringement, a court has the power to issue an injunction to prevent people from making or distributing further copies of a work. A court may also impound all copies claimed to have been made in violation of the owner's copyright. The copyright act also states that the copyright owner can collect either one or the other of the following monetary awards:

- Any actual damages the copyright owner has sustained, as well as any profits the copyright infringer has made.
- An amount of money to be determined by the court, which can range from $500 to $20,000 for an infringement of any one work. If the court finds that the infringer acted willfully, the court can increase the award to $100,000. If the infringer was unaware that he or she was violating someone else's copyright, the court can award as little as $200.

Fair Use

The Fair Use provision of the Copyright Act allows reproduction and other uses of copyrighted works under certain conditions for purposes such as criticism, comment, news reporting, teaching (including multiple copies for one-time classroom use), scholarship, or research. Additional provisions of the law allow uses specifically permitted by Congress to further educational and library activities.

Under the Copyright Act four factors must be considered to determine whether a specific action is a "Fair Use."

- The purpose and character of the use, including whether such use is of commercial nature or is for nonprofit educational purposes
- The nature of the copyrighted work
- The amount and substantiality of the portion used in relation to the copyrighted work as a whole
- The effect of the use upon the potential market for or value of the copyrighted work

The distinction between Fair Use and infringement may be unclear and not easily defined. There is no specific number of words, lines, or notes that may safely be taken without permission. Acknowledging the source of the copyrighted material does not substitute for obtaining permission. Nowhere in the Copyright Act is it suggested that Fair Use includes the republication of a copyrighted work, even publication on an educational web page when that page is available to the public on the Web.

Photocopying Under the Fair Use Doctrine

The legislative history of the Copyright Act of 1976 and subsequent amendments in 1998 provide teachers and librarians with guidelines for the Fair Use of copyrighted materials reproduced from books and periodicals for classroom use. A single copy may be made of any of the following by a teacher for his or her scholarly research or use in teaching or preparation to teach a class: a chapter from a book; an article from a periodical or newspaper; a short story, short essay or short poem, whether or not from a collective work; or a chart, graph, diagram, cartoon or picture from a book, periodical, or newspaper. Multiple copies for classroom use (not to exceed in any event more than one copy per pupil in a course) may be made by or for the teacher giving the course for classroom use or discussion, provided that: (a) the copying meets the tests of brevity and spontaneity as defined below, (b) the copying meets the cumulative effect test as defined below, and (c) each copy includes a notice of copyright.

Brevity
Length:
- Poetry: (a) A complete poem if less than 250 words and if printed on not more than two pages or, (b) from a longer poem, an excerpt of not more than 250 words
- Prose: Either a complete article, story or essay of less than 2,500 words, or an excerpt from any prose work of not more than 1,000 words or 10 percent of the work, whichever is less, but in any event a minimum of 500 words

Each of the numerical limits stated above may be expanded to permit the completion of an unfinished line of a poem or of an unfinished prose paragraph.

- Illustration: One chart, graph, diagram, drawing, cartoon or picture per book or per periodical issue

Spontaneity
- The copying is at the instance and inspiration of the individual teacher.
- The inspiration and decision to use the work and the moment of its use for maximum teaching effectiveness are so close in time that it would be unreasonable to expect a timely reply to a request for permission.

Cumulative Effect
- The copying of the material is for only one course in the school in which the copies are made.

- Not more than one short poem, article, story, essay or two excerpts may be copied from the same author, nor more than three from the same collective work or periodical volume during one class term.
- There shall not be more than nine instances of such multiple copying for one course during one class term.
- Normally, all copies of the copyrighted work must be collected when the students are done using them, so further copying, or use outside the educational environment, is prevented.

Works in the Public Domain

Works in the public domain include those whose copyright has expired, or those whose author has expressly declared to be in the public domain. If a work is in the public domain, it may be distributed freely in both electronic and print form. But do not assume that a work is in the public domain simply because it is popular or ubiquitous. For example, the song "Happy Birthday" is not in the public domain.

As of 2003, U.S. federal law states that all works created on or after January 1, 1978, and works that still had copyright protection in effect in 1998 when the copyright law was revised, have copyrights that last until 70 years after the death of the author, or 95 years after the work is produced by a company. If an author has been dead for 70 years, then any materials produced by that author are considered to be in the public domain. In practice, the revision of the law means that from 1999 until 2019, no new works will enter the public domain due to expiration of copyright in the United States.

If authors explicitly state that they intend for their work to enter the public domain, there are no restrictions whatsoever on the distribution, duplication, or other manipulation of their work. Be wary, however, of harboring the mistaken assumption that the lack of a copyright notice means that a computer program, an image, a piece of writing or a recording is in the public domain. If you do not see language to that effect, you should assume that the program, image, writing, or recording is under copyright protection and you should refrain from using it in ways that would infringe on the author's rights. (The language above relating to Fair Use is from an official U.S. publication in the public domain.)

Copyright Law in the Creation of Curriculum Webs

Because most curriculum webs are created by teachers for educational, nonprofit purposes, the inclusion of copyrighted materials created by others would seem to fall under "Fair Use," provided that only a small portion of the original work is used and it is in some way modified or enhanced by new additions by the creator of the curriculum web. However, the "Fair Use" provision was enacted before the development of the World Wide Web, and seems to apply only when an educational resource is made available to a defined group of students, say within a single classroom. Web pages that are readily accessible by the general public do not meet the limitation on the "cumulative effect" of copying something, because the number of copies that can be made of it is potentially unlimited. Therefore, if your curriculum web will be accessible to everyone on the World Wide Web, then you should *not* assume that "Fair Use" protects you even if you are engaging in an educational, nonprofit activity.

If your curriculum web will be hosted on a secured network that is accessible only to the students, teachers, and parents of your school (a so-called **intranet**), or particular pages of your curriculum web are password protected (see *curriculumwebs.com* for information on how to do this), you may be able to use materials and have the "Fair Use" provision apply. The primary issue in whether such use constitutes "Fair Use" is the extent of such use when compared to the amount of information given in the original. This comparison is made in light of the purpose of the copying. In other words, different purposes will justify different amounts of copying. If you are a teacher researching the history of baseball as part of the process of creating a curriculum web for your students, you are certainly justified in photocopying entire articles or chapters on the topic from journals and books in your public library, for your own use. But that is different from copying them into your own web site! Similarly, you may make multiple copies of an article to be read in class by your students (provided you meet the require-ment that such copying is "spontaneous") but it is not okay to copy even a single page from a workbook for your students to fill out, since the whole purpose of a workbook is for it to be filled in once by a single student.

The most important thing to remember about copyright is that you cannot take something that someone else has created and include it in your web site (unless the person has explicitly placed that something in the public domain). This extends to the use of graphics, tables, text, examples, backgrounds, diagrams, and so on. All such copying, unless you have explicit *written* permission, is illegal and unethical.

If the curriculum web you are building will require you to include resources from many locations, it might be helpful to develop an e-mail template so you can quickly request permission at the time a useful resource is located. Your template should include information about the work in question (including its title, URL, copyright holder, and date of publication), as well as information about how you plan to use the work (including the title of your curriculum web), as well as assurances that you will include proper citation with the work. You should ask the copyright holder to send you an e-mail in reply that includes the sender's name and title, explicitly describes the work that you want to use, and gives you permission to use it as part of your curriculum web. See David Warlick's *landmark-project.com* for a web-based template that can be used for sending out multiple permission letters.

What about Linking to Copyrighted Materials?

Building links to copyrighted resources should be both legal (given current copyright law) and ethical (given the structure of the World Wide Web), provided that the owner has not explicitly asked you *not* to link to it. In this sense, a URL is like a person's name; it is not ordinarily illegal to include someone's name in a list of people belonging to a certain organization, for example, but if a member explicitly requests that he or she not be included in the list, then the organization should honor that request. Similarly, including a linked URL in a web page should be considered okay unless a specific request has been made to exclude that URL.

For example, the owner or creator of a web site may not want you to create a link to a page deep inside that site. Rather, the owner may want the site to be viewed whole, in its entirety, rather than piece by piece. The creator should have the right to say how the site should be viewed (and in fact has said so in how he or she created the web page), and you should not violate that intent.

If you include more than a link to the URL in your curriculum web—for example, a summary or description of the contents of the page—you should probably also include the name of the author or the owner of the page. If you include any quotations or extracts from the page you are linking to—no matter how short the quotation—be sure to include a proper citation as discussed above.

Another issue is whether it is okay to build a frame that contains entire pages from another person's web site. (See Chapter Eight, Page 173, for more on frames.) This is probably not ethical, because it hides the actual location of the content, and it may confuse the reader into thinking that you created the content, when it actually belongs to someone else.

Alternatives to Obtaining Permission

If you want to include certain images on your curriculum web but do not have the time or inclination to request permission to use someone else's images, consider creating them yourself, or having your students create them for you. In our "Who Am I?" curriculum web, we have used a number of photographs of people as "decoration" for our activities about self-identity. We used our personal photographs, and supplemented these by going out and about in public places in Chicago, where the people in the pictures could have no reasonable expectation of privacy, taking some pictures, and then scanning these pictures to create digital photos for our site. You can also purchase collections of photographs and clip art that you may use for your web sites. Such collections typically include hundreds or thousands of photographs organized by topic or subject, and usually include a provision allowing the purchaser of the collection to use them without obtaining separate permission. Alternatively, you can work with your local art teacher to obtain thematic art created by students at your school. The idiosyncratic or local character of such collections may greatly offset any issues of quality that may be involved (Grabe and Grabe 1998). Your school's Acceptable Use Policy probably requires you to get release forms to use the students' art in this manner.

ACTIVITY 7I ■ Self-Testing Your Understanding of Copyright

1. Visit the companion web site at *curriculumwebs.com* and click on Chapters and then Chapter 7.
2. Toward the bottom of the page you will find a link to a Copyright Quiz.
3. Take the quiz. If you missed any of the questions, go back into this chapter and reread relevant sections.

Chapter Summary

This chapter:

- Lists and explains the tools available on the Web to assist in information searches
- Provides means to evaluate web-based resources for accuracy, bias, relevance, and so on
- Details issues surrounding copyright laws, the "Fair Use Doctrine," and the use of existing web materials on your own curriculum web and for your students

Questions For Reflection

Recently, technologies have been developed that make it possible to copy and distribute almost any artistic or literary work at little or no expense, using peer-to-peer sharing networks such as Kazaa and Internet Relay Chat, or IRC. These technologies threaten to undermine copyright protections, especially for popular music and videos.

What would be different about our society if there was no copyright protection? Think in terms of the life of artists, writers, and other holders of copyright as well as the life of others who are interested in their works. Would the world have more art in it, or less? More creativity, or less?

We think the obvious or most common answers to these questions are not necessarily the right ones. (If you are taking a class that is using this book, this might be a fun topic to debate with others.)

Your Next Step

Download Hands-On Lesson 7. This lesson uses the bookmarks you have gathered in the activities in this chapter as the basis for the development of a web-based lesson.

If you have not already read the Appendix (An Overview of Web Technologies), now might be a good time to do so. Chapters Eight through Ten will assume that you are familiar with the contents of the Appendix. As you read Chapters Eight through Ten, you should be thinking how the principles and procedures of web design that we discuss can be applied to the learning activities that you selected in Chapter Four and Chapter Six.

For Further Learning

. . . .

- *Curriculumwebs.com* provides a number of useful links to evolving information about copyright as it applies to the creation of web sites.
- Brunner and Tally 1999 provide a good general introduction to media literacy—including the evaluation of existing web materials.
- Lists of educational web sites worth visiting are provided by Leu, Leu, and Coiro 2004.
- Hill 1997 and Ackermann and Hartman 2002 provide good introductions to search techniques. Leshin 1998 provides a useful appendix on how to find a web site that has moved. Sherman and Price 2001 is a good introduction to the invisible Web.

CHAPTER 8

DESIGNING AN EFFECTIVE WEB SITE

Overview

At this point you have gathered and created a lot of the components of your curriculum web: a teaching guide, activities for your learners, lists of supporting resources, lists of materials and equipment, rubrics, and assessment plans. You may have created web pages for some or all of these parts of your curriculum web. Now it's time to put them all together!

This chapter focuses on the design of a web site. We discuss designing for your audience, using a visual metaphor or other clues to create a consistent look, creating navigation tools to enable your user to find his or her way around in the site, breaking your materials up into individual pages, and designing an overall site structure.

THE STEPS OF WEB SITE DESIGN

Organizing your web site as a whole is vital. Providing a consistent look and feel, using a familiar metaphor, and providing easy-to-use navigation elements will help your users find the information they are looking for. "Look and feel" refers to exactly what it seems to refer to. Every page in your site should have a similar look, so that the user knows when he or she is still within the site, and the pages should all have the same feel, or user interface, so users have to figure out only once how to move within and between the pages.

The process of designing a web site can be broken down into several steps. These steps apply whether your web site is a curriculum web or another kind of web site. The steps are:

1. Decide who your audience will be.
2. Choose an appropriate visual metaphor or theme.
3. Break up your information into appropriately sized chunks.
4. Create the site structure and consistent tools for navigation within the site.
5. Design each page.

After you have designed your site, you'll publish it, test it, publicize it, and then maintain, revise, and update the site. These are covered in subsequent chapters, as are additional enhancements you might want to consider, such as interactivity and multimedia.

STEP 1: PLANNING FOR YOUR AUDIENCE

As with any design process, it is important in web-page development to keep your intended audience in mind. Just as the appearance of a book—its size and shape, the pictures and colors used, and even the size of the text—depends on whether the book is written for preschoolers or college students, curriculum webs also vary depending on their intended audience.

Your curriculum web's primary audience is its learners. These are the people who will be working through the individual pages and using the web site over an extended period of time. However, your curriculum web has secondary audiences, such as the teachers who browse through the site trying to decide whether to use it with their students and the parents who may want to see what Junior has been up to in school. Generally, you should design for the primary audience, but then spend some time thinking about whether the secondary audiences of your curriculum web will need additional clues or tools to help them use the site. (The teaching guide can offer additional explanations or suggestions for teachers considering using the site. If necessary or helpful, you might also consider including a page for parents.)

A web site for primary school children will probably include very small blocks of large type, lots of colors, animations and other images to attract interest, and only a few navigational choices, whereas a site for high school students will rely more on words than on extraneous graphics or animation to sustain interest, and include more navigational choices, perhaps based on an expectation that the users will generate their own plans for completing their learning activities. Don't fall into the trap of building a site that is mostly made up of text to read. People generally don't like to read a lot of text on screen. (You might want to create PDFs of any longish reading passages so users can read them offline. See page 195.) Be sure to break up text passages with images, examples, or activities. Think about using text to discuss illustrations and examples, rather than using images to illustrate text. This approach is more in tune with the needs of many visual learners.

ACTIVITY 8A ■ Thinking About Your Learners' Needs

1. In Chapter Three you described the learners for your curriculum web. At this point, go back and look at your description and see if there are specific ways that you need to design the web site to support those learners. Make a list of some ways that you can help these learners to success while using the curriculum web. Be sure to consider the following (Lachs 2000):
   - Reading level
   - Appropriate sounds and images
   - How specific and detailed instructions and information should be

- Whether you should include humor or entertaining elements
- What kind of navigation is appropriate
- Amount of interactivity appropriate for the audience and subject matter
- Number and type of illustrations (see Chapter Nine for more guidance)

2. Think also about what secondary audiences may exist and how you can help them better utilize the site. Are there groups such as parents who might benefit from having a separate page to introduce the curriculum web? Are there secondary groups of learners who might have different needs than your primary group? Do any of your learners have special needs? (See page 89.)

3. Plan to revisit these questions reflectively throughout the design and implementation of your curriculum web.

STEP 2: GATHERING INFORMATION AND MATERIALS

Before making any further design decisions you should have at hand all the information that will make up your curriculum web. This includes any activities you designed in Chapter Five, the draft teaching guide, background information and supporting documents for the reader (if any), relevant web sites found in Chapter Seven, and so on. You should also decide what graphics and other multimedia elements you intend to include (sounds, movies, etc.). (Multimedia is discussed in detail in Chapter Nine.)

Every element in your web site should convey content, particularly if it significantly increases download times (see the discussion on this topic later in the chapter). *Never* include a graphic that adds nothing to the lesson you are creating. Design elements should not be merely decorative; they should always have an instructional purpose. The four major instructional purposes of images are to foster attention, increase retention, enhance understanding, and create context (Duchastel 1978). Before adding an image or sound, a block of text, an animation or a movie, ask yourself whether it adds any of these to the page. If not, do not include it, no matter how tempting. Let learning drive the design, not the other way around!

STEP 3: ESTABLISHING A VISUAL METAPHOR OR THEME

Visual metaphors are good for providing a consistent look to a web site, by providing something familiar and making the learners feel at home. "A good metaphor puts the light switch where you expect to find it" (Siegel 1997, 23). Consistent repetition of a well-executed visual metaphor makes it difficult for the visitor to get lost, whereas poorly chosen metaphors can be confusing.

The "Our United States" curriculum web extends its geography theme by using the atlas as a visual metaphor. Each page looks like a map, with latitude and longitude lines in the background and a compass rose in the upper-left corner for navigation. These simple elements, repeated page after page within the web site, provide a comfortingly familiar environment for the student.

Another example of a visual metaphor is shown in Figure 8.1. This page, which uses the metaphor of a bulletin board, was the home page of one section of WIT 2003. The page contains a host of information helpful to the participants in the section, including a schedule, an image-map photo of the participants, and some relevant resources, each appearing to be a piece of paper tacked to the board. The navigation buttons on the left under the WIT logo were common to all of the site's pages, but were modified slightly to look like they were on a piece of paper hanging on the board.

Other visual metaphor possibilities include:

- galleries (such as a museum or art gallery)
- comic strips
- TV channels

FIGURE 8.1   A web page for one of the sections of the Web Institute for Teachers 2003. Notice the use of a bulletin board as a visual metaphor.

- magazines and newspapers
- inside the human body
- the interior of a building
- a classroom
- a highway
- a town
- a cupboard
- a safari
- the periodic table of elements
- a computer, video game, or some other electronic gadget

Some visual metaphors imply wide freedom of exploration (a safari, for example); others, such as a highway or a periodic table, imply more directed learning activities. Aim for a metaphor that works well within your subject area: maps for geography, newspapers for history, and so on. (See the Questions for Reflection at the end of this chapter for more about metaphors.)

A consistent visual theme can work just as well as a metaphor. A site can be photographic or hand-painted, primitive or futuristic, art deco or gothic, juvenile or mature. The "Who Am I?" curriculum web uses a photographic theme to reinforce the human dimensions of the lesson.

At this point in the design process you may need to create or gather more elements, particularly graphics that will support your choice of metaphor. (Be sure to pay attention to the copyright status of visual elements you find on the Web. Many designers allow you to use their creations, but some want explicit statements of credit and others do not allow it at all.)

ACTIVITY 8B ■ Brainstorming Visual Metaphors

Taking your learners, subject matter, and curricular goals into consideration, list three possible visual metaphors (or visual themes) you could employ in your curriculum web. If you are having trouble with this task, explore some of the curriculum web examples found at *curriculumwebs.com*. These may inspire you. From the three candidates, choose the one you feel best suits your audience. Why is this one the best? How does it relate to your learners, the subject matter, and your goals? Discuss these questions with another person familiar with the development of curriculum webs.

STEP 3: CHUNKING

The concept of **information granularity**, or **chunking**, relates to putting just the right amount of information in front of the user at any one time. By the time you reach this stage in the design process you usually will have divided your curriculum into manageable pieces, if only in your own mind. Now is the time to formalize those divisions. Sometimes it is obvious how your material should be divided and sometimes it is not so obvious—and sometimes you must create artificial divisions. Each activity in a lesson will probably be on its own page or group of pages; similarly, the teaching guide, background information, links to outside resources, suggestions for further study, and so on, will each be on a separate web page within your site.

Textbook pages are sometimes cluttered, with too much information, graphics, charts, and maps on each page. This is because textbook costs increase with the number of pages in the book. Your curriculum web does not suffer from this limitation! Create as many separate web pages as you need in order to present a clean and uncluttered user interface.

How much information is too much? Present the user with only two or three new ideas per page. Limiting page length has the added benefits of reducing the amount of scrolling the user must do and of decreasing download times. A popular rule of thumb suggests that six screens of information per page should be the maximum. In other words, the user should not have to scroll down more than six screens to see everything on the page.

ACTIVITY 8C ■ Creating a Concept Map of Your Subject Matter

One way to break the information in your site up into chunks is to create a concept map or outline of the material. (An example of a concept map is shown on page 54.) Each separate bubble on the map or separate entry on the outline can represent one page in your site. You can also get some help from a person who has not participated in the development of your curriculum web. Ask them to create an outline of the material you want to present, with each entry representing the amount of information that should go on each page.

STEP 4: PLANNING SITE NAVIGATION

Once you have settled on a visual metaphor or theme that is the basis of the look and feel of your curriculum web and have divided up your curriculum material into appropriately sized chunks, it is time to consider the overall architecture of your site. In other words, it is time to decide how the bubbles of your concept map of Activity 8C are connected.

A particularly important step in the design process is deciding how your visitors will navigate through your curriculum web. In what order will the information on your web site be presented? Sequentially? Nonlinearly? Hierarchically? Is it important that the learners progress through your curriculum web in a predetermined order, or should the learner choose where to go in order to complete a learning activity?

Well-designed web sites take advantage of the properties of hypertext to present information differently than in traditional media. For example, you might want some information to be presented in a star or hub-and-spoke pattern, where the user starts at a menu and clicks on each choice one-by-one, visiting a page or set of pages relevant to that choice and then going back to the menu page to click on the next choice, and so on. If this is how you want your users to travel through the site, you'll need to build in the navigational elements (buttons, links, instructions) that will naturally lead them to

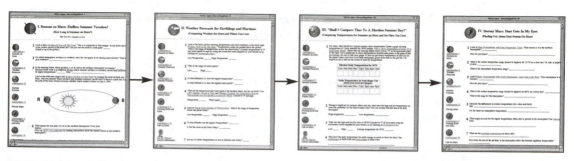

FIGURE 8.2   A linear navigation scheme.

make the choices you intend. It is very important that the user know how to proceed at each step. Do not simply include on each page a set of buttons linking the user to all the major sections of your site. You might not want your learners to visit the "Activities" page until after they have finished reading the "Background Information" pages. The navigation should be determined by the learning sequence, not the other way around!

If you are designing a series of activities intended to be followed in sequence, you might set up your web site so that the user could only go to activity 3 after completing activity 2. See Figure 8.2. In that case, a "Next Activity" link on the bottom of the page would be best.

If, on the other hand, the activities could be completed in any order, non-linearly, then it would be more appropriate to include links to all of the activities on each page. See Figure 8.3.

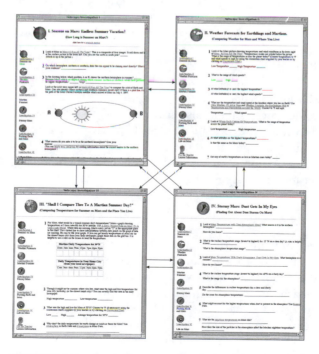

FIGURE 8.3   A nonlinear navigation scheme.

You can build more than one navigation structure into your curriculum web. You can direct learners to move linearly through certain sections of the site but travel more independently at other times using a site's site map, index, or a site-specific search engine. In the "Who Am I?" web, we have built in a drop-down navigation menu that has a different set of choices than the buttons that lead the learner through the curriculum web in a predetermined order. Another useful tool is a cascading menu, in which pop-up windows show increasing detail at each level of a menu, allowing them to choose the specific page they are looking for. See Hands-On Lesson 8 for more about different menu structures.

When designing your navigational elements, be they text links, clickable images, rollover buttons, and so on, there are a few points to remember:

- *Organization/presentation.* Include a clean, clear direction and structure of navigation, and limit the number of links. Cluttered pages with lots of links only confuse your users. Choose to have a limited number of links from the starting page and include more links within each subsection. The best designed sites offer only a handful of links off the main home page. In turn, the rest of the links lie within specific category pages. This allows you to better control the direction your users will go.
- *Naming convention.* Use intuitive names for different areas of your site. Avoid technical jargon in navigational elements unless you are sure your audience understands it.
- *Hierarchy.* What links should be listed first? Either the most important links or the ones you want your visitor to go to first, if web page order is important. Remember, as a general rule, most people read things left-to-right and top-to-bottom. When designing your navigation interface, have the most important links appear first because, more often than not, those will be the first things people choose to click on.

In addition to navigation tools that users use to actively wend their way through a web site, designers should also include ways to provide information as to where the user is within the overall site. Such passive navigation tools, or **wayfinding elements,** include page titles, buttons that stay highlighted to show the current page, a visual representation of the directory path from the home page to the current page, and breadcrumbs (see page 204).

Major Parts of a Web Site

The interior of your curriculum web is made up of the pages that you have thus far determined are vital to your curriculum. Consider also creating an **entry-point** and **exit-point** for your curriculum web. These provide definite starting and ending points for your curriculum and are a great way of extending the visual metaphor that you have chosen to use.

The entry-point should entice visitors and welcome them in. It should give an idea of what the web site is about, but should not be loaded with information; it should lure the user in, but not tell everything about the web site. Sometimes implemented as a splash page, the entry-point should, above all, load quickly; longer than a 10- to 15-second wait will drive away visitors. Include a menu of options on the entry page (with links to key areas of your web site), or at least a strong visual clue to the user where to go first. Include notes like "Teachers, visit the teaching guide!" or "If this is your first time visiting this curriculum web, click here." The last thing you want is someone staring at the entry page thinking, "Now what do I do?"

The exit-point, if included, should be reached naturally at the conclusion of a user's visit to your web site. It provides a feeling of completion, letting the user know that he or she has come to the end and (most likely) has not missed anything major on the site. You can include a summary of the learning objectives as a sort of mental checklist for the departing learner. Many exit-points also contain links to further resources.

In addition to an entry and an exit, curriculum webs also include: a page (or pages) for the teaching guide; perhaps a page for parents; pages related to each of activities that you have planned (including a culminating activity if you have one); as well as pages of information, lists of resources, and assessments. You can also add a page containing a site index or site map. See Figure 8.4 for an example of a site map that provides an overview of the structure of the "Our United States" curriculum web. This could be implemented as an image map on a web page.

ACTIVITY 8D ■ Weaving Your Web

Create links on the concept map you created in Activity 8C by drawing lines between the various bubbles of information. Use one color for links that a teacher might follow and a separate color for links that a student might follow, numbering the links if order is important. Are the paths different? How might that affect your navigation scheme? Be sure to consider the possibility of multiple pathways.

STEP 5: BUILDING SITE STRUCTURE AND NAVIGATION TOOLS

Once you have determined what your navigation scheme or schemes will be, you will want to use it consistently. Whether you are placing the navigation links at the bottom, top, or side of your page, put them in the same place on every page. Setting up a template from which you create your individual web pages is helpful in this regard. (We discuss this process in Hands-On Lesson 8, which you should follow at the conclusion of this chapter.)

Before you can actually build your tools for navigation, you will have to begin to create your site structure. This includes deciding whether you will need to create a set of folders to store individual pages and other elements such as graphics, and whether the pages of your site will all be in the same folder or separated by topic, activity, or other criteria. Each page in the site will be stored as a separate file. On a smaller web site, all of

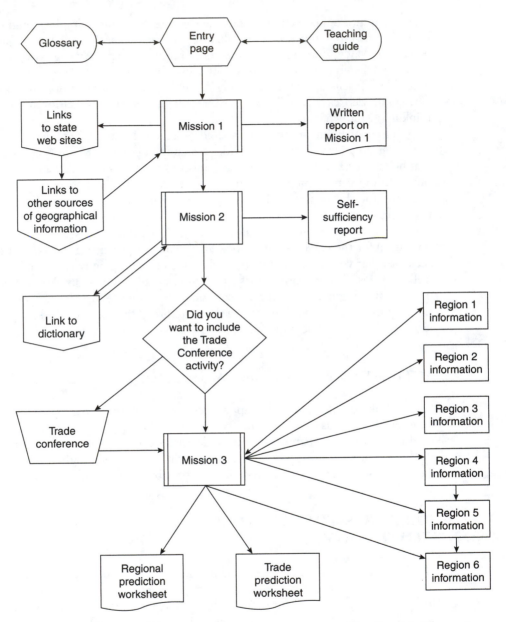

FIGURE 8.4   A visual representation of the "Our United States" curriculum web.

these files can be in the same directory. However, your life may be easier if you divide the files into a directory structure that makes sense for your particular curriculum web. This structure may be similar to the structure you created for your bookmarks in Chapter Seven, reflecting the subject matter structure of the curriculum. Alternatively, it could be more of a functional categorization, with subdirectories for activity pages, resource pages, and multimedia. What's important is that you as the designer of the web site know where everything is, so you can find individual pages or multimedia elements when you need them, and so you don't accidentally end up with two versions of any given page.

The web editing and site management software packages that we discuss in the Hands-On Lessons provide tools to help you to build your site structure. Because it is much easier to learn about site structure and navigation tools by actually building them than by reading about them, we have left most of our discussion of these topics to the lessons.

Frames Versus Tables

At this point in the planning process it is time to think about implementation details that will affect your site's file structure. One of these is the choice between using frames and using tables to create areas on your web pages for navigation that are separate from content.

A great many web sites place navigation links at the left-hand side or top or bottom of the page; you have probably noticed this while surfing, and in Figure 8.1. The pages in Figure 8.3 also have a navigation bar at the left-hand side. There are two primary ways of implementing this: using tables and using frames. Each has its advantages and disadvantages.

- *Persistence.* Frames offer the advantage of persistence of certain parts of the page layout, such as a navigation bar. When one frame is scrolled, the other frames are not affected. In a page laid out using tables, the entire page scrolls as a single unit. See Figure 8.5 and Figure 8.6.

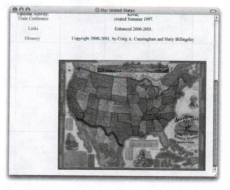

FIGURE 8.5   The entry page of "Our United States," implemented using tables. Notice that when the user scrolls down to see the map, the navigation elements scroll up almost out of sight.

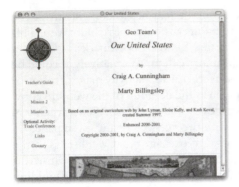
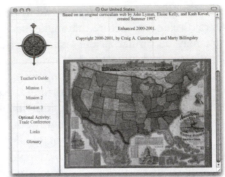

FIGURE 8.6   The same page as shown in Figure 8.5, implemented using frames. The navigation bar stays in place, even when the user scrolls the page down to see the map.

- *Download times.* Frames also offer the advantage of decreased download times when the user selects a new page within the web site. Because only part of the page is replaced by new content, fewer and smaller files are downloaded from the server. When the user follows a hyperlink within the site, only part of the window has to load new content. This leads to faster download times.
- *Screen real estate.* A disadvantage of using frames to lay out a web page is that often the navigation bar uses up screen space that could be put to better use. See Figure 8.7.

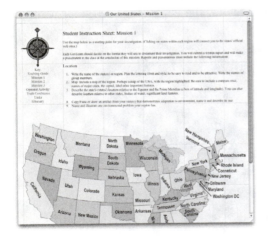
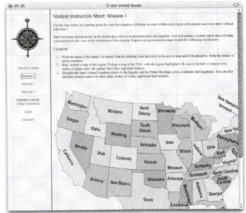

FIGURE 8.7   A web page implemented using tables (left) and frames (right).

Notice that in the left side of Figure 8.7, which is implemented using tables, the large map at the bottom can span two cells of the table, allowing the student to see the whole map without scrolling sideways. In the right side of Figure 8.7, which is implemented using frames, the map has to be displayed entirely in the right-hand frame; it cannot cross over into the navigation bar. A potentially beneficial piece of screen space is wasted.

How to Implement Frames

Frames are implemented with a set of HTML files, rather than a single file. The main file specifies the layout of the frames within the browser window. The HTML for the layout in Figure 8.6 of "Our United States" is:

```
<FRAMESET COLS="150,*" ROWS="*">
    <FRAME SRC="navbar.html" SCROLLING="no">
    <FRAME SRC="main.html" NAME="content_frame">
</frameset>
```

The `<FRAMESET>` tag specifies that there will be two frames side-by-side, the first one 150 pixels in width and the second one the remaining width of the browser window. The first `<FRAME>` tag specifies that the first frame (the left-hand one) will display the contents of the HTML file `navbar.html`. Because the navigation bar is not very long, a scroll bar will not be displayed (thus saving some screen space). The second `<FRAME>` tag specifies that the second frame (the right-hand one) will display the file `main.html`. It is given a name, `content_frame`, for future reference. Links in the navigation bar will use this name to load new pages into the right-hand frame.

See our HTML Reference on *curriculumwebs.com* for more information on the HTML tags used to create frames. Many of the WYSIWYG web editors have features that allow you to create frames (see Hands-On Lesson 8) but some do not (for example, Mozilla Composer), in which case you will have to create the HTML tags yourself.

ACTIVITY 8E ▪ Implement Your Site Structure

Download Hands-On Lesson 8, which leads you through the steps of setting up a new web site. Create a web page for each of the chunks of information you currently have in your curriculum web. If you have chosen to use frames, create the framesets now. If you have decided to store images or other resources in separate folders, create those folders now. (You will add most of the content in Activity 8F.)

Implement a rudimentary navigation system that mirrors the map you created in Activity 8D with links that are simply text for now. Even though your curriculum web is stored locally on your computer and is not yet published on the Web, you can test all the links by viewing your pages in a web browser. Make sure all links work. Don't worry for now about the way your links look. As you learn more about graphics and multimedia in subsequent chapters, the look of your navigation links will change.

ACTIVITY 8F ■ Insert Content Into Your Site Structure

In the course of the first seven chapters of this book you created and gathered much material for your curriculum web: a teaching guide, activities for your learners, lists of supporting resources, lists of materials and equipments, rubrics, assessment plans, and so on. Some of these may exist only on paper; others have already been created as web pages. For each page that you have created for your web site, insert the appropriate content. This may involve some copying and pasting from a word-processing document, typing in content that you had written down on paper, or inserting already existing web pages.

As you learn more about interactivity, instructional supports, and assessment in the chapters that follow, you may want to add content to your pages, or even pages to your site plan. By the time you are finished with Chapter 11, the site's structure and look and feel will be complete (at least until you decide to start improving the curriculum web, which could be an ongoing process).

Chapter Summary

This chapter:

- Outlines the steps to consider for organizing and planning your web site
- Emphasizes the importance of metaphor for conveying information and making visitors feel comfortable
- Discusses the overall architecture of your site, focusing on choosing an easy-to-use navigational scheme
- Points out the differences between using frames and tables to present information
- Describes how to use chunking to better present information
- Lists the major components that you might want to include in your web site

Questions For Reflection

In his book *Experience Design*, Nathan Shedroff (2001) writes:

> Metaphors are one way to build a *cognitive model*, and they can be very powerful in orienting people to help them understand an experience; but they can be equally

disastrous if they aren't applied well. Metaphors use references to already known experiences as clues to new ones. The 'desktop' metaphor of most personal computer operating systems is an attempt to help people create and use files, store and arrange them, delete them, and work with them. It has mostly worked well, but only because the metaphor isn't totally consistent with the real experience—the operating system doesn't *really* work like a person's desk. Too close of an adherence to the theme either limits the functions of the system, or creates confusion when the two don't work together consistently.

In actuality, most metaphors used in this sense are actually similes. The difference is subtle. . . .

Metaphors are not required and can be crutches for poor ideas and design. Used well, however, they can be illuminating for users and quickly orient them to the functions and interactions of an experience. (102)

We can define *simile* as a comparison of two unlike things. A computer operating system is like a desktop in some ways, and unlike it in others. The WIT section home page shown in Figure 8.1 is like a bulletin board in some ways but unlike it in others. By concentrating on the differences, and building explicit cues to help the user bridge those differences (for example, using images of thumbtacks), the simile becomes a useful metaphor.

Consider the difference between a simile and a metaphor in reference to the metaphor or theme you developed in Activity 8B. What are some explicit cues you can use in your curriculum web to bridge the difference between the curriculum web and the thing or system you are going to use as a metaphor? Make a list.

Your Next Step

At this point, you have reached a milestone in your web design. You have gathered much of the information, data, activities, pictures, sounds, and movies that you will display on your web site. You have chosen a theme or metaphor to support your curriculum. You have divided all your materials into logical pieces that are of a manageable size, and have decided how your visitors will move from piece to piece. You have created the skeleton of your web site, with a page for each chunk of information and rudimentary navigation elements in place.

In Hands-On Lesson 8, which you should complete now if you haven't already, you will begin to construct the web site that will support the curriculum you have planned. You will create the file structure for the site (based on the chunking you learned about in this chapter), and create some navigation tools.

In the next two chapters, you will learn more about two of the most important ways that web sites can be different from (and better than) textbooks: multimedia and interactivity.

For Further Learning

■ See *curriculumwebs.com* for some links pertinent to the topics in this chapter and for our extensive online HTML and CSS references.

■ The process of building a web site is well explained in layman's terms in Hixson and Schrock 2003 and Williams and Tollett 2000.

■ A good review of developing a metaphor and a look and feel for a web site can be found in Siegel 1997.

■ For more about wayfinding elements and other aides to navigation see Shedroff 2001.

CHAPTER 9

USING MULTIMEDIA

Overview

The most exciting feature of the Web is its ability to deliver many types of content in addition to text. This chapter helps you to go beyond text in your curriculum web. It defines multimedia, describes graphics file formats, gives procedures for acquiring and creating images and placing these images on web pages, discusses image maps, shows you how to incorporate sound and video into your web pages, and suggests a rationale for the use of PDF format.

WHAT IS MULTIMEDIA?

Multimedia is defined as information that involves or encompasses several **media.** In the world of the Web, multimedia tends to mean a combination of text, pictures, movies, and sound on web pages. In the future we may see this expand to include smell, touch, and even taste. In this chapter our discussion is limited to pictures, movies, and sound. We discuss some technical details of file formats, talk about how to create or acquire images, and show how to incorporate images into a web page. (You will learn more about this in Hands-On Lesson 9.) Then we move on to **animations,** movies, and sound.

Why include graphics, movies, and sound in a curriculum web? In the 1950s, Marshall McLuhan said that the "medium is the message." Whereas graphics previously were an aid that reinforced the message communicated through text, over time the reverse has become the norm. Contemporary learners, influenced by music videos and the sound-clip culture, increasingly perceive text as an aid to support audio and visual messages. You will need to embrace this shift if you hope to create a truly engaging learning experience.

GRAPHICS FILE FORMATS

All file formats for the Web have one thing in common: compression. Compression is the key to making small graphics. By small, we mean small file sizes that download quickly rather than graphics that are small in dimension. Unfortunately, sometimes compression is accompanied by loss of quality.

FIGURE 9.1   A photograph saved in JPEG format (left) and GIF format (right).

The format you choose for an image depends on the type of image. Full-color photographs generally yield the best results when saved as **JPEG** files. JPEG compression can preserve the broad color and tonal range in photographic images better than other compression formats can. **GIF** is usually the best file format for graphics with areas of solid color such as logos, cartoons, or illustrations. GIF format compresses files by reducing repetitive areas, such as large areas of solid color, which photographs do not contain.

Figure 9.1 shows a photograph saved in two different file formats. Notice the degradation in image quality when the photo is saved in GIF format (the image on the right). The file sizes are identical at 12K apiece; no size advantage was gained in converting to GIF.

Figure 9.2 shows a graphic saved in different file formats. The top image, which was saved as a JPEG at the lowest quality, has a file size of 15K and very poor image quality. The middle image, which was saved as a JPEG at the highest quality, has a file size of 24K and the quality is just fine. The bottom image, which was saved as a GIF,

FIGURE 9.2   A banner headline saved in JPEG format at the lowest quality (top), in JPEG format at high quality (middle), and in GIF format (bottom).

has a file size of only 9K and sacrifices nothing in terms of picture quality. Thus we see that GIF formatting is the best choice for this type of graphic; it results in the smallest file to download while maintaining great quality.

The moral of the story is: use JPEG format for photographs and GIF format for text, logos, and cartoons.

There are other graphics file formats available for the Web, notably PNG, short for Portable Network Graphics. Designed to replace the simpler GIF format, PNG is a **lossless** compression scheme that allows more colors to be included in an image and more than one color to be transparent. This file format is not yet in widespread use but will become more so as web designers become more familiar with it.

JPEG Details

JPEG is the image format defined by the Joint Photographic Experts Group, and is the most common way to compress photographs and other images with subtle gradations. Because of the overhead involved with even small images saved in this format, it does not work well for small images or line art. But because JPEGs can represent millions of colors, they work very well for photographs.

JPEG is a **lossy** process—information is always lost in the compression. Once compressed with JPEG, even using the highest quality settings, the image will not be identical to the original. To the human eye the difference may or may not be discernible, but the file will be smaller. At the higher compression ratios (lower quality settings), the image is noticeably different. Use the highest compression (lowest quality) that you can without making the image look bad. This usually involves saving several copies of the image at different compression ratios to see what is the highest compression that produces an acceptable image. Many graphics editors, such as Adobe Photoshop, include tools to help you choose the optimal setting.

Always end your JPEG filenames with the suffix ".jpeg" or ".jpg," as in "photo1.jpeg." This is similar to HTML files, which are always saved with the suffix ".html" or ".htm." As with HTML, choose one format to use throughout your site (either ".jpeg" or ".jpg") and stick with it to avoid confusion.

Progressive JPEGs.   Normally, files in JPEG format are stored in such a way that the pixels at the top of the image download first and the pixels at the bottom of the image download last, and they are shown to the user in that order. A "progressive" JPEG stores pixels out of this linear order; they arrive at the user's browser in evenly spaced blocks. You may have seen these images; they show up out-of-focus and gradually come into full focus. The idea is to show the user a rough version of the whole image first, to be filled in as the details of the image arrive. This is a good technique to use for impatient surfers or those with slow Internet connections, or for very large images. However, images that are being used for navigation or text that must be read need to fully load before they can be used, so this technique should only be used for nonessential information. To implement this, select the "Progressive" option when saving your JPEG file in a graphics editor.

GIF Details

The GIF format uses a compression algorithm called Lempel-Ziv-Welch, or LZW, which was designed specifically for online delivery. This compression scheme is lossless, which means that the resulting decompressed image looks exactly like the original. In general, use GIF formatting for anything that is not photographic or highly shaded, such as type or line art such as logos, cartoons, or illustrations. The downside to GIF formatting is that images are limited to 256 colors, so photographs usually do not look good in this format.

Always end your GIF filenames with the suffix ".gif," as in `button1.gif.`

Interlacing.   Interlaced GIFs are similar to the progressive JPEGs discussed above. Interlaced GIFs show up out-of-focus and gradually come into full focus. Again, this is a good technique to use for impatient surfers or those with slow Internet connections. To implement this, select the "Interlaced" option when saving your GIF file.

There are two additional issues that are germane to GIF file formatting that do not crop up with JPEGs: transparency and animation.

Transparency.   Images on the Web are always rectangular. You can get around this limitation through the use of transparent GIFs, which can create the illusion of irregularly shaped graphics. One color within the image is designated as transparent; the user's browser will make all pixels of that color in the image transparent, allowing the background to show through. Be warned, however, that only a single color can be chosen; any pixels that are very close but not exactly that color will be displayed. Search the help file of your graphics editor to learn more about how to create transparent GIFs.

Animated GIFs.   An animated GIF is a sequence of images, or frames, stored in a single GIF file. Each frame differs slightly from the preceding frame, creating the illusion of movement when the frames are viewed in quick succession. At the time you create an animated GIF, you can choose certain options, such as for continuous play or a slide-show effect. Once the image file downloads into the client's memory, it can continue to run.

Animated GIFs are the simplest form of animation on the Web; they require no **plug-ins** on the user's browser, and the authoring tools used to create them are often free and easy to learn. They are inserted in a web page just like any other GIF: by means of the <IMG> tag. These GIFs tend to be fairly simple; more complex animations are normally implemented using Flash, which we discuss in Chapter Ten.

To animate photographs that are in JPEG format, you must first change each frame to GIF format and then create the animation. Sometimes the quality of the image as it is reduced to 256 colors is unacceptable to most web designers. Other times it looks fine. For example, Figure 9.3 shows a web page that displays an animated GIF of the phases of the moon. The lack of color depth doesn't really matter for these images.

Figure 9.4 shows some frames of the animation itself. Although the images used to make up the frames of the animation had to be converted from JPEG to GIF, the

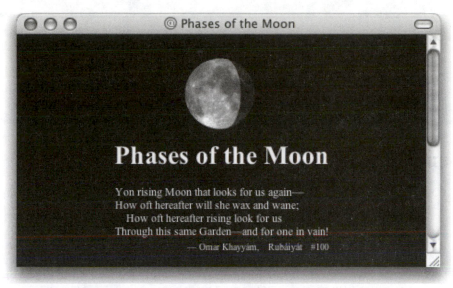

FIGURE 9.3   Web page displaying an animated GIF of the phases of the moon.

Source: Courtesy of Ed Stephan, *ac.wwu.edu/~stephan.*

image quality is perfectly adequate. Most software packages that meld these GIF frames into animation do some additional compression or other tricks to reduce the file size of the finished animation. In this case the file, which is made up of 59 frames, is only 39K in size and downloads very quickly.

FIGURE 9.4   Snapshots of frames that make up an animated GIF.

Source: Courtesy of Ed Stephan, *ac.wwu.edu/~stephan.*

■ ■ ■ ■ ■

"GIF" OR "JIF"?

GIF is the acronym for Graphics Interchange Format, one of the two ubiquitous image formats found on the Web. Because the first word in the acronym is "graphics," the acronym is pronounced with a hard g (not like the peanut butter brand).

ACQUIRING IMAGES

Many people choose to use images that have been created by others instead of creating their own for use on their web sites. There are plenty of resources available, both off- and online. Please be sure to consult Chapter Seven's discussion of copyright issues before using graphics created by others.

There are lots of web sites that have clip art and photographs freely available for use. See *curriculumwebs.com* for an up-to-date list of some of these sites. When you find an image you like, you can download it to your computer for later use:

- On a PC, right-click on the image itself. You will get a menu allowing you to "Save Image As . . ." or "Download Image to Disk." Specify a location and a file-name and save the image.
- On a Mac, click and hold the mouse button down on the image itself. You will get a menu allowing you to "Save this Image As . . ." or "Download Image to Disk." Specify a location and a filename and save the image.

Clip art is also available for sale on CD. The images might not be in either JPEG or GIF format; you might have to open them up in a graphics software package and convert the format. Be sure to check the licensing on any source of clip art to make sure you are allowed to publish the images on your web site!

CREATING IMAGES

You may choose to create your own images for your web page. In order to do this, you will need some image-making software. Many software packages are available, including Photoshop, Illustrator, Painter, Photo Deluxe, Paint Shop Pro, Freehand, and Photo-Paint. Any of these programs can be used to create text headlines or line drawings from scratch, or to manipulate scanned artwork or photos. Digital images that you create or modify might include headline text, scanned artwork or photographs, or pictures taken with a digital camera.

Adobe Photoshop is the most popular graphics software among professional designers on any platform, for almost any purpose; it has the most depth and features of any graphics software package. The latest versions come with a tool called ImageReady that makes the creation of almost any format for the Web (including animations) a snap. A product with similar functionality, Fireworks, is available from Macromedia. This book does not propose to provide a tutorial on using Photoshop, Fireworks, or other tools; there are several other admirable books available that provide such instruction. See For Further Learning at the end of this chapter. Our web site at *curriculumwebs.com* also has links to online tutorials for several graphics programs.

The key thing to remember when creating your own images is that they should be in JPEG, GIF, or PNG format, and you should pay particular attention to the size of the file. A great graphic is no good if it takes minutes to download. It is a good idea to experiment with different image settings to see how these affect file size. ImageReady's "optimization" feature will help you to do this.

Using Images for Headlines

Headline type is typically larger than the bulk of the written text on a web page. It is designed to quickly draw the user's eye it, help define a page break, or organize multiple ideas. This headline text can either be implemented using the <FONT> or <H1> through <H6> tags in HTML, or can be an image that contains type.

The advantages of using an image for headline text is that you can use fonts that may not be available on the client's computer, gradations of color, drop shadows, and other graphics techniques. The primary disadvantage has to do with increased download time. Other problems creep in if you are trying to place this text over a background pattern; you'll have to use a GIF image with a transparent background, and the text might have a white shadow or look more jagged than if saved in JPEG format.

Scanned Artwork and Photographs

You might consider using scanned imagery instead of clip art or images that you have downloaded from the Web. You can use a scanner to include your students' art work, to include photographs that you have taken, or to include works from other publications. Make sure to review the discussion on copyright law in Chapter Seven before using work that others have created.

There are many types of scanners available, and each operates in slightly different ways. Some have their own software to control the scan and save the resulting image, while others allow you to scan from within a graphics program like Photoshop. Consult your scanner's manual for information on using your particular scanner. There are two technical things to remember when scanning for the Web:

- Scan your image at a **resolution** of 72 dots per inch (dpi). This is the resolution of most computer monitors. Any higher resolution in the image will be wasted (unless the image is intended for printing onto paper).
- Save photographs in JPEG format and line art or cartoons in GIF format. These are the optimal applications of these two formats.

Digital Photos

The other way to create your own images for your web site is to take photographs with a digital camera. Again, there are many different cameras and many different ways to transfer the photo from the camera to your computer; consult your camera's manual for more information. Keep in mind that newer, better cameras can take pictures at a much higher resolution (or size) than is necessary for web applications. If you know that the pictures you are taking will be displayed only on the Web, set your camera to "Basic" or "Low Resolution" mode. Of course, you can always take your pictures at high resolution and use a software package to reduce the file size to acceptable levels.

Most digital cameras come with software that will perform simple tasks such as cropping, reducing size and resolution, rotating photos, and removing red-eye.

PLACING IMAGES

After you create or acquire your images, the next step is to decide where they fit within the layout of your web page. See page 78 for a discussion of this issue. The HTML to include an image is fairly simple, but there are several attributes worth mentioning. Your favorite web-page editor may or may not have the capability to include all these attributes; you may have to add some of them manually. See our HTML Reference at *curriculumwebs.com* for more details.

The tag for including an image on your web page is the `<IMG>` tag. (There is no closing `</IMG>` tag.) This tag requires at least one attribute, `SRC`, which specifies the source of the image (i.e., the file where the image is stored). If the graphics file is in the same folder as your HTML file, then the filename will suffice. Otherwise you will have to provide a path to the image file. (See the Appendix—An Overview of Web Technologies—for details.)

For example, say that you are creating a web page about graphing. You have several images that you want to include, so you grouped them in a folder called "images" that is located in the same directory as your HTML file. To include a bar graph with the filename "bar-graph.gif," the tag would look like this:

```
<IMG SRC="images/bar-graph.gif">
```

If your image is to be a link, surround the image tag by an anchor tag:

```
<A HREF="destination.html"><IMG SRC="images/
bar-graph.gif"></A>
```

By default, a border will show up around the image, in the link text color. To eliminate this border, add the `BORDER` attribute to the `<IMG>` tag.

```
<A HREF="destination.html"><IMG SRC="images/
bar-graph.gif" BORDER="0"></A>
```

Perhaps you would like a border around an image that is not a link; the `BORDER` attribute can do that too:

```
<IMG SRC="images/bar-graph.gif" BORDER="1">
```

The border color will be the same as the default text color.

As mentioned in Chapter Four you can specify the alignment of the image with regard to surrounding text. The ALIGN attribute has five different values: left, right, top, middle, and bottom. The left and right values make text flow around the image, which is moved to the corresponding margin; the remaining three align the image vertically with respect to the surrounding text, but the text is not wrapped.

Manually set the widths and heights of your images so that other page content can be displayed while the images are downloading. By adding the WIDTH and HEIGHT attributes to your <IMG> tag, you tell the browser how much room to set aside for the image so it can start to display the text around the image before it actually gets the image itself. This gives the user something to look at other than an empty page. Fortunately, most web-page editors will put in the image dimensions for you. If you want to include them yourself, you will have to open up the image in a graphic editor like Photoshop and look at the height and width as specified in pixels or points (these are in general the same thing). Then include the HEIGHT and WIDTH attributes to your image tag.

```
<IMG SRC="images/bar-graph.gif" WIDTH="300" Height="210">
```

Widths and heights are always specified in pixels, not in inches or centimeters. This photo is 300 pixels wide and 210 pixels high, which will be displayed as about 4″ × 3″ on most monitors.

You can use HTML to change the size of an image by specifying new WIDTH and HEIGHT attributes. The same size file will be downloaded, but shown in new dimensions. There are two reasons to avoid doing this:

- If the dimensions specified are larger than the actual image, the picture will probably be too grainy.
- If the dimensions specified are smaller than the actual image, the image will display properly, but the file will take just as long to download than if it were displayed at full size.

In either case, it is much better to open the image in a graphics editor such as Photoshop to resize it. You end up with the best quality picture with the smallest file size.

The HSPACE attribute specifies how much white space is to be added to the left and right of an image. Similarly, the VSPACE attribute can be used to put white space above and below an image. The values are given in pixels.

```
<IMG SRC="images/bar-graph.gif" HSPACE="5" VSPACE="5">
```

The ALT attribute provides information about the graphic to people who are viewing your page with a text-only web browser or who have turned image loading off in their browser preferences (while surfing the Web via a modem, for example). The information you provide here will help the user determine if it is worthwhile reloading the page with full graphics. Computer setups for the visually impaired also make use of this attribute to speak the image's information to the user. (See Chapter Twelve for more on helping special needs leaners.)

```
<IMG SRC="images/bar-graph.gif" ALT="example of a bar
graph">
```

The LOWSRC attribute of the <IMG> tag shows the user an image with a smaller file size and less detail while the user is waiting for a picture with a larger file size to load. This works rather like interlaced GIFs or progressive JPEGs in placating users who are impatient for a final image to load. To do this, a low-resolution version of the image must be stored in an alternative file.

```
<IMG SRC="images/bar-graph.gif" LOWSRC="images/
bar-graphLoRes.gif">
```

IMAGE MAPS

Image maps are graphics in which different areas of the image are linked to different locations. An example is the U.S. map on the "Our United States" curriculum web that links students to informational web sites about different areas of the country. Looking at the status bar as the mouse pointer passes over the different states, we can see that they are links to different web sites. See Figure 9.5.

It is possible to manually create the HTML tags necessary to define an image map, but it is tedious and unnecessary. Some web-page editors include tools for creating image maps (we discuss this in Hands-On Lesson 9), and there are some good shareware programs that will create the tags for you as you point-and-click to outline the different areas of the map. Once the tags are created, all you have to do is copy and paste them into your HTML document where you want the image to go. See *curriculumwebs.com* for pointers to the latest shareware for making image maps.

You can also create the effect of an image map by breaking down a large picture into smaller sections, making each one a link, and tiling them together by using a table. Make sure that in each <IMG> tag you have included the attribute BORDER="0", or you will get a colored line around each segment of the image map. Also include the attributes HSPACE="0" and VSPACE="0" in the table tags to ensure that the images abut each other with no white space between. The advantage of this technique is that

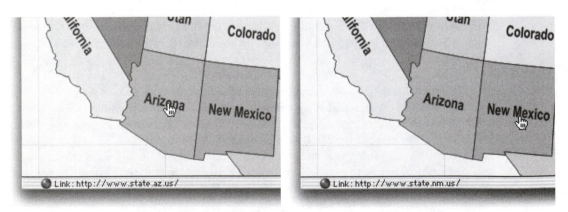

FIGURE 9.5   Detail of an image map in which each state is a link to a different web page.

the smaller images will load more quickly. The disadvantage is that each clickable area is limited to a rectangular shape; this would not work very well for a U.S. map.

ACTIVITY 9A ■ Add Images

Assemble all the images that you have acquired or created for your curriculum web. Examine each one for the following:

- *Relevance:* does the image either contribute to the content of your subject matter or extend the metaphor or look of your web site? If neither, discard the image.
- *Resolution:* is the image saved at 72 dpi? If not, use graphics software or a file conversion package to reduce the resolution.
- *Format and filename:* is the image in the appropriate format (GIF, JPEG, or PNG)? Does the filename extension accurately reflect the image's format? Does the file have a useful, descriptive name? If not, make the necessary corrections.

Add the image files to your web site. If you created one or more separate folders to hold images, put the image files there. *It is important to put the image files in the right place within your site before using them in any of your web pages.* If you move an image file after inserting the image in a web page, the page will no longer display the image properly.

Insert the images into the pages of your curriculum web. Use the techniques you have learned to design an effective layout for each page.

INCORPORATING SOUND

There are many ways in which sound can enhance your curriculum web. Excerpts from speeches, sound bites from historical events, examples of dialects, foreign language tutorials, sound effects that play whenever the mouse pointer rolls over a link (this is great for the visually impaired), samples of music, examples of different animal noises; these are all aural aids that can be put to good use on a web page. Sound can be used in annoying or inappropriate ways as well; there exist educationally oriented web pages on which background music that has nothing to do with the subject matter plays continually at top volume. It is very difficult to use these pages in a classroom (unless each computer has one or two headphones attached to it). Make your sounds count; do not add sound just because it is an exciting technology and you know how to do it.

As with some of the other sophisticated technologies, the details of how to create sound files are beyond the scope of this book. We will focus instead on incorporating these files in your web page in various ways, but begin with a brief overview of sound file formats.

There are two basic kinds of sound files: wave files and instruction files. A wave file is a compressed version of a sound wave, like a human voice or notes from a piano. The most recent browsers have built-in support for the AIFF, AU, and WAV audio formats; however, the most popular technology for playing these sounds are the

RealAudio Player and Windows Media Player plug-ins. In software that is built into web browsers, the entire sound file must be downloaded before it begins to play. RealAudio Player and Windows Media Player, however, use streaming, so you hear it as it comes in over the Internet. (See the sidebar on streaming AV on page 194.) Streamed audio can be used for music, distance learning, and even for two-way conversations. This is a technology that is becoming more prevalent.

Instruction files work in a different way. MIDI files transmit musical-instrument instructions that are then synthesized in software on your computer and sent to your speakers. The QuickTime plug-in includes a good MIDI player, as do several other audio plug-ins. MIDI files are very small, even when several instruments are playing at the same time, and the sound quality is very good.

There are many software packages available to help you create or capture sound and store it in a web-compatible file format. See *curriculumwebs.com* for further information on the latest technology in this area. You can acquire sound files by capturing your own voice, live music, music from a CD, or other sounds. You can download sound files from other web pages; in fact, there are lots of web sites and CD-ROMS that include royalty-free music and sound effects. Remember that sound is protected under copyright law, just as text and images are; it is not legal to take a recording from your favorite band and stick it on your web site. Check out the copyright status of every sound you intend to use.

One way to include sound files in an HTML document is through the <A> tag. When the user clicks on the text or image located between the <A> and </A> tags, the sound is downloaded and played. For example, the following line of HTML will display clickable text that is linked to the AIF sound with the filename "sound1.aif."

```
<A HREF="sound1.aif">Click here to play this sound</A>
```

Browsers depend on the filename suffix (like ".aif" or ".midi") to determine the file format and hence what software to use to play the sound. Make sure to label your files carefully!

You can use an image, such as a picture of an ear, that the user clicks on to get the sound:

```
<A HREF="sound1.aif"><IMG SRC="ear.gif"></A>
```

The more advanced web-page editors have options that allow you to easily add sound to your web page; in fact, some of them will automatically produce JavaScript that checks to see if the user's browser has the necessary built-in capacity to play the sound. This is by far the easiest way to embed sound into your HTML document. See Hands-On Lesson 9 for specific procedures. Sounds can also be embedded in a web page along with user control buttons by using the <EMBED> tag. (See Table 9.1.)

Inline sound, or sound which is played without the user having to click on anything, is incorporated with the <BGSOUND> tag. The tag

```
<BGSOUND SRC="sound1.aif" LOOP="5">
```

will repeat the sound "sound1.aif" five times when the web page is opened or refreshed.

The tag

```
<BGSOUND SRC="sound1.aif" LOOP="infinite">
```

will play the sound "`sound1.aif`" forever and probably drive your users mad—or at least elsewhere.

ACTIVITY 9B ▪ Brainstormig Sounds

Consider the subject matter of your curriculum web. Make a list of sounds that could enhance the content of your site. (Pay no attention at this point to whether the sounds you list exist or not, or are available to you or not.)

Consider your audience. Are there ways in which sound could be used to help convey the subject matter or instructional plan of your curriculum? Write down a list of the sounds you would need.

If feasible, create or acquire the sounds and incorporate them into your site.

INCORPORATING VIDEO

Videos that incorporate both moving pictures and sound can enhance your curriculum web. However, movie files tend to be large and can take a long time to download. Also, to play a movie, it must be held in the client computer's memory; a computer with a small amount of **RAM** will not be able to show the movie properly. Beware of creating content that only the elite few with fast Internet connections, loads of RAM, and high-end computers can view—you may be excluding a large segment of your target set of learners. Make sure your medium fits the message and use multimedia wisely and sparingly. Just because you *can* add video clips to your web site does not mean you should!

One way to avoid the long download times on video is to use streaming. This works similarly to the audio streaming we discussed above. Again, very few schools will have streaming video servers to support this technology. Eventually, we expect there will be commercial web sites that will offer this as a service to schools. The details of incorporating streaming video are beyond the scope of this book; however, we have provided some information in the sidebar "Streaming AV."

Movie formats for the Web include QuickTime, AVI, and MPEG. MPEG was the early Web standard, but has been surpassed by QuickTime because, unlike MPEG movies, QuickTime movies combining both moving pictures and sound can be created without special hardware. The QuickTime browser plug-in shows movies right on the web page, unlike earlier technology in which a helper **application** opened up a separate window. It can handle several different movie formats and is included with most popular web browsers these days.

There are many movie-making software packages available, some of which are very simple for the novice to use. See our web site for an update on the latest technology in this field. With movie-making software you typically can edit digital video, taken from videotape footage or from a digital video camera, or you can create pure animation from still images. For example, you can turn a panoramic picture into a video of a pan or sweep from one side of the picture to the other. Video editing software also allows you to add titles to your movies. Another source of video clips is to download them from other web sites. These are covered by copyright law, so be sure to check their status before using them!

If you are going to make your own videos, you should know that the standard size for movies on the Web is 240 by 180 pixels. (That is about 3 $\frac{1}{3}'' \times 2 \frac{1}{2}''$ on a computer whose monitor is set to a screen resolution that you might find in a classroom.) This looks better than you might think; web audiences are used to looking at these small movie screens and do not expect movie-theater quality. If you decide to include titles or graphics in your movie, create those elements at a bigger scale than you would if you had the full screen to play with. Fonts should be at least 30 points in size to be readable once the move is shrunk to thumbnail size.

Web-based movies look good at anywhere from 5 to 15 frames per second. However, if the video includes audio the frame rate must be closer to the high end of this scale. The choice will probably be dictated by the length of your movie; even at 5 frames per second a half-hour documentary will result in a file size that is simply too big for web delivery. Movies on the Web are typically less than one minute in length. When saving your movie in a web-based file format, use the lowest frame speed and the highest compression setting that still results in a decent-quality picture (and comprehensible audio).

Once you have created or acquired a movie, you can include it on your web page in one of two ways. You can use the <A> tag surrounding some text or a graphic that users have to click on to get to the movie. In this case the HREF attribute specifies the name of the movie file. Here is an example of the tag for a web page that plays the movie "webTour.mov" when the user clicks on the text "Click here to take a web tour":

```
<A HREF="webTour.mov">Click here to take a web tour</A>
```

The advantage of this method is that it does not need a plug-in on the client computer in order to work; the disadvantage is that the user must click on the movie to start the process going, and then wait until the movie downloads from the web server before it plays.

Much nicer is to use the <EMBED> tag. This tag is used to include files on a web page that are to be handled by a plug-in on the user's computer. QuickTime movies and other video format fall into this category. The advantages to this method are that the movies are shown inline, that is, within the context of the web page, and that the download begins as soon as the web page is opened, lessening the waiting time for the user. A control panel appears below the movie, allowing the user to play, fast forward, rewind, and stop the movie.

The <EMBED> tag has several attributes, some of which are reviewed in Table 9.1.

Figure 9.6 shows a web page with a QuickTime movie embedded with the following tag:

```
<EMBED SRC="webTour.mov" WIDTH="240" HEIGHT="180"
AUTOPLAY="FALSE">
```

Note the player controls at the bottom of the QuickTime window.

TABLE 9.1   Attributes of the <EMBED> Tag

SRC="filename"	The filename of the movie or sound file. If the movie is on a different web server, the complete URL must be given.
PLUGINSPAGE="URL"	If the necessary plug-in is not installed in the user's browser, this attribute will take the user to the appropriate page to download the plug-in.
WIDTH="size"	The width of the movie must be given, unless the movie is to be hidden (which is only useful if the movie contains only sound and no pictures). The width is given in pixels; the Web standard is 160. Note that giving a bigger number will not make the movie any bigger; it will be centered in a bigger space.
HEIGHT="size"	The height of the movie, given in pixels; the Web standard is 240.
HIDDEN	This hides the movie. Usually it is only useful when the movie is nothing but sound.
AUTOPLAY=TRUE AUTOPLAY=FALSE	If set to TRUE, this attribute causes the movie to start playing as soon as it is downloaded. The default value is FALSE.
CONTROLLER=TRUE CONTROLLER=FALSE	If set to TRUE, the movie controls are shown; if set to FALSE, the movie controls are hidden from the user. The default value is TRUE.
LOOP=TRUE LOOP=FALSE LOOP=PALINDROME	If set to TRUE, the movie plays over and over. If set to FALSE, the movie plays once. If set to PALINDROME, the movie plays alternately forward and backward.
HREF="URL"	This provides a link to another page when the movie is clicked on.

FIGURE 9.6   A web page with an embedded QuickTime movie.

Another interesting video technology is QuickTime Virtual Reality (QTVR). QTVR is a type of QuickTime movie that makes it possible to see and navigate through 360-degree panoramic images without any external gadgetry. The file can be created so that to the user it looks as if he or she is standing in the center of the picture, able to turn around and see the view in all directions, or it can be made to look as if the user is walking all the way around an object. Clickable "hot zones" can take the user to another place, presumably another QTVR clip. This technology has been successfully used to create online museum exhibits where the user can examine artifacts from all angles.

ACTIVITY 9C ■ Brainstorming Video

Consider the subject matter of your curriculum web. Make a "wish list" of movies, with or without sound, that could enhance the content of your site.

Consider your audience. Are there ways in which movies could be used to help convey the subject matter or instructional plan of your curriculum? Write down a list of the videos that could enhance the teaching of your site.

If feasible, create or acquire the movies and incorporate them into your site.

STREAMING AV

Streaming is a technology for playing audio and video files, either live or prerecorded, from a web page. Data is *streaming* when it's moving quickly from one computer to another and doesn't have to be all in one place for the destination computer to do something with it. When audio or video is streamed, a small buffer space is created on the user's computer, and data starts downloading into it. As soon as the buffer is full (usually just a matter of seconds), the file starts to play. As the file plays, it uses up information in the buffer, but while it is playing, more data is being downloaded. As long as the data can be downloaded as fast as it is used up in playback, the file will play smoothly. Sound and picture quality will be determined by the user's available bandwidth (download speed) and the speed of the user's computer. Users with older processors and slower modem connections will have more dropped frames and pixelization, or pauses in the audio.

With streaming, learners can access lengthy prerecorded audio and video clips to enhance and enrich their study of a topic. Students can also watch or listen to a live event remotely. In the case of distributed learning, streaming audio and video can serve as the primary mode of content delivery.

There are several utility programs that will take standard video files and convert them to a streaming format. See *curriculumwebs.com* for a list of these utilities. Most video editing software will also allow you to export video in a streaming format. There are currently three common media formats for streaming:

- Real Media files (files ending in .ra or .rm), played with the RealPlayer plug-in
- QuickTime (files ending in .mov), played with the QuickTime plug-in
- Windows Media format (video files ending in .wmv, audio files ending in .wma or .wm), played with the Windows Media Player plug-in

CONTINUED

You can play streamed media from any web server. However, to get the best results you really need a dedicated streaming media server or one that has streaming media server software installed that allows for smoother transmission.

PDF FILES

A specialized file format, known as Portable Document Format, or PDF, has been developed by Adobe. This format allows document designers to specify the formatting of their documents precisely. When readers access PDF documents, they see the documents exactly as the designer wanted them to appear. (Note that this is quite different from web pages, where the settings on the browser often thwart the designer's original intent.)

Developers of curriculum webs may want to use PDF when they have reasons to want their formatting to appear exactly as intended. Examples include worksheets or instructions that will be printed on the user's printer, or tables that require precise column widths or row heights. The printing of web pages produces varied and uncontrollable results; however, printing PDF documents almost always results in documents that look like the original, in terms of font, color (if the printer is color), placement of items on the page, page breaks, and so on. One solution that has worked for many web designers is to include both Web and PDF versions of certain documents, which allows the users to see it on the Web and also (if they desire) to see it or print it with its original formatting.

In order for readers using a PC to view a PDF file, they must have the Adobe Reader (formerly called Acrobat Reader) application or plug-in installed. These are available from the Adobe web site, at *adobe.com*, or via a link on *curriculumwebs.com*. It is always a good idea to include a link to Adobe's web site when including PDF documents in your curriculum web, so that readers who do not have the plug-in can go and get it. (Nearly all browsers now come with this plug-in preinstalled.) Macintosh OS X users can view PDF files either with Adobe Reader or with Preview, an application that comes installed with the operating system.

Creating PDF files to include in your curriculum web requires some additional software if you use a PC. The Adobe Acrobat program will convert a document in almost any electronic format, such as Microsoft Word, to a PDF file. Macintosh users using OS X can create PDF files simply by choosing the "Save as PDF" option in the print dialog box of any application.

Chapter Summary

This chapter:

- Defines the graphics file formats used on the Web
- Discusses the creation and acquisition of images

- Explains how to place images on your web page
- Reviews how to avoid some common problems encountered by web designers in using images
- Explains how to incorporate video and sound into a web page, including using streaming technology
- Describes the Portable Document Format and discusses its use in curriculum webs

Questions For Reflection

Read the excerpts from *Visual Literacy, Languaging, and Learning* by John L. Debes and Clarence M. Williams, found via a link in the Chapter 9 section of *curriculumwebs.com*.

What does this article tell you about the ways that thinking and learning may be changing in the twenty-first century with the rise of a visual culture? Can you think of examples that illustrate these changes from your own experience as a teacher, student, or curriculum developer? What implications do these changes in thinking and learning have for the development of curriculum webs? Add any relevant principles to the list you created at the end of Chapter Four.

Your Next Step

Download Hands-On Lesson 9, which shows steps for incorporating multimedia with your specific software. Follow the procedures, even if only for practice to help you retain the concepts found in this chapter.

For Further Learning

- See *curriculumwebs.com* for links to current shareware packages designed to edit images and create animations.
- For an in-depth review of graphics creation and use see Weinman 2003.
- See both Weinman 2003 and Siegel 1997 for more information on anti-aliasing and other technical issues related to creating images for the Web.
- Also see Weinman 2003 and Pirouz 1998 for discussions of web-based sound and video.
- See Lundsten and Spancer 2001 for discussion of how to integrate streaming audio or video into your web page.

10

CONSTRUCTING INTERACTIVITY

Overview

This chapter describes how to make the pages in your curriculum web **interactive** through the use of navigation aids, forms, interactive animation, and online editing tools such as blogs and wikis. JavaScript, CSS, and Flash are also discussed, as are techniques for sending users to alternate pages when they do not have proper computer hardware or software to handle your interactivity.

Because the needs of each curriculum web vary widely there are no set activities for this chapter. Readers are strongly encouraged to review each type of interactivity and consider how it might help their curriculum webs, and to try out those that seem interesting or worthwhile. Hands-On Lesson 10 covers some interactive techniques.

WHAT IS INTERACTIVITY?

Interactivity is back and forth communication between a user and a computer. Adding interactivity to a curriculum web creates a dialogue between the site and the learner, which helps the learners to immerse themselves in the subject matter. The simplest interactivity occurs when a web server delivers a web page to a user after the user clicks on a link. More complex interactivity involves more than a click and a response. Some web sites allow their users to input certain preferences that determine how the site responds to that particular user. Other sites allow the user to submit information to which the web server responds. Interactivity can be useful in engaging the readers' attention, in imparting more information than a static web page, or in gathering information from the user. It can be used to give immediate feedback to the user and long-term feedback to the web designer. Interactivity might be used in a curriculum web in the following ways:

- As an aid to navigation
- To collect feedback from the user through the use of forms
- To enable a collaborative process in which students can create journals or group projects

- To deliver interactive information, such as animated graphics or text that respond to the user's mouse movements, clicks, or other behaviors
- To provide online assessments that are automatically graded and that give immediate feedback
- To password-protect areas of the curriculum web for student confidentiality

It is important to distinguish between what is possible and what is easy to implement on a web page. Some interactive technologies are beyond the scope of this book; we will describe them but refer the reader to additional resources for help in implementing them.

Don't use technology just for technology's sake. The technologies discussed in this chapter should be used to enhance the content and navigability of your web site, not to overwhelm users with senseless features that may not work with their browsers. For each element of your design, ask yourself, "Do I really need to add this to my site? Will it truly add value to the flow and presentation of my content? Will it help foster learning?" Because not all web browsers can handle the technologies covered in this chapter, we also discuss how to provide low-tech alternative web pages for users with older or slower browsers.

JAVASCRIPT

Some of the techniques described in this chapter can be implemented using CSS, which was introduced in Chapter Four. Other techniques use JavaScript. JavaScript is often confused with the programming language **java.** Although the names are similar, there are fundamental differences between these two technologies. Java is a full-featured programming language that is compiled into machine code before execution. It is used for building independent, full-featured applications that can run without any other program on the user's machine. JavaScript, as its name implies, is a scripting language designed to work within an HTML document to manipulate elements of a page. Although it borrows much of its syntax from java and the programming language C++, JavaScript is always interpreted at download time, rather than compiled in advance. Therefore, JavaScript is dependent on the browser to interpret its commands.

One of the great advantages of JavaScript is that users familiar with HTML can get started using it with no prior programming experience. JavaScript code sits inside HTML documents and, like HTML, you can view it in the source code. Then you can copy the code, paste it, and personalize it as much as you like. There are several web sites that make scripts available for people to use; see *curriculumwebs.com* for an up-to-date list of these resources. (The more advanced web editors also help you to create JavaScript. See Hands-On Lesson 10.)

JavaScript can be used in many different ways, such as displaying a slide show, showing information about the HTML file such as its size or who created it and the last time it was updated, creating interesting interactive effects such as rollover buttons (discussed later in the chapter), making jump menus, displaying the current date and

FIGURE 10.1   A typical JavaScript segment. This segment displays a quote selected at random from a list of quotes.

```
<script language="JavaScript">

<!-- returns a random number between 1 and num (inclusive) -->
function randNum (num) {
        rand = Math.floor(Math.random() * num) + 1
        return rand;
}


<!-- prints a quote pulled at random from the list of quotes in the
function -->
function printRandomQuote()
{

    quotenumber = randNum(6)

    if (quotenumber == 1) document.write("A teacher affects eternity;
he can never tell where his influence stops.<br>-Henry Brooks Adams");
    if (quotenumber == 2) document.write("The highest result of
education is tolerance.<br>-Helen Keller");
    if (quotenumber == 3) document.write("A child's education should
begin at least 100 years before he is born.<br>-Oliver Wendell
Holmes");
    if (quotenumber == 4) document.write("The secret of education is
respecting the pupil.<br>-Ralph W. Emerson");
    if (quotenumber == 5) document.write("If there is anything
education does not lack today, it is critics.<br>-Nathan M. Pusey");
    if (quotenumber == 6) document.write("To be able to be caught up
into the world of thought--that is being educated.<br>-Edith
Hamilton");

}

</script>
```

time, timing how long a user has been looking at a particular page, finding out information about the user's browser and computer settings, creating calculators of various types, making pop-up windows, and so on. We discuss a few of these JavaScript applications a little later.

In Figure 10.1, we have reproduced a typical segment of JavaScript. This particular segment displays a quote selected at random from a list of quotes. Each time the page is reloaded a new quote appears.

Again, like HTML, you do not need to know a lot about JavaScript in order to use it. Full-featured WYSIWYG editors such as Dreamweaver and FrontPage include tools to enable you to create scripts, or use scripts you have copied from other web pages, without knowing any programming at all. The only caution is that you need to copy and paste entire scripts at a time, and not try to copy portions of scripts, unless you take the time to learn something about JavaScript syntax. If you want to learn more about JavaScript, see the resources listed at the end of this chapter.

COOKIES

Cookies were created to enable a server to store client-specific information on the client's machine, and to use that information when that server is accessed again by the client. Cookie technology allows servers to personalize pages for each client without having to use a complicated **CGI** or database system on the server's side.

Cookies are put to every conceivable use by web servers. For example, *tvguide.com* uses them to remember where you live and what cable service you have, thus allowing their server to show you the correct TV listings. *My.cnn.com* uses cookies to remember what types of news you want to see and how you'd like it presented.

Notice that because cookies remain on the client machine, the information is not available if the user sits down to work at a different computer. Many large sites, such as *amazon.com* and the *New York Times* site at *nyt.com*, choose to keep the information in a database on the server, which entails asking the user to log in when he or she goes to that site.

Cookies could be used in inventive ways in curriculum webs. For example, cookies could be used to remember where in a lesson a given user is, or to provide a review based on the results of an online quiz. Implementation of this technology is beyond the scope of this book; we refer the reader to a manual on CGI programming. See resources listed at the end of this chapter.

AIDS TO NAVIGATION

One way that you can use interactive features on your web site is to support navigation. The more intuitive and useful your navigation scheme is, the easier it is for the user to find the information he or she is looking for. Rollover text, rollover images, and text status messages can give the user feedback while browsing.

Rollover Text

Rollover text, which changes when the user's mouse rolls over it, adds interactivity without using graphics. The advantage of using rollover hyperlinks as opposed to rollover buttons is that the web-page designer doesn't need to upload images for the rollover effect. Rollover text is created solely through the manipulation of the code with CSS styles.

Implementation.   There are four states to a CSS rollover:

1. *Link* is the normal, unclicked state of a hyperlink.
2. *Active* is a the state of a link when the user clicks down on it.
3. *Visited* is a link to a page that has been visited recently (how recently depends on the browser settings).
4. *Hover* is the hyperlink when the user's mouse cursor is held over the link, but not yet clicked.

In the following example the normal link text has normal weight, dark blue color, with an underline. Visited links are the same except for the color, which is maroon. A hyperlink in the hover state has a very different formatting, with bold, bright red text, with no underline (text-decoration: none). In addition, the a:hover rule defines a light gray background color, which creates a box around the hyperlink text, with a one-pixel black border and four pixels of padding to separate the border from the text. An active link has the same formatting as the hover state except that the text is white and the background color is maroon.

```
<style type="text/css">
a:link {
    font-weight: normal;
    color: #0033FF;
    text-decoration: underline}
a:visited {
    font-weight: normal;
    color: #990000;
    text-decoration: underline}
a:hover {
    font-weight: bold;
    color: #FF0000;
    text-decoration: none;
    background-color: #CCCCCC;
    border: 1px solid #000000;
    padding: 4px;
}
a:active {
    font-weight: bold;
    color: #FFFFFF;
    text-decoration: none;
    background-color: #990000;
    padding: 4px;
    border: 1px solid #000000;
}
</style>
```

Remember from Chapter Four that this code can be inserted in the HEAD of an individual web page or continued in a separate, linked style sheet.

Rollover Images

A rollover image changes when the user's mouse rolls over it. You can use these to create navigation buttons that respond with a different graphic, or even a sound, when the user's cursor passes over it. This immediate feedback can help the user know exactly where his mouse is pointing, and can also be used to provide additional information about each link. Well-chosen images or icons add to the visual metaphor of the web site.

FIGURE 10.2   **Rollover images used in a navigation bar can change color when the mouse is over them.**

Implementation.   A rollover or "picture swap" causes a graphic to switch to another graphic when the mouse rolls over the image. Thus, a rollover actually consists of two images: the primary image (the image that is displayed when the page first loads) and the rollover image (the image that appears when the pointer moves over the primary image). When you create a rollover, the two images must have the same height and width.

The JavaScript for the example shown in Figure 10.2 is too lengthy to be included here. Look at the page source for a web page that uses rollover images, such as *curriculumwebs.com*. JavaScript functions are defined that will replace one image with another. Then the `<A>` tag for the rollover button is given two extra attributes: `onMouseOver` and `onMouseOut`. When the user's mouse moves over the primary image, the `onMouseOver` attribute will call the JavaScript function to replace the primary image with the rollover image. When the user's mouse leaves the area in which the rollover image is displayed, the `onMouseOut` attribute calls the JavaScript function that replaces the rollover with the primary image. Similar effects can be created with background colors of table cells that change as the mouse rolls over the cells.

Some web-page editors, such as Dreamweaver, will create the JavaScript for rollovers; with other editors, such as Mozilla Composer, you must insert the JavaScript manually. You will learn how to do a picture swap and also create a set of rollover navigation buttons in Hands-On Lesson 10.

Text Status Messages

Many web surfers rely on the bottom status bar of the browser window to let them know where the link will take them. Normally when you point to a link on a page (but don't click the link), the URL of the linked-to page appears in the status bar. (Try it.) Why not take it a step further and tell your users something about the page they are going to rather than just showing the URL? A simple JavaScript addition to your HTML will allow you to show a customized message when users roll over a link. You will have to add this manually by editing the HTML code; most web editors will not add this for you. Note that this technique will work whether the navigation link is text or an image, because it is the <A> or anchor tag that contains the status bar information.

Look at the following tag that defines a text link to "`mission1.html`":

```
<A HREF="mission1.html">Mission 1</A>
```

The results of this tag are displayed in Figure 10.3. The status bar lists only the URL that the user is about to go to.

Now add just a bit of JavaScript to the <A> tag:

```
<A HREF="mission1.html"
onMouseOver="window.status='Mission 1: Finding out about a
region of the United States' ; return true">Mission 1</A>
```

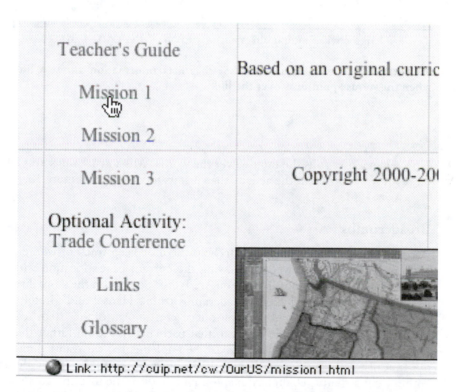

FIGURE 10.3   Detail of the status bar of a web page when the mouse pointer is over a link.

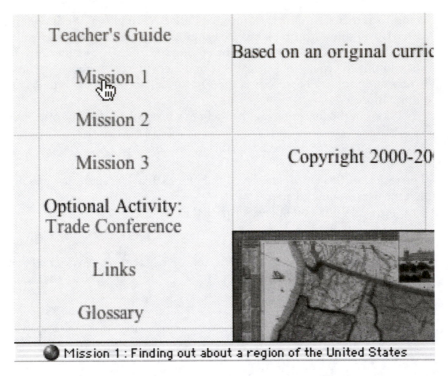

FIGURE 10.4   Detail of a status bar that lists information about a link when the mouse pointer is over the link.

Now when a user rolls the mouse over the words "Mission 1," the status bar will give more information about the activity than just its filename. See Figure 10.4.

Breadcrumbs

Breadcrumbs are a method used to help the user keep track of where he or she is within your curriculum web by showing the current page's location within the web site's structure. It functions like a "You Are Here" pointer on the store directory at the mall, or like leaving a trail of breadcrumbs (think Hansel and Gretel) in order to be able to backtrack and find your way out of a forest. Any of the "steps" can be clicked on and the user will be taken back to that particular location, rather than having to back up page by page. Breadcrumbs can be implemented with static links, or created dynamically with JavaScript. Figure 10.5 shows an example of breadcrumbs used within a curriculum web on health and fitness (look at the text immediately below the images). For simpler sites, leaving a navigation button highlighted shows the user what section of the web site they are in.

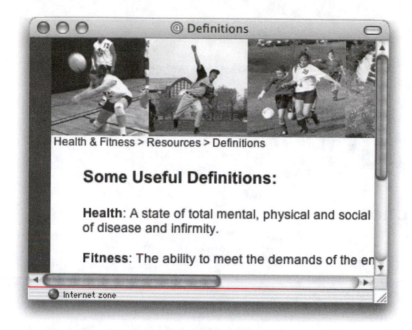

FIGURE 10.5   An example of breadcrumbs used to show location
of a web page within a site.

Jump Menus

Another aid to navigation that you can create with JavaScript is a type of drop-down
menu known as a jump menu. This is a great way to allow your users to quickly access
a page deep within your web site without having to click through a set of buttons that
may not lead directly to individual pages. More advanced web-page editors such as
Dreamweaver include tools for creating these menus quickly and easily. The "Who
Am I?" curriculum web includes a jump menu, shown in Figure 10.6. You will learn
how to do this in Hands-On Lesson 10.

FORMS

Forms are used in web pages to gather feedback from the user. In a curriculum
web, this feedback might contain the results of an activity or information about
your learners in order to update and maintain your curriculum web in appropriate
ways.

There are two aspects to adding forms to a web page: the HTML tags and the
forms processing. The HTML tags are fairly straightforward to implement. In addition
to `<FORM>` and `</FORM>` tags that indicate the beginning and ending of the form,

@ Who Am I?

✓ Home
My Generation
Values and Consumerism
Just for Boys/Girls
Family/Teen Issues
Sports/Hobbies/Recreation
Pages by Teens for Teens
My Ethnicity
My Neighborhood
Personality
Summary
My Career
Career Possibilities

duction

Vho Am I? module, yo   ur
." This includes how y   tu
orhood/city/state/coun   ob

rst Investigation, you will explore how teenagers these
e themselves. In the second Investigation, you will explore

FIGURE 10.6   Screen shot showing a jump menu, used for navigating quickly within a web site.

HTML also includes tags that create elements such as text fields, multiple-line text fields, check boxes, radio buttons (in which only one of a set of buttons can be chosen at any one time), and submit and reset buttons. Most web-page editors allow you to insert these elements without having to edit the HTML directly. (You will learn how to do this in your web-editing software in Hands-On Lesson 10.)

Forms processing is more complicated, and is what happens to the data once your user enters it into the form and presses a submit button. Typically the processing is done by the web server, not by the user's computer. An exception to this is the simplest type of forms processing: e-mailing the data to an e-mail address. More complex data processing is done by scripts and programs that run on the web server.

Form Elements and Layout

The HTML for various form elements is fairly easy to use. Consult the HTML Reference at *curriculumwebs.com* for details on the various tags. We'll give only one example here. In Figure 10.7 we have reproduced a form that is used in WIT to collect feedback from users of a curriculum web. Here is the HTML for the first question in the feedback

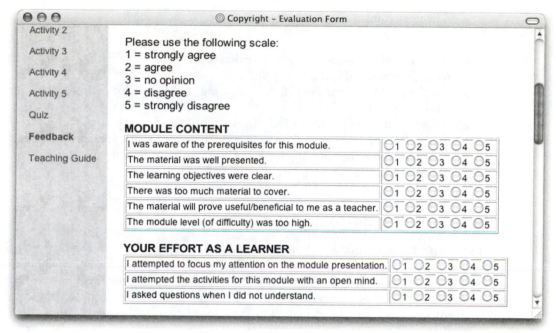

FIGURE 10.7   Part of a feedback form.

form. Note that these form elements are aligned in table cells, so those table tags are included:

```
<TD>
   I was aware of the prerequisites for this module.
</TD>
<TD>
   <INPUT TYPE="radio" NAME="q1" VALUE="strongly agree">1
   <INPUT TYPE="radio" NAME="q1" VALUE="agree">2
   <INPUT TYPE="radio" NAME="q1" VALUE="no opinion">3
   <INPUT TYPE="radio" NAME="q1" VALUE="disagree">4
   <INPUT TYPE="radio" NAME="q1" VALUE="strongly
   disagree">5
</TD>
```

The <INPUT> tags define a form element, in this case of the radio button type, named "q1." Depending on which button is pressed by the user, the value of q1 will be "strongly agree," "agree," and so on. When the user presses the submit button at the bottom of the form, this value, along with those selected for the other questions, will be sent to a specified destination: either someone's e-mail address or a script or program that will process the data.

When designing a form layout on your page, consider the following points:

- Use tables with invisible borders to structure an underlying grid into which form fields, graphics, and text can be placed.
- Use the BGCOLOR attribute of the <TD> tag to create color behind your form fields.
- Make sure that the look and feel of your form stays consistent with the overall look and feel of your curriculum web, and is in keeping with the visual metaphor.
- Incorporate graphics in your form structure to make it more interesting or to reinforce your visual metaphor.

Forms that E-mail Data

The simplest way to process a form is to have the data e-mailed to a specified e-mail address. No scripting or programming is needed to implement this procedure. There are two disadvantages to e-mailing the data. The first is that you must specify the e-mail address at the time you are creating the web page; it is more difficult to select an e-mail recipient at the time that the data is being collected. The second is that for the form to work, the user's computer must have valid e-mail setup information in its browser preferences. Many computers in labs are not set up to do this, and school security software often prevents users from changing this information themselves. Thus, e-mail forms are a fine tool to use in collecting feedback from individual home users on the design and content of a curriculum web, but not such a good tool for collecting assessment information on students (unless, of course, you know that the computers those students are using have valid e-mail setup information).

Figure 10.7 shows an example of part of an e-mail form used at one time to collect information at WIT.

The complete HTML for this form is too lengthy to include here; for now, look only at the tags that create a button to submit the feedback and a button to clear the form.

```
<FORM METHOD="post" ACTION="mailto:WITfeedback@cuip.
uchicago.edu"ENCTYPE= "text/plain">
  <!-- The HTML for the different form elements that
  make up the feedback questions should go here -->
  <!-- Here are two buttons, one labeled "Finished" that
  emails the data; the other clears all the input from
  the form -->
  <INPUT TYPE="submit" VALUE="Finished">
  <INPUT TYPE="reset" VALUE="Clear Form">
</FORM>
```

When the submit button is clicked, the browser e-mails the data from the form to the e-mail address listed in the ACTION attribute of the <FORM> tag. When the user clicks the reset button, all the entries or choices previously made are erased, and the user can start over.

Remember that e-mail forms will only work if the user's browser has been properly configured. A better way to handle forms is to have your web server process forms using a CGI script, although your success with this process will depend on the support of your web server administrator and the script processing resources available.

Processing Forms with CGI Scripts

CGI (Common Gateway Interface) is a type of scripting that connects web pages to external applications. The scripts gather information sent from a web browser to a web server (via a form) and make that information available to a program that is on the web server. They also send information back to the web browser after the program has processed the data. These scripts run on the web server and are usually found in a directory called cgi-bin. A few web servers have public cgi-bins directories into which you, as a web designer, can upload CGI scripts from other sources to use with your web pages. However, most web servers prohibit the public from uploading their own scripts, thus forcing the web designer to go through the server's administrator or webmaster to add new CGI scripts to the server's cgi-bin. Many web server administrators are wary of adding public domain CGI scripts to their servers because of security issues; a poorly written script can cause the server to crash. Consequently, the scripts you will have available will most likely be commercial ones for which your institution has purchased a license; these scripts are usually well written, useful, and very powerful.

It is not possible to view the source code of a CGI script from within a browser in order to deconstruct how these scripts are written. Further, CGI scripting is not something the beginner can learn overnight; see your webmaster for help in creating and using CGI scripts, or refer to the sources listed at the end of this chapter.

The web server used by WIT has a CGI script called FormHandler that is designed to process forms and distribute data in easily configurable ways. Feedback information from a curriculum web, for example, can be collected into a log file instead of being e-mailed to the web designer. That way the designer can review all the feedback information at one time and perhaps feed it into a database for further analysis. You can find out more information about FormHandler and other form handling tools on *curriculumwebs.com*.

Figure 10.8 shows a sample web page that incorporates a simple form handled by a CGI script. This form is a simple guestbook application that asks visitors to a web page to input some information about who they are.

Here is the HTML used to create this form:

```
<H1>Please sign my guestbook!</H1>
<FORM METHOD="GET" ACTION="/cgi-bin/guestbook.pl">
  First Name: <INPUT TYPE="TEXT" NAME="firstname"><BR>
  Last Name: <INPUT TYPE="TEXT" NAME="lastname"><BR>
  <BR>
```

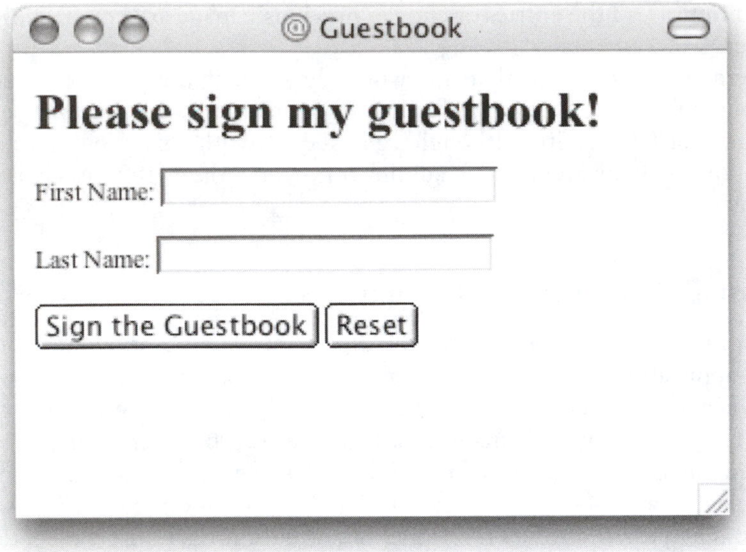

FIGURE 10.8   A simple guestbook form.

```
<INPUT TYPE="SUBMIT" VALUE="Sign the Guestbook">
<INPUT TYPE="RESET">
</FORM>
```

Notice that the ACTION specified in this form is to call the CGI script named guestbook.pl. If this script is not located in the server's cgi-bin, this form will not function properly, and will return an error message to the user. Contact your webmaster to find out what CGI scripts are available for you to use.

Even if there are no CGI scripts available on your server, you can use scripts that are placed on public servers for this purpose. See this book's accompanying web site at *curriculumwebs.com* for a partial list of sites that remotely host such scripts. These scripts can provide such functionality as counting the number of visitors to your web site, providing drop-down navigation menus, implementing web-based bulletin-board systems, displaying banner advertisements, protecting parts of your curriculum web with passwords, and even implementing a shopping cart.

Processing Forms with PHP

PHP (a recursive acronym for "PHP: Hypertext Preprocessor") is a scripting language used to create dynamic web pages. Like JavaScript, it can be embedded directly into HTML, but unlike JavaScript the code is executed on the server rather than on the user's computer. (One side effect of this is that the user can't view the code.) PHP can perform most tasks that CGI programs can do, such as collect form data, generate dynamic page content, or send and receive cookies, but its strength lies in its compatibility with many types of databases. If you are creating forms to accumulate data that will go in a database,

PHP may be your tool of choice. The advantage over a CGI script is that PHP scripts do not have to reside in the cgi-bin and you do not always need system administrator privileges to install them.

The learning curve on PHP is steep, but there are web sites with PHP scripts that you can copy and paste, rather like JavaScript. Some things you can do with PHP include all sorts of forms processing, creating slide shows, counting visitors to your site, building an interactive calendar, a guestbook, a calculator, a bulletin-board message system, games, even a shopping cart and check-out system. See *curriculumwebs.com* for a list of sites with ready-to-use PHP scripts.

Processing Forms with JavaScript Functions

Another way to process forms is to use JavaScript functions. Figure 10.9 shows a web page that is part of an online HTML tutorial, in which a user can test out his or her knowledge of HTML by typing some HTML code into the text box. The form contains two elements: a text box named "htmltext" and a button called "Test HTML". When the "Test HTML" button is pressed, a new browser window opens and displays the web page generated by the user's HTML.

Here is the HTML used to create the form shown in Figure 10.9:

```
<H1>HTML Tester</H1>
<SCRIPT LANGUAGE="JavaScript">
   function blankWin() {
      var win = window.open("", "win");
      win.document.open("text/html", "replace");
      win.document.write("<HTML><HEAD><TITLE>New Document
      </TITLE></HEAD>
      <BODY BGCOLOR=FFFFFF>");
      win.document.write(document.htmlform.htmltext.value);
      win.document.write("</BODY></HTML>");win.document.
      close();
   }
</SCRIPT>
<FORM NAME="htmlform">
   Type your HTML here: <br>
   <FONT SIZE=-1>(You can periodically test the HTML by
   clicking on the button that says "Test HTML".
   A new browser window will open, showing you what your
   HTML looks like in a browser.)</FONT>
   <br>
   <TEXTAREA NAME="htmltext" COLS="60" ROWS="15">
   </TEXTAREA>
   <br><br>
   <INPUT TYPE="button" VALUE="Test HTML" onClick=
   "blankWin()">
</FORM>
```

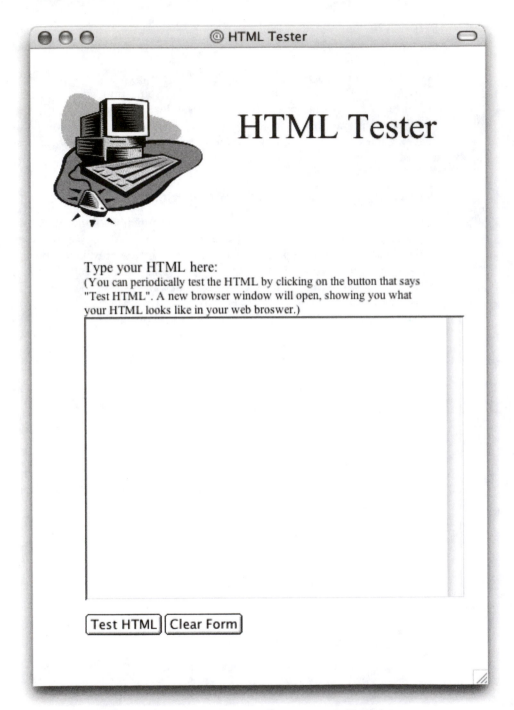

FIGURE 10.9   A form that allows users to try out various HTML tags.

Looking at the HTML, we see that there is a JavaScript function named "blankWin" whose job is to open a new browser window, write the HTML tags for the beginning or head of a web page, include the HTML tags that the user has typed into the text box, and then write the HTML tags for the end of a web page. The function is invoked when the user clicks on the button called "Test HTML" (as specified by the button attribute `onClick="blankWin()"`) Notice also that the form itself has a name, which is used within the JavaScript function to help locate the form element "htmltext" whose contents are imported into the new browser window.

Creating Interactivity with Layers and Behaviors

Straight HTML can be used to create layers on a web page that move, show, or hide depending on the user's actions. These layers can contain text, images, even movies. These interactive layers can give contextual information to students, such as the definition of a word or a photo of an object, at the time that the student needs the information. Figure 10.10 shows a web page with layers that appear when a user clicks on a part of the body. The layers contain textual information about the body part, and disappear when the user moves the mouse away from that body part. Showing/hiding layers, or using pop-up windows, is a good way to display more information without moving the learner off the page; it's better than sending the user to another page and making him or her use the back button to get back to where she or he was. This method is best for short pieces of information only (one or two sentences; a single image).

Layers can also be used to allow users to rearrange elements on a web page. Matching exercises are easy to create this way. Figure 10.11 shows a web page used in an art class to allow students to explore the composition of a piece of art by experimenting with the shapes. Each shape is on its own layer and can be moved from the palette on the right side into the composition on the left side. (This is pretty neat!)

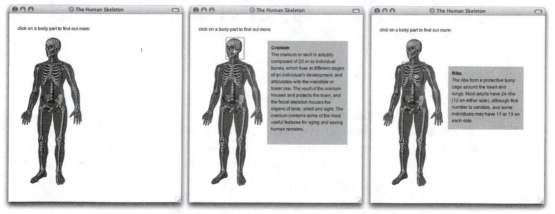

FIGURE 10.10 An example of layers and behaviors in which layers with explanatory text appear when the user clicks on different parts of the body.

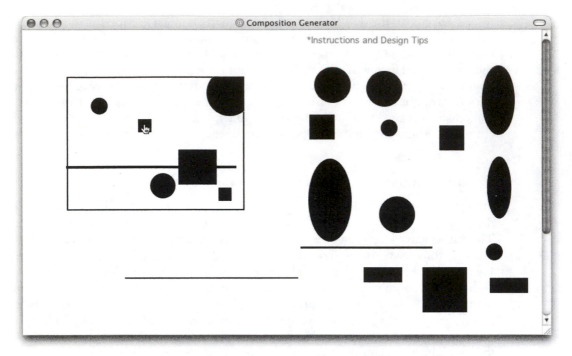

FIGURE 10.11   A web page used in an art class to allow students to experiment with the arrangement of shapes.

Source: Courtesy of Phyllis Burstein, *webinstituteforteachers.org/~pburstein/2003/cgdirections.html.*

Layers are easiest to implement using a full-featured web-page editor, as the JavaScript that controls the behavior of layers is tedious to type by hand. It can be done, however, or the JavaScript can be copied and pasted into your web page from the source listing of a page on another site. See *curriculumwebs.com* for some JavaScript examples and other resources, and Hands-On Lesson 10 for some procedures specific to your software.

Interactive Cursors

CSS styles can control what the cursor looks like as it moves over various web page elements. Typically, a Web browser's cursor looks like an arrow except when it passes over a link, when it changes to a hand. If certain links lead to extra help, you could indicate this to students by having the cursor change to a question mark. See Figure 10.12.

To implement this, place the following code in the head of your HTML document:

```
<style type="text/css">
.questionMark {
  cursor: help;}
</style>
```

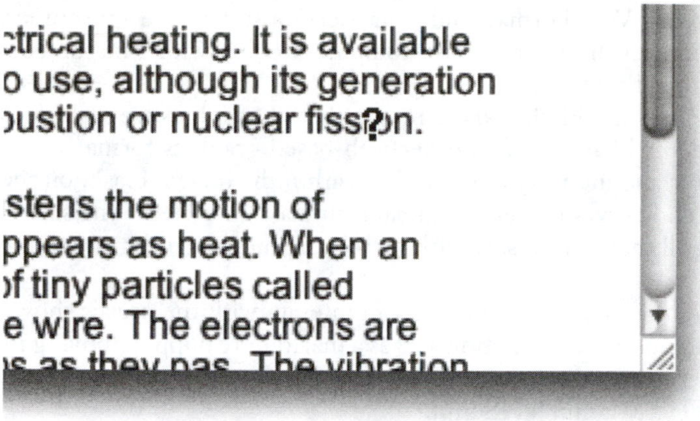

ctrical heating. It is available
o use, although its generation
)ustion or nuclear fiss?on.

stens the motion of
ppears as heat. When an
)f tiny particles called
e wire. The electrons are
s as they pas. The vibration

FIGURE 10.12 **Using CSS to change the browser's cursor to a question mark.**

Then in an <A> tag, assign the style to the text (or image) that links to further help:

```
<a href="definitions.html#fission" class="questionMark">
nuclear fission</a>
```

When the user moves the mouse over the words "nuclear fission" the cursor will change into a question mark, indicating that a definition is available for that word. Clicking would take the user to the definitions page. You could also use layers and behaviors to cause a layer with the definition to pop-up when the user passes the mouse cursor over or clicks on the words "nuclear fission."

INTERACTIVE ANIMATION WITH FLASH

Flash is a web development environment that goes way beyond the capabilities of HTML; it is one of the most powerful animation and interactivity tools for the Web. Although it is a proprietary technology created by Macromedia, its use is widespread. Flash is used to create **scalable** interactive animation for the Web; some uses of this animation include animated logos, navigation controls, and slide shows. With this added power comes a steeper learning curve. You cannot see the source code for a Flash project, as you can for a JavaScript, so it is impossible to see how others have implemented the technology. Learning Flash involves purchasing the program from Macromedia (or downloading a 30-day trial version) and reading the manual or taking a course or online tutorial; it is beyond the scope of this book.

That said, there are some considerable advantages to learning to use Flash technology. It can let your students interact with your curriculum web in ways difficult or impossible to implement using HTML, JavaScript, or CGI technology. Flash files have a file suffix of .swf (Small Web Format) and your users must have the appropriate plug-ins installed on their web browsers. Most computers come with Macromedia Flash Player already installed these days.

(The key technology behind Flash and the reason that its graphics are scalable is the use of **vectors** instead of **bitmaps.** The other web-based graphics formats, GIF and JPEG, define the color and intensity of each pixel within the image. Flash, on the other hand, defines lines and curves by mathematical formulas. To increase the size of a graphic by 100 percent, all that is necessary with vector graphics is to multiply all the values by two.)

A stunning example of how Flash animation can interact with the user is shown in Figure 10.13. The skeleton in this animation acts as a marionette puppet, moving its body and limbs as the user moves the strings. This type of interaction with the user is impossible using straight HTML and JavaScript.

Flash applications require the installation of a plug-in to the user's web browser. Most up-to-date web browsers come with the Flash plug-in already installed. If your users will be using older browsers, it will be helpful to provide them with a link to the *macromedia.com* web site where they can download the plug-in. Your web page can also check the user's computer for the appropriate plug-in. See the discussion of alternate pages on page 219. Remember that in many computer labs users will not be allowed to install plug-ins; if you plan to use a curriculum web in a restricted environment, check to see that the computers have the necessary software already installed.

BLOGS AND WIKIS

A **blog** (web log) is a journal that is available on the Web. The activity of updating a blog is *blogging* and someone who keeps a blog is a *blogger*. Blogs consist of chronologically organized entries submitted by the blogger, containing text, links to other web pages, and sometimes images. Only the blogger can add entries to the web page. Blogging software allows people with little or no technical background to update and maintain a journal—this is perfect for students! Some blogs invite reader feedback, which is posted to the web site—also useful for students, as no e-mail is required. There are lots of ways to use blogs in the classroom, including:

- student journaling
- blog kept by a fictional character (in one third-grade class it was a teddy bear) who responds to student questions
- long-term communication with a student who is sick or who has moved away
- record of what is happening in the classroom (for parents)
- teaching journal (a teacher's self-reflections)

A wiki is a weblog-like system that allows anyone to edit anything on the page. (*Wiki* is the Hawiian word for *fast*.) Unlike a blog, which is typically the work of a single author making diary-style entries in chronological order, a wiki is the collective work of many authors. The best-known example is the Wikipedia (*wikipedia.org*), a

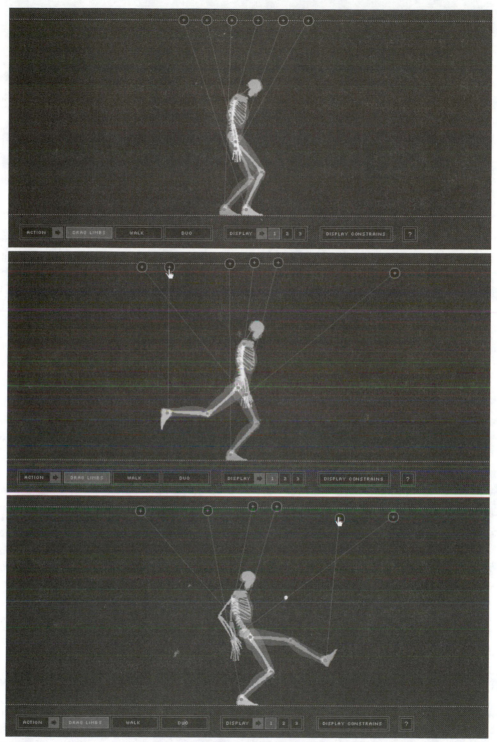

FIGURE 10.13   Screen shots of an interactive Flash animation that reacts to user input.

Source: Courtesy of Andries Odendaal, *2flashgames.com/f/f-220.htm.*

collaborative public effort to develop a free online encyclopedia. Here are some examples of using a wiki in the classroom to facilitate student collaboration:

- collaborative glossary
- group-editing a story or novel
- publishing an electronic magazine across classes and subjects
- creating a class bookmark list
- creating a collaborative FAQ or help page
- joint puzzle-solving
- student-curated galleries
- restaurant, book, or and movie reviews

To implement either a blog or a wiki, you need to install some software. Some of the available software is free and PHP-based, which means you may not need system administrator privileges to install or use it. There are also sites that host blogs and wikis, some of which are also free (but you might have to put up with some advertising). See *curriculumwebs.com* for a list of programs and hosting sites.

RSS AND PODCASTING

Really Simple Syndication (RSS) is a format designed for sharing headlines and other Web content. It has evolved into a popular means of sharing timely content between web sites. Think of it as an automatically-distributed "what's new" for your site. RSS a set of HTML-like tags for sharing news. Each RSS file contains both static information about your site and dynamic information about your new stories, all surrounded by matching start and end tags.

Most curriculum webs are not dynamic enough to warrant broadcasting frequent updates via RSS except, perhaps, the posting of student work. RSS may be useful, however, in displaying up-to-date news from other sites within your curriculum web. To do this, you use a program known as a feed reader or aggregator, which can check RSS-enabled webpages and display any updated articles that it finds. Encyclopedia Britannica's "this day in history," for example, can be displayed in a window on the entry page of your curriculum web. Lots of online publications distribute information via RSS, from the New York Times, Reuters, the Associated press and BBC News, to Discover Magazine, Scientific American and Nature, to *Dictionary.com's* "word of the day," and even several popular comic strips. Check *curriculumwebs.com* for links to sotware that make it easy to use these RSS feeds.

A specific type of RSS is Podcasting, which is a way of publishing sound files to the Internet, allowing users to subscribe to a feed and receive new audio files automatically. All sorts of audio files are available for student use: poetry readings, storytelling, news and sports broadcasts, educational lectures, foreign language broadcasts, and, of course, music files.

Podcasting is reasonably easy to set up (with some help from your webmaster); if your curriculum web includes the production of audio files, consider using poscasting to share them with your parent population.

ALTERNATE PAGES

There are several technologies that older browsers will not be able to view properly, if at all. These include JavaScript, frames, and Flash animations. It is important to know your audience, and to give those users with older browsers and/or a low-bandwidth Internet connection low-tech alternate implementations of your web page. <META> tags can be used to automatically transfer users to these alternate pages.

For example, let us look at the HTML of a page that incorporates JavaScript, but makes allowances for those users whose browsers cannot interpret this technology:

```
<SCRIPT LANGUAGE="JavaScript">
  <!- put your JavaScript code here ->
</SCRIPT>
<NOSCRIPT>
  <META HTTP-EQUIV=REFRESH CONTENT=5
  URL="noJavaScriptPage.html">
</NOSCRIPT>
```

The above code, which goes in the HEAD of your page, will test to see if the user's browser is capable of running JavaScript and, if not, after five seconds would load the page "noJavaScriptPage.html."

Similarly, the <NOFRAMES> tag can be used to provide an alternative page for those browsers incapable of displaying frames. This is used within the <FRAMESET> tag of a frame document.

If a Flash animation is a vital part of your page, it would be wise to test to see if the user's browser has the Flash plug-in installed. The following JavaScript performs the test and sends the user to a page called shockwave-enabled.html if the plug-in has been installed and to a page called no-shockwave.html if the plug-in is absent.

```
<SCRIPT LANGUAGE="JavaScript">
  var plugin=navigator.plugins["Shockwave Flash"];
  if (plugin) {
    window.location=('shockwave-enabled.html');
  }
  else {
    window.location=('no-shockwave.html');
  }
</SCRIPT>
```

There are similar scripts to redirect the user to a simpler page if his or her browser is not java-enabled, to choose a page based on the user's platform (PC or

Mac), and even to redirect a user to one of a number of pages depending on what language the browser is set to read. See *curriculumwebs.com* for details on these scripts.

Because alternate web pages are often intended for users with older browsers, who might well have slow Internet connections, keep the following design tips in mind when creating such pages.

- *Keep the graphics small and simple.* If people with older browsers or text-only browsers are being sent there, it does not make sense to load them down with lots of graphics.
- *Always use the* `ALT` *attribute in your* `<IMG>` *tags.* This allows text-only web browsers to give the users some idea of what images were intended to be displayed.
- *Tell the viewers why they have been sent to this page.* Tell them what functionality their browser is lacking. If they are missing a plug-in, point them to a site where they can download and install the plug-in.

Chapter Summary

This chapter:

- Discusses ways in which interactivity can be used in a web site
- Reviews the techniques used to implement various types of interactivity
- Gives instructions how to implement the simplest interactive techniques: rollover buttons, status bar messages, and forms
- Points you to software packages and other resources that will help you implement the more complex types of interactivity: online assessments, image maps, and Flash projects
- Discusses the wisdom of providing alternate pages for users with older technology

Questions For Reflection

According to the *mediascope.org* web site:

- Ninety percent of households in the United States with children have rented or owned a video or computer game.
- Young people spend an average of 20 minutes per day playing a video game.
- Frequent eighth-grade video game players tend to be those who also watch a lot of TV and do poorly in school.
- But there seems to be little difference in the academic performance of college students who play or don't play video games.

- Computer-based training has been shown to be an effective way to increase performance on standardized tests.
- In fact, greater gains in reading scores have resulted from use of a computer-based training program than from a teacher training program.
- Frequent video game players tend to be more extroverted and less achievement-oriented than infrequent players.

In other words, the evidence is truly mixed about whether the educational influence of video games in our culture is negative, positive, or neutral.

Considering this, reflect on whether or not you think your learners would benefit from *more* or *less* use of interactivity such as that which is discussed in this chapter. Does it help or hurt learning to make educational materials more like video games and less like textbooks? Can you find evidence to support your position? If you are using this book in a class, you might want to debate these questions with your classmates.

Your Next Step

Download Hands-On Lesson 10, which takes you through the steps necessary to create a navigation bar with rollover buttons and several other interactive technologies.

You are almost finished building your curriculum web. Before you start using it with students, you will want to test the site and develop a plan for evaluation. Chapter Eleven discusses these topics.

For Further Learning

- See *curriculumwebs.com* for some links pertinent to the topics in this chapter.
- The definitive reference guide to JavaScript is Flanagan 2001.
- A short instruction manual on CGI programming is Spainhour and Eckstein 2002.
- See Sather et al. 1997 for more ideas on using interactivity in a web page.
- Many useful JavaScripts can be found in Pirouz 1998. JavaScripts for public use can also be found on several web sites; see *curriculumwebs.com* for links to these.
- You can find out how to use Flash by reading Yeung 2004 (a basic introduction) or Capraro et al. 2004 and Rebenschied 2004 (for more advanced techniques).

CHAPTER 11

EVALUATING AND MAINTAINING CURRICULUM WEBS

Overview

This chapter discusses issues relevant as you complete your curriculum web, including methods and criteria for evaluating your curriculum, and testing, maintaining, and publicizing it. Implementing your curriculum web with students is covered in Chapter Twelve.

PLANS FOR EVALUATION

We use the term **evaluation** to refer to judgments made about inanimate objects such as curriculum webs, oral presentations, educational programs, or textbooks. These judgments often result in a decision whether to adopt, discard, or change a curriculum web or other product. Evaluation can apply to the product itself or to how it is used or implemented with learners. We don't believe in "evaluating" learners; rather, we "assess" learning.

When evaluating a curriculum web, you will want to determine whether the web works in the way that it is intended to work. The most important way to determine this is by assessment of student learning. Thus, the results of learning assessments provide data for evaluating curriculum webs. If the learners have mastered the learning objectives, the curriculum web has met the basic criterion for success. However, additional levels of success are determined by additional criteria, discussed in this chapter.

Many books on educational evaluation make a distinction between **formative evaluation,** which is used to guide the process of developing and improving a curriculum, and **summative evaluation,** which is used to provide a final judgment on a curriculum after it has been completed. This distinction is not especially helpful for curriculum webs, because they are almost always in the process of improvement. Even an evaluation of a curriculum web *after* it has been used by a group of learners can be formative if it is used to generate modifications for the next group of students. So almost all evaluation of curriculum webs is formative. (However, an evaluation could certainly be called summative if as a result a teacher or learner decides the curriculum web is not worth trying to improve!)

Because curriculum webs are both curriculums *and* web sites, the criteria for evaluating them have to be taken from both the curriculum development field and the field of web design.

Curriculum Evaluation

Curriculum evaluation should be an ongoing and essential part of the curriculum development and teaching process. Reflective educators consider the possible consequences of all of their actions and then collect data continually to test their predictions and modify their curriculum plans, curriculum webs, web sites, and instructional strategies to maximize learning. Effective evaluation requires a variety of methods of collecting and analyzing data, including anecdotal records, observation checklists, rating scales, self-assessments, peer assessments, learner products and presentations, learner surveys, and learner journals. Setting forth plans for evaluation in the curriculum plan and teaching guide allows students and others to comment on the evaluation plans and suggest additions or improvements. Ideally, evaluations of curriculum webs will avoid bias, cultural insensitivities, and inequalities. When the person doing the evaluation of the curriculum web is the same person who developed it, there may be a tendency to produce too rosy an evaluation; involving objective peers and learners in the evaluation can help to avoid this.

Once the basic criterion of whether students have mastered learning objectives is met, additional criteria can help to determine whether the curriculum web is just an adequate support for student learning or an excellent one. One important issue is whether the curriculum web works as well as or better than more traditional methods of achieving the learning objectives for the intended learners. Comparative evaluations of traditional methods and your curriculum web may be difficult and expensive to carry out, but you certainly can use your own memory and experience as a guide for making judgments about the value of alternative approaches. Another important criterion is whether the learners enjoyed their use of the curriculum web. While enjoyment is not ordinarily the primary function of an educational tool, it certainly increases motivation and often engagement. Table 11.1 lists additional questions that are relevant to evaluating curriculum webs. Still more criteria can be gleaned from our discussion of each element of the teaching guide in this book, especially in Chapter Three, Chapter Four, and Chapter Six, and from the rubric for evaluating a teaching guide, found at Table 6.1 on page 123.

Techniques for evaluating curriculum webs include:

- Outside review by teachers, subject matter specialists, or potential learners
- Observing how learners of different abilities and dispositions respond to the curriculum web
- Having learners fill out a questionnaire during or after their use of the curriculum web
- Examination of the learners' work produced while using the curriculum web

TABLE 11.1   Questions to Consider While Evaluating a Curriculum Web

■ What are the curriculum web's underlying purposes and assumptions?

■ Did the learners seem to be able to find their way around within the curriculum web, according to the intentions listed in the instructional plan?

■ Was the statement of prerequisites adequate, or were there skills, knowledge, or attitudes that should have been included as prerequisites that were not?

■ Did learners appear to be engaged in the learning activities? Did they spend most of their time on task?

■ Did the curriculum web provide adequate opportunities for learners to seek further information about topics that interested them? Did the curriculum web provide room for enrichment for advanced or motivated students while also including step-by-step options or modifications for slower learners?

■ Did other aspects of the curriculum web cause any confusion or frustrations? If yes, could these confusions and frustrations be avoided by modifications?

■ Did all groups of learners who used the curriculum web experience similar results? If not, what can the differences tell us about how to improve the curriculum web?

■ Were the rubrics adequate for describing the performance criteria for assessing learning?

■ Were the learners able to use the rubrics to self-assess the quality of their work?

■ Is the level of writing appropriate for the intended learners?

■ Did the embedded and authentic assessments provide useful feedback to the teacher about student learning?

■ Are instructions to learners clear?

■ Does the curriculum web use appropriate instructional supports to scaffold the learning activities throughout?

■ Is the teaching guide clear and concise? Are all of the necessary elements present and complete? Is each element clear and concise?

■ Are the learning objectives clear and attainable?

■ Do the learning activities work for all intended learners?

■ Is the subject matter accurate, relevant, or interesting?

■ How does the curriculum web work in classrooms or computer labs? How does it work for individuals working alone?

■ Does the curriculum web support local, state, or national standards? Are the connections to the standards clear? Did the developer use standards or performance descriptors to develop the learning objectives? Is this explicitly stated?

■ How does the curriculum web compare to other methods for learning similar content?

■ Does the curriculum web build on the special features of the Web, such as multimedia, hypertext, and available modes of communication?

■ Analysis of learners' journals or weblogs produced while using the curriculum web

■ Pilot testing with a small number of learners in different settings to learn how and when it works well

■ Field testing in several different classrooms with different teachers and learners

The last of these is unlikely to be feasible with a curriculum web developed by an individual teacher for use in his or her classroom; however, field testing might be worthwhile if the curriculum web is considered for adoption by an entire school district or is developed for multiple classrooms. It may be easier for an individual teacher who has developed a curriculum web to find a colleague at the same grade level and in the same subject area to try out the curriculum web and offer comments on how it works relative to the techniques that he or she had previously been using.

Students can help with evaluation by giving written feedback about the curriculum web as they work through it. For this reason, it is helpful to put an e-mail address or link to a feedback form on each page. Having a contact e-mail address also allows others who happen on the curriculum web to contribute to its future development or to find out more about the curriculum web.

Web-design Evaluation

The web-design aspect of a curriculum can be evaluated according to a wide variety of criteria. Each of the following aspects is important:

- *Navigation scheme*. Invite some people who have never seen your web site to try it out. If your site is intended for students of a certain age, have your test audience be of that age group. Look over the users' shoulders without offering advice and see if they are able to navigate your site without difficulty. This will ensure that your embedded instructions and supports are clear to the user.
- *Platform*. Test your site on both Macintosh and PC machines. Images will often look darker on a PC and lighter on a Mac; make sure they are acceptable on both platforms. Also, form elements such as text boxes and pull-down menus often take up more space on the page when displayed on a PC than on a Mac. You may end up having to change the layout of your page slightly to accommodate this.
- *Different screen sizes and window sizes*. Particularly if you designed your web site on a large computer monitor, test to see how it looks on a small monitor (15″ or less). Make sure it still looks good on a big monitor (21″); in particular, make sure your background image is not repeating if you did not want it to. (If the image is smaller than the window, it will repeat from left to right, creating a "tile" effect.) Make your browser window as big as possible, and as small. Check that each page in your curriculum web is acceptable in all these configurations.
- *Color depth*. While most computers these days are capable of displaying images in thousands or millions of colors, recognize that some people are still using 256 color systems and (especially) projectors. Set your monitor to a low number of colors and make sure your images look all right.
- *Browsers*. Make sure your page looks good on all the major browsers that you anticipate your visitors will use. This includes Mozilla, Internet Explorer, Firefox Safari (for the Macintosh), and Opera. Test out older versions of these browsers if you anticipate that your learners will be using older software. If your site includes alternate pages to accommodate older web browsers, make sure these pages are functional.

- Other things should be tested after publishing to the server:
  - *Images*. After publishing your site on your web server, check to see that all the images load properly. If they do not, one problem might be that the filenames in your `<IMG>` tags are not the same as the names of the actual files on the web server, or the cases are not identical. Another problem could be that absolute path names were used in the `<IMG>` tag, and these paths changed when the site was uploaded to the web server. Another good test to run is to turn off image loading in your browser (via the Preferences) and check that the `ALT` text—if you used it—works properly. (Some browsers display the `ALT` text when you point the mouse at the image.)
  - *Links*. Make sure all your links work! Obviously, going through every page and testing every link can be a time-consuming process, but it is worth the time to fix broken links and avoid frustrating your users. Some web-page editors include a feature that allows you to check all the links in your site automatically. This is especially important if for some reason you have to move your curriculum web to another server or another location on the current server.
  - *Forms*. If you use forms in your web site, test out each form to make sure the submission process works as expected. If a CGI or PHP script is involved, test it thoroughly.
  - *JavaScript and other technologies*. Check all rollover images, pop-up windows, and other scripts to make sure they are working. Try out all your java applets and Flash and Shockwave images as well.

Heuristic Evaluation of Curriculum Webs.   **Heuristic evaluation** is a professional method of evaluating the usability of curriculum webs and other web sites. The method relies on a carefully defined set of design principles (the heuristics, or rules of thumb). In practice, a small group of people with knowledge of these principles is asked to look individually at the curriculum web and fill out an evaluation form that lists the principles, provides a rating scale, and has room for comments and recommendations. Then the group comes together and develops a consensus document that lists their issues or concerns and perhaps includes recommendations for improvement. Jakob Nielsen has shown that increasing the size of the group doing the evaluation by only a few has huge dividends in terms of the number of usability problems that are found. (See Nielsen 1994 and Tognazzini 2003.)

Example Plan for Evaluation

Evaluation plans can range from a simple one-line statement to elaborate field testing and revision testing plans such as those used by commercial software developers. How elaborate it needs to be is determined by how widely it will be used, and whether the learners and teachers are local to the developer or more remote. The more widely used it will be, and the more remote the learners are from the developer, the more elaborate the plan has to be.

At a minimum, the plan should include some means for the learners to provide feedback to the developer. The evaluation plan for the IQ WebQuest (shown on page 27) and the "Building a Curriculum Web with Dreamweaver" meet this minimal requirement. A more elaborate plan will include additional strategies such as those already discussed. Plans for evaluation of "Our United States" and "Who Am I?" are available at *curriculumwebs.com*.

"Building a Curriculum Web with Dreamweaver" Plan For Evaluation.   A feedback form is available (link provided). Participants with other comments or concerns about the curriculum web should send the author e-mail (link provided) or, to remain anonymous, can e-mail same to John Doe (link provided), asking that he pass along the anonymous feedback.

ACTIVITY 11A ■ Writing Your Plan for Evaluation

Write a plan for evaluating your curriculum web. Include methods for evaluating both the effectiveness of the curriculum and the design of the web site. The following strategies may be helpful:

- Test the site with a small group of users similar to the target audience or learners.
- Have a subject matter expert review the curriculum web.
- Ask other teachers to evaluate the curriculum web according to criteria similar to those listed on page 224.
- Field-test the curriculum web with a whole class in a school setting.
- Use additional methods suggested by the list of web-design evaluation issues found on page 225 or by the discussion of heuristic evaluation on page 226.

MAINTAINING, REVISING, AND UPDATING

If you are going to use your curriculum web more than once, you should plan on doing maintenance on a regular basis—at least once a year. It is important to make sure that content is up-to-date; to check all links, especially to pages outside of your curriculum web; and to determine whether anyone is actually using the site.

Update the Content

If you want people to use your curriculum web, do not let it get stale; keep its information up-to-date. If it looks outdated, modify the design. If appropriate, post examples of recent learners' work to encourage other learners. Remember, one of your aims is to make your curriculum web as attractive and engaging to the learners as possible. Use the information you gather from watching students learn with your curriculum and from the feedback forms that you provide. Modify your curriculum web to make it as easy as possible to use.

Links

Test all links that you have made to external web sites to be sure that those sites are still up and functional, and that they still contain information that is useful for your curriculum web. For broken or outdated links you will have to find replacement sites or rewrite parts of your curriculum. (Sometimes a broken link has merely moved to a new location as part of a site redesign. Before you assume the worst, do a little digging around. If the primary domain name is still operational, it could be that the content you want is still on the site at a different location.)

Some web-page editors include a feature to check links automatically. However, these tools rarely check external links. Rather, they merely flag the links as external, leaving it up to you to check them manually. There are web sites that will check your external links, once you submit your site's URL. Often, these services are free if used once, but a small fee is charged for subsequent use. See *curriculumwebs.com* for links to such utilities.

Tracking Site Usage

Ever wonder how many people have been to your site? Consider putting a counter on your page to keep track of visitor traffic. If a counter is available in your CGI directory, use it! Otherwise, there are web sites that will keep track of this visitor count for you. Curriculumwebs.com lists some of these sites, as well as sources of CGI and PHP scripts for counters.

Some search engines offer the capability of performing a reverse search, that is, a search for pages that link to your own. For example, suppose your site's URL is *http://cuip.uchicago.edu/CurriculumWebs*. If you enter a search for "*link:cuip.uchicago.edu/CurriculumWebs*" at *google.com*, the search engine will return any web sites that include this string in any links. After your site has been publicized for a while, try out one of these searches to see if other sites are linking to your curriculum web.

Publicizing Your Curriculum Web

Many teachers who develop curriculum webs will use these webs primarily with their own students, and will have little or no interest in attracting other users to their web site. However, some developers, especially those who work for nonschool institutions with educational goals, will be very interested in attracting users to their curriculum web. This section gives some pointers for what to do to increase the number of people who see your curriculum web.

The first step is to get listed by the major search engines. According to some estimates, no search engine or directory on the Web today indexes or searches more than one-third of all web sites. Therefore, it is necessary to take active measures to get listed by as many different search engines as possible in order to maximize your exposure.

An important and simple thing to do is to include in your HTML a description of your curriculum web. The <META> tag's attribute KEYWORDS is used to list a number of key words, separated by commas, that are related to your page's contents.

These keywords are picked up by many search engines and used to determine the subject matter of your web site. The `DESCRIPTION` attribute is used to list a one-sentence description of your web site. Some search engines display this description when they display your site in a list of search results. See the HTML Reference at *curriculumwebs.com* for more information about how to use these attributes.

As discussed in Chapter Seven, there are two major types of search tools: search engines and directories. The major difference between the two is that directories are manually updated, whereas search engines are indexed automatically. There are different techniques to getting your web site listed by these two types of searching tools.

Publicizing with Directories.   The Yahoo directory (*yahoo.com*) is an example of a site whose content is kept up-to-date by real people. In order to be listed by Yahoo, you must fill out their online registration form and wait until a human has manually added your site in the appropriate part of their database of web sites. The form asks you to provide not only the URL but also the title and a description of the contents of your site, and may ask you to suggest which category your site should be placed in. Registration forms for most web directories can be accessed from their web sites. Many of them are free, but some charge a listing fee.

Publicizing with Search Engines.   Search engines such as Google (*google.com*) will add your web site to their databases automatically when you submit your URL. The search engine will send out a spider or robot to investigate the submitted URL, collect any `<META>` tag keywords and descriptions, and add them to the search engine's database.

Here is an example of the `<META>` tags used in the "Our United States" curriculum web. Notice that they go in the Head of an HTML file.

```
<HTML>
<HEAD>
<TITLE>Our United States</TITLE>
<META NAME="keywords" CONTENT="geography, curriculum,
curriculum web, map, mapping, atlas, compass, United
States, environment, human activities">
<META NAME="description" CONTENT="Geography lessons
based around the United States. Good for 4th-6th
graders. Student activities and teaching guide
included.">
</HEAD>
```

When a user searches a search engine, it compares the search request with the millions of keywords it has on file and then brings up pages containing keywords similar to or identical to the search request. Pages are displayed with the description that was submitted along with the keywords. This is why the description is so important. Note that most search engines will display only the first two lines of a description, so keep it short.

Some spiders ignore the <META> tags, but will pick up the same information if it is included as an HTML comment in the Head of the document. Comments begin with `<!--` and end with `-->`. Just to be on the safe side, "Our United States" also includes the following HTML:

```
<!-- Geography lessons based around the United States.
Good for 4th-6th graders. Student activities and
teaching guide included. geography, curriculum,
curriculum web, map, mapping, atlas, compass, United
States, environment, human activities -->
```

Many web-page editors allow you to edit these tags without having to directly alter the HTML.

You need to have <META> tag information only in your web site's main or home page, because most search engines will look only at your opening page. It cannot hurt, however, to include the tags on all the pages of your site. One way to do this is to add them to a site template. If your web site is designed using frames, make sure that the <META> tags containing the description and keywords are in your index.html file, as search engines often have a difficult time accessing data past the index.html pages in sites that contain framesets.

It is essential that you include a <TITLE> for the home page of your curriculum web, as many search engines present the results of a search by listing the titles of the pages that were found. A well-thought-out title that describes your curriculum web well will attract visitors.

There are specialized web sites that will submit your curriculum web to several or many search engines at once. Some of these sites are free, while others charge for the service. See *curriculumwebs.com* for links to some of these useful sites.

Getting Listed on Educational Web Sites.   There are lots of web sites that were created for and are used by teachers. Many either maintain lists of online curriculum or periodically feature curriculum webs that they think will be of interest to other teachers. Do your best to bring your curriculum web to the attention of these educational sites by either registering with them or e-mailing their creators. Consult *curriculumwebs.com* for a list of these educational web sites.

ACTIVITY 11B ■ Adding Metatags

Write down as many keywords as you can think of that describe the content matter of your site. Now consider your audience and write down keywords that will attract that audience, words like *education, teaching,* and *learning*. On the entry page to your web site, add a <META> tag with the KEYWORDS attribute that includes all of the words on your list.

Write a sentence or phrase describing your site that contains as many of your keywords as possible. Add another <META> tag, with the DESCRIPTION attribute, that contains your paragraph.

ACTIVITY 11C ■ Telling the World

On *curriculumwebs.com*, you will find a list of links to the URL submission pages for a variety of search engines and directories. Register your curriculum web with as many search engines and directories as you can using the keywords and description you generated in Activity 11B.

Chapter Summary

This chapter:

- Introduces several important concepts about evaluation
- Provides means to evaluate your curriculum web
- Suggests questions to ask yourself as you evaluate the results of a curriculum web for your students
- Discusses writing a plan for evaluation
- Helps you to fully test a web site
- Explains how to list your web site on various types of search engines
- Discusses how to keep your web site up-to-date

Questions For Reflection

Jakob Nielsen has distilled the large number of possible principles for evaluating a web site or other system into 10 principles that he refers to as the "heuristics" of usability design.

1. Access the heuristics at *useit.com/papers/heuristic/heuristic_list.html* or via a link at *curriculumwebs.com*.
2. For each of the 10 heuristics, write a translation that puts the principle into words that can be applied to the evaluation of your curriculum web. (Not all the principles may be applicable.)
3. Apply these principles to your plan for evaluation in Activity 11A.
4. Make any necessary modifications to your plan for evaluation.

Your Next Step

Download Hands-On Lesson 11, which teaches you some advanced features of your software including some techniques related to this chapter.

   You are almost done! The final step in developing your curriculum web is to write an "Implementation Plan" that discusses the context in which learners will use it. This is the focus of Chapter Twelve.

For Further Learning

- See *curriculumwebs.com* for some links pertinent to the topics in this chapter.
- General information about evaluation is given by Pratt 1994, Madaus and Kellaghan 1992, and Eisner 1985.
- For in-depth coverage of <META> tags, see Spainhour and Eckstein 2002, or Musciano and Kennedy 2002.
- For more on heuristic evaluation, see Nielsen 1994 and Nielson Undated.

CHAPTER 12

TEACHING WITH CURRICULUM WEBS

Overview

This chapter is about the organizational issues—school, classroom, networks, computer hardware and software, and student grouping—that are affected by and that affect the use of curriculum webs. It also includes information on preparing students to use curriculum webs and some general advice on how to make sure that the students' experience with your curriculum web is successful.

Each teaching situation is unique, involving a specific configuration of time, hardware, software, students, teachers, computers, desks, networking, printers, scheduling, and grouping. Each of these factors affects how you will manage the use of the Internet with your students, or how you will use a particular web-based resource.

The curriculum planning and web design discussed in previous chapters must take into account certain contextual issues involving the actual mix of human and computer resources available in the teaching classroom. It is possible to develop curriculum webs without much attention to local contexts by making certain assumptions about the classrooms in which the curriculum will be used. However, if you are developing a curriculum web for your specific classroom, you will want to consider the specific issues involved in your classroom. How many computers are available? How many Internet connections? What are the options regarding furniture in the room? Is there a projector or other system that allows everyone to see the output from one computer? Is there a very wide range of abilities or experience, or is the group relatively homogenous?

This unique combination of these factors determines how you can use your curriculum web or other resources from the Internet. Here, we discuss the teacher or teachers, then the students or learners, then the physical classroom itself, the computers in the room, those special classrooms we call "computer labs," network and Internet connectivity, and two issues concerning software: filtering and student e-mail.

PEOPLE

Teacher(s)

The teacher (or teachers) is the most important single resource for using curriculum webs. He or she is the one person who can know what the students need and how to help them learn. When technology is involved in the delivery of instruction or is the medium in which activities take place, the teacher must not only know about teaching, but also about the technology, and how to teach about the technology while simultaneously teaching the subject matter.

An additional factor in the use of curriculum webs in teaching and learning is the availability of teaching assistants in a computer lab or classroom. When an entire group of students is using a curriculum web, they may have a lot of questions and need one-on-one or small-group assistance. Students may have questions about the use of the software (creating bookmarks, saving graphics or text files, copying and pasting information). It is possible for them to get lost (both within the curriculum web if it is poorly designed or out on the Web at large). They may wonder about the best way to approach a given assignment. The best solution to the proliferation of student questions during their use of computers and curriculum webs is to have more than one teacher in the room at a time. In WIT, we place two mentors with about 20 teacher-learners. This is an almost ideal situation that you may not be able to duplicate in your school. However, there are other sources of assistance. Parents may be willing to come in to assist on particular days in which you are trying out a new technology-based approach. Local universities may be willing to supply students who can help out in schools as part of their community service requirement or work-study assignment. Your school's librarian, media specialist, or technology coordinator may be able to assist you or make suggestions for how you might get extra help when needed.

If you have access to the Internet only in the computer lab, and the computer teacher is the most Internet-savvy teacher in the school, then see if you can serve as his or her assistant next time your class is scheduled in the computer lab. Your principal might be willing to give you some other time for class preparation if that is what you usually do when you drop off your class in the lab. Or you might see if the computer lab teacher is willing to serve as your assistant for a lesson that is subject-centered or otherwise related to your classroom curriculum but uses the Internet as a tool.

If you are the only teacher in a roomful of students with computers, you will want to institute some kind of system to prevent an overwhelming rush of questions or demands for assistance. Many experienced lab teachers provide students with small paper cups that they can place on top of their computer monitors when they have a question. This way, the teacher can help the students one by one, and the other students do not have to wait with their hands up for the teacher to notice them.

If you are using a curriculum web that you have not used before, or that you designed a while ago, you will need to check the external links in the curriculum web before you begin using it with the students. Some links may have moved or disappeared entirely. Make sure that the links that are most important for the learning activities are live and still contain the expected and relevant information.

Learners

The teacher must make sure that the learners or students have mastered the necessary prerequisites of a given learning activity. Teachers should be sure to read the teaching guide of the curriculum web before they decide to use it with their students, and they should plan on spending a few minutes, or up to an hour, preparing the students before they use the curriculum web. Most students, for example, will need explicit instruction on how to use bookmarks and guidance on how to conduct effective searches.

One issue regarding students' use of curriculum webs focuses on the minimum age at which it makes sense to have them use the Web for learning. Most experts claim that the Web is useless for students who cannot read. However, there remains the question of whether such young students are better off using the computer or using more tangible learning materials. Jane Healy, author of *Failure to Connect* (1998), claims that few students will benefit from computer use until they are in the fourth grade. Given that young students have so many needs (learning to write and to read, basic math skills, people skills, delaying gratification, cooperation, listening, etc.), she may be right. While this is true in most cases, some teachers have successfully designed curriculum webs that do not require reading. (For an example that uses audio to provide instructions, see Figure 12.1.)

In any case, younger students will likely be unable to use the keyboard effectively and will be overwhelmed by the conceptual and logical demands of search engines.

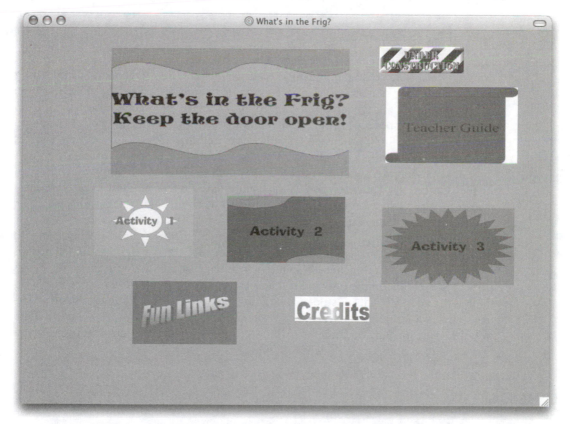

FIGURE 12.1   **The home page of a curriculum web that uses audio to provide instructions.**

Curriculum webs designed for students in kindergarten through third grade should be self-contained and should require very little, if any, typing. Most small children quickly learn how to use a mouse, however, so building in navigation tools that are big and bright and graphical works well. Keyboarding skills can generally be learned in fourth grade or beyond; curriculum webs designed for these age groups can incorporate activities that require keyboarding.

Most search engines are designed for adults; however, a few search engines such as *yahooligans.com* and *ajkids.com* will work well even for younger students. The danger when students use general-interest search engines built for adults is that they may find themselves confronted with inappropriate materials. It is generally wise not to expect students younger than 10 to find their own web-based materials using search engines, but rather to direct them to sites that have been previously reviewed and approved by the teacher. Even for those 10 to 14 years old, it may be best to provide ongoing guidance to ensure that searches do not become huge time-wasters.

The characteristics of your learners will determine what you will plan to accomplish in your curriculum, as well as what you will want the learners to do. Some curriculum webs are very closely targeted to a specific group or type of learners. These curriculum webs may indeed have no usefulness outside of those target learners.

Special Needs Learners

During the past two decades, considerable work has been done to make computer technologies accessible to students with special needs. The newer versions of operating systems such as Windows and MacOS contain provisions for enlarging the type on the screen, using special keyboards and adaptive input devices, and generating speech from text or text from speech. Further discussion of these provisions and devices is beyond the scope of this book; interested readers are invited to look at some of the resources listed at the end of this chapter or on *curriculumwebs.com* for more information.

Curriculum webs can be used to individualize instruction, allowing choices of subject matter and activities that can accommodate diverse student needs. Students who read very slowly can take their own time to work through a set of web pages, or can go back and reacquaint themselves with earlier materials if they forget what they learned. As many districts move from self-contained special education classrooms to mainstreaming students, special education teachers are often assigned to small groups of students as resource teachers, helping them as necessary to thrive in the regular class work at the school. These resource teachers can create curriculum webs specifically for their assigned special-needs students, building in appropriate reading levels and activities so that the students can learn. See Figure 12.2 for a screen shot from a curriculum web designed for autistic students. Also see page 89 for more about making curriculum webs accessible for all students.

CLASSROOMS

Your classroom puts limitations on how you can use the Internet. Its size and layout, furniture, electrical power, and connectivity all play a role.

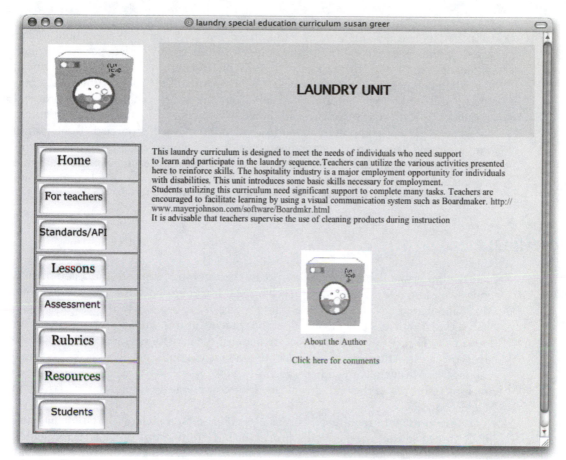

FIGURE 12.2   A curriculum web designed to teach sequencing to severely autistic students through the steps of doing the laundry.

Source: Courtesy Susan Greer, *http://webinstituteforteachers.org/~sjgreer/laundry/laundryhome1.html.*

Classrooms differ widely in terms of their size and layout. Some classrooms are really just boxes with barely enough room for several rows of desks. Such rooms tend to offer few options for rearranging or for the placement of computers. In these situations, it might be best to have computers placed on mobile carts that can be stored elsewhere and brought into the classroom as needed. This also provides the computer with its own furniture, which may avoid the problem of where to put the computer so students can access it comfortably.

Some schools have taken the route of purchasing an entire classroom set of wirelessly networked laptop computers, stored on a cart that also serves as a recharging station for the laptop batteries. The set of laptops becomes an instantly networked computer classroom that can be used at any time anywhere in the school building. Schools that do not have elevators may need to purchase a mobile cart and set of laptops for each floor. Another issue to consider is the charging time that may be necessary between uses.

An important factor in putting computers in classrooms is the availability of electrical outlets and also the amount of electrical power available to the school. Older school buildings rarely had more than one or two electrical outlets per room, often placed near the front of the room for use by the teacher. Such classrooms will need upgrading before computers can be placed in other parts of the room. While it is sometimes possible to power multiple computers from one outlet using extension cords and splitters, this is often a fire hazard and should be avoided. Also, many older outlets are not grounded, and computers, monitors, and printers need grounded (three-prong) power to avoid damage to the equipment. Do not use adapters designed to plug a three-prong plug into a two-hole outlet. Static electricity is a real issue with computers, so that ground is important! It is probably a good idea to check even three-hole outlets for a ground with a tester before installing expensive equipment.

COMPUTERS

The computers available in your classroom—their number, sophistication, and peripherals—will also affect the kinds of teaching and learning that can go on in the room. With about one computer for every four students, it is possible to design learning instructional activities that involve all of the students using computers at once, working in teams of four. While teams of two are better if the activity is more computer intensive, you can structure activities so that one student at a time actually uses the keyboard and mouse. Meanwhile, the other students can take notes, make search decisions, keep track of resources as they are downloaded, or communicate results to the class or to the teacher.

The minimum requirements for a classroom should include a multimedia computer linked to the Internet and a projector. Indeed, just this one instructor station may be more valuable than having a computer for every single student. It is usually possible to find room for one computer, even if it is on the teacher's desk or against the back wall. Even if it is not projected, if the computer is linked to the Internet, it may be quite useful as a classroom resource, used by one or two students at a time as part of a whole class project. Projectors remain, unfortunately, somewhat expensive. Most schools will not be able to afford a computer projector for each room. But projectors can be shared by placing them on mobile carts, with or without a computer. Newer projectors are very small and easily carried from place to place.

A projector turns a single computer into whole-class learning tool. It can be used for presentations, demonstrations, and direct instruction on various computer techniques. Both teachers and students should be involved in using this instructor station to demonstrate techniques, show resources, give instructions, and display work products (web pages, images, data, etc.). Some companies are bundling computers, projectors, software, cameras, and microphones to create mobile presentation stations that can be used for videoconferencing, document scanning, and other functions in a package that is easy to use and maintain. (Note that the screen resolution or color depth supported by your projector may differ from that of your monitor. Test your curriculum web with the projector in advance of using it with students.)

If you are an elementary school teacher in a self-contained classroom with only one Internet-connected computer, it may be helpful to create a schedule that gives each student in the class 20 or 30 minutes at the computer each week. You can easily manage this time by creating a computer "lesson plan of the week" that guides the student toward your learning objectives while you are teaching the rest of the class. (If creating a weekly web-based lesson plan seems like a lot of work, a simpler option is simply to set a bookmark or bookmarks in the web browser and provide a single sheet of paper—perhaps taped to the desk—with instructions on how to use the resources.) If you use this strategy, vary the schedule each week so students do not always miss the same part of the weekly routine. It also is a good idea to partner the students: they can help each other understand the assignment and deal with problems as they arise. Partners should be rotated so students get to work with many other children during the course of the year (Leu, Leu, and Coiro 2004).

High school teachers will be less likely to find successful ways to integrate one nonprojected computer into the classroom routine. In this case, the computer may be most fruitfully used as a reference source, in which one student per class period is assigned the job of discovering information that may be needed by the class.

If two or three computers are placed in the room, management becomes more challenging. Who gets to use the computers, and at what time, and in what groups? One common strategy is to use the computers as one or more "centers" in a classroom with a variety of activities going on at once. Each computer can have a separate activity, and groups of two or three can easily work together at one computer. Teaming students into pairs or trios works well if the task at hand requires several roles: keyboardist, recorder, navigator. A group will be more difficult to manage if the task only really requires one person to "run the computer," such as typing up a report or creating a digital image. The other students will either be getting in the way or itching to have their turn. Better to give them something relevant to do: take paper-based notes, plan the next step in the search or project, or work on noncomputerized projects elsewhere in the room.

Many classrooms are burdened with a number of older computers that may not be capable of running today's software. Such computers may be useful as word processors or for running stand-alone software such as "Math Blaster," "Reader Rabbit," or "Where in the World is Carmen Sandiego?" But their limited memory and slow speed make them somewhat useless as Internet machines. Students accustomed to video games and fast computers that generate graphics and load programs very quickly may become impatient while their older computer loads up an Internet browser or graphics editor. It's hard to blame them!

One potential solution for schools with lots of older computers is creating a so-called "thin client," or server-based environment, in which the computers act merely as dumb terminals, letting a newer, faster computer handle the processing. These solutions are sometimes challenging to implement, requiring expert assistance for installation and maintenance, but they can result in a much more rewarding experience for students at somewhat less cost than purchasing all new individual computers. Web access is greatly improved, especially if caching is implemented on the network server. (When one student loads a page or image from the Web, the cache temporarily stores a copy of that page, and so when another computer accesses the same resource, it only has to come from the cache instead of the Web. This is an easy way to increase the apparent speed of Internet access in a school, especially when whole classes are working on the same curriculum web or other web site.)

The minimum configuration for a computer used for the Internet is a 333 **MHz. Pentium** or Mac processor, 128 **MB** of RAM, and a 2 GB hard drive. The memory is needed in order to successfully use a web browser or web-page editor and to handle the content of more elaborate web pages. The hard-drive space is necessary to handle the size of the operating system, the Internet browser and web editor, and productivity software.

Computers should be able to provide sound so that students get the most from web-based resources such as sound clips, videos, and some animations. Ideally, each computer should have a sound card and speakers, along with headphones to allow students to listen without disturbing others. Some computers come with multiple headphone jacks, or you can purchase a headphone splitter that will allow two or more students to listen at once.

A printer in the classroom enables students to print some of what they find and to access materials when they are not sitting at the computer. This allows you to divide the class into at least two groups, one of which is working at the computers while the other works with printed materials or on other aspects of a learning activity. However, printers can be easily abused. Students should be taught NOT to print everything they find on the Web, but, rather, to skim through the materials and either take notes or save relevant information to a disk. Further, printing from web browsers does not always have the desired effect. Often, web pages are much longer than they seem, and one web page might turn out to be many printed pages. Also, many printers do not handle web-based images and graphics correctly. (If there is something in your curriculum web that you want the students to print—for example, a worksheet—create a PDF file so that it prints correctly. See page 195.) Reserve printing for documents that are especially useful and that include either long text passages or charts with lots of data, or for the finished products or draft products that students create themselves. (Teachers whose students have e-mail may want students to e-mail finished products to them, saving paper and perhaps also making feedback easier.) We also urge you to consider the environmental impact of excessive printing.

Additional peripherals such as scanners or digital cameras allow students to supplement web-based resources with other pictures, data, and text that they find in books or in the local environment. If you know that such equipment is available to your students, plan on having them collect local information or images and use these in completing the learning activities supported by the curriculum web. Nothing is more motivating to students than to see their own drawings or photographs incorporated into their work, especially when it is online where they can show it to friends or family members!

COMPUTER LABS

The next best thing to Internet access in the classroom is the availability of a computer lab with Internet access. Labs are ideally suited for whole-class direct instruction or allowing the entire class to work on a curriculum web at once.

Many computer labs have servers that can cache files that are most recently accessed from any computer in the lab. This is a great boon when using curriculum webs, especially if an entire class is working on the same web site at once, because once the page has been accessed once, the rest of the class will only be copying it from the server's cache, rather than downloading it from the Internet. Some schools have such caching software running on schoolwide networks. Schools that do not may find things slowing down considerably during periods of lots of web activity. If you notice pages loading very slowing when your entire class is using the Web, talk to your school's technology coordinator about setting up a caching system.

The great advantage of using the computer lab for teaching specific computer skills is also its biggest disadvantage. Computers rather than subject matter seem to take center stage in a computer lab. This is why David Jonassen (2000, 278) writes, "I believe that computer labs are one of the major impediments to meaningful integration of technology in schools." Jonassen advocates integrating computers into meaningful activities in the regular classroom, making them "mindtools" for student learning.

Many schools, unfortunately, reserve the computer lab for using specific software packages or for instruction in computer skills, rather than letting subject matter teachers use the labs to enrich classroom teaching and learning. If your school limits the use of the computer lab in this way, then it might be necessary to convince the principal that there are other options. Even worse is when regular classroom teachers drop off their classes in the computer lab once or twice a week and then take a preparation period or otherwise do not participate in the lab time. Unless the lab time is used for the teaching of computer science, the class should bring subject area projects to the lab with them. Computer lab should not be isolated from subject matter learning. Without practicing computer skills in the context of subject matter or classroom learning, students see the computer only as an add-on rather than as a real tool for learning.

Computer skills (such as the use of a word processor, presentation software, spreadsheets, or Internet browsers) are best learned while participating in an activity designed to teach writing, reading, history, science, or foreign language. If there are separate computer teachers, these teachers and the classroom teachers should work closely to tie skills directly to ongoing classroom learning. One solution to the mutual isolation of computer skills and subject matter is to have computer teachers and classroom teachers jointly develop curriculum webs and then work together to implement them with students. The computer teacher can take the lead while students are learning computer-specific skills necessary for completing the curriculum web, and the subject matter teacher can take the lead in teaching subject matter skills. Also, when both teachers are in the room they can learn from each other and circulate among the students, alternately offering assistance and leading the class.

CONNECTIVITY

One issue involving servers and curriculum webs is the issue of where you, as a teacher, will put your curriculum web so that students can access it. The ideal situation is one in which your school runs a **file server** or web server and provides you with an account on that server where you can put files to be accessed by students. If the server is within the school's **local area network,** you may be able to put files onto your account merely by saving them to a **network drive.** The school's web site may be housed on the same file server, in a separate directory, or you may have a "web account" on the server in which you can place your curriculum webs. Find out from your school's technology coordinator or webmaster what the procedure is at your school to publish files to the school's web server. Your school may require you to submit proposed web pages to a person or committee for approval, and then have the pages published by the webmaster. Because the school as a whole may be judged by the quality of such publicly available materials, this makes some sense, provided such approval and publication happens quickly.

With luck, you can also access your own personal web account from home, where you may be doing most of your curriculum development and lesson planning work.

If your school does not have a web server, you may need to use an external web account for your curriculum webs. Most **Internet Service Providers** (ISPs) give web space along with e-mail addresses. Find out from your ISP how to publish files to your web account, which should be accessible from within the school. If you can see your web pages from outside the school but not within it there may be an issue with the **firewall** or filtering software. Your school's technology coordinator should know whether these factors need to be considered in your particular situation.

Eventually, we believe, every school will want its own web server, both for external use (by parents and the community, by teachers and students working from home), and for internal use. Most schools will try to control what goes onto the school's web site, but despite these efforts, schools should support the notion that teachers should be able to "publish" web-based materials easily and regularly, and be able to update these materials as needed, from school or from home, so their students are well served.

SOFTWARE ISSUES

Filtering Software

During the 1990s, as the Internet became more popular, many parents, teachers, and public officials became concerned about Internet content that is inappropriate for young people. Certainly during the early popularity of the Web, pornography sites as well as sites advocating hatred or violence were fairly common, and these sites would occasionally be accessed by innocent persons seeking more wholesome experiences. The federal government responded by trying to make certain content illegal with the Communications Decency Act. In a landmark case in Philadelphia, a federal appeals court found that this act violated the free-speech provisions of the First Amendment to the U.S. Constitution. Subsequent efforts to control Internet content were also voided on free-speech grounds.

In 2000, a new effort began in the U.S. Congress to require schools and libraries with Internet access to install and maintain filtering software to protect students from adult-oriented material. Many school districts adopted such programs in advance of the federal requirement. However, other school districts and (especially) libraries resisted this demand, claiming that it was impossible to create a filter that would allow everything educational in while keeping everything inappropriate out. At the time of publication of this book, Congress still had not fashioned a bill acceptable to the broad majority of educators and librarians. Consequently, schools are pretty much on their own to make decisions about filtering.

There are several filtering approaches, each with advantages and disadvantages. One approach is to list all the sites that are to be accessible from within the school, blocking any sites not on the approved or "include" list. But there is no way for an individual school or district to know, in advance, what kind of information or images might be educational in all contexts. The lists must be reviewed and updated constantly to reflect the availability of new content on the Web. One solution is to hire outside firms to maintain the list of approved sites, and to rely on this outside firm to understand both what might be inappropriate and what might be educational. (There are, of course, some more difficult cases where content might be both inappropriate *and* educational. A school district needs to be sure that any firm it employs reflects the district's values regarding the relative importance of shielding kids and opening minds.)

Another approach is for schools or outside firms to create a list of excluded sites. This does not work very well because the providers of adult-oriented and potentially inappropriate content are constantly creating new URLs or setting up new servers to attract new users, and exclude lists simply cannot be kept up-to-date. Another variation is to set up a list of words that block access to a web page if they appear. Nearly everyone would agree that some words—curse words, racial slurs, and the names of body parts or illegal drugs—should be on this "exclude" list. They will agree, that is, until a situation arises in which web pages containing such words may be educational. If students are conducting research on breast cancer, or producing a report on the slang names associated with certain illegal drugs, or investigating Jim Crow laws and their effects on African Americans, there may be web sites containing the words "breast," "marijuana," or "nigger" that are educationally appropriate but which nonetheless would be blocked by filtering software.

Yet another approach taken by some schools is to purchase proprietary content that can serve as an Intranet, or pseudo-Internet, allowing free access within the web space but no or limited access beyond it. This approach treats the Internet access as the school would treat the school library: not every book or magazine available in the outside world gets placed in the library, but students generally have free access anywhere within the library. Although this is a defensible position for schools to take, and is certainly better than keeping all Internet resources out, this is not the approach that we believe will result in students learning how to deal with a complex world in which materials and content of all descriptions is readily available outside the school walls.

We prefer that the teacher, rather than some outside group (the government, the district, a filtering firm) make decisions about what should be accessible or not, because in most cases only the teacher knows what kind of content is appropriate and educational for the students in his or her classroom. If districts or governmental authorities do not trust teachers to make these kinds of decisions, then how can they trust the teachers to make other decisions about what is or is not worth doing in the classroom? Teachers should receive training in the selection of appropriate Internet content, learning how to apply criteria such as those listed beginning on page 150, and they should be empowered to teach students how to select appropriate content while avoiding inappropriate materials.

E-MAIL

Many school districts routinely provide e-mail accounts to their teachers and use e-mail for school management and districtwide communication. It is best for these e-mail accounts to be handled by a server accessible from outside the school, so teachers can use the same accounts from home. Some school districts do not allow teachers to access their district-provided accounts from outside the schools for various reasons, often having to do with the security of student information. Teachers in these districts can set up their own e-mail account with another e-mail provider.

Getting home access to e-mail requires two somewhat different types of access. The first is access to the Internet, through an ISP. This access will be either through a dial-in connection or some kind of dedicated broadband connection such as a **digital subscriber line** (DSL) or **cable modem.** Monthly fees for dial-in access range from around $10 to more than $30, depending on usage levels. Dedicated lines typically cost $40 or more. The second type of access is access to your e-mail. Almost every ISP will provide subscribers with e-mail accounts. It might be possible to have your home e-mail account access your school account, if the school e-mail server is accessible from outside the school. (Technically, if your school is not protected by a firewall, and the e-mail server is **POP3** or **IMAP,** you can usually access it from outside the school or from anywhere linked to the Internet. However, if your school e-mail server uses a proprietary e-mail standard—such as that used by **Microsoft Exchange** Servers—you may not be able to access it from anywhere but within the school district's LAN).

Another option is to set up one of the many free **web-based e-mail accounts** available from big web portal sites such as *yahoo.com* or *hotmail.com*. These accounts are usually supported by advertising, but they have the advantage of being accessible from any computer with unrestricted access to the Web. In addition, some of these free web-based e-mail accounts will allow you to connect to other e-mail accounts, such as the one provided by your school, if those accounts use POP3 or IMAP e-mail protocols.

Student e-mail accounts are useful as a support for web-based learning because they allow students to contact web-based authors and experts, participate in listserv discussions with students around the world, and e-mail work or questions to the teacher. Many progressive school districts provide e-mail to every student. These accounts are often not accessible to the student from home, presenting some of the issues just discussed regarding teacher e-mail accounts. The biggest fear of school administrators is that students will use their school e-mail accounts to get into trouble (for example, by communicating with people who may not be looking out for the student's best interests). For this reason it may be necessary for any students wishing to contact outsiders to use the teacher's e-mail account. Students prepare drafts of their messages, which the teacher must approve before they are sent. This is not a bad idea when liability and safety are primary concerns.

Another alternative is for the students to set up web-based e-mail accounts (described previously) with an outside providers. Some districts have banned this practice, fearing that if the student gets into trouble with the account (whether in school or out of school), the school will be held liable if a teacher helped the student to set up the account initially. Because web-based accounts often use servers outside the control of the school, it is very difficult to prevent the student from sending and receiving inappropriate messages during school time. However, see *gaggle.net* for one very useful approach to student e-mail.

ENSURING SUCCESSFUL TEACHING WITH A CURRICULUM WEB

Before you begin using your curriculum web with students, consider the following preparatory activities:

- Do a "dry run." Go through the curriculum web yourself. Then, ask someone else (a friend, colleague, family member) to go through the curriculum web. They will be able to tell you if the instructions are clear, if there are any broken links, and how long the curriculum web took to complete.
- Poll your students to find out who has computer access at home, and who has Internet access at home (you may be surprised at how many do). This will not only indicate a potential higher skill level for those with at-home access, it will also save lab/computer time as the students may be able to use your curriculum web at home.
- You may need to prepare your students technologically for working with computers. If students do not have the skills necessary to perform basic computer functions, both they and you may get frustrated while using the curriculum web. It will save time in a lab situation if you can go over the skills in the classroom first and then partner the more technologically advanced students with those who are less experienced.
- Prior to allowing your students to begin on the curriculum web, take the time in the classroom to prepare your students. Find a way to connect the curriculum web's focus and activities to previously covered material, their activities in other classes, and/or to the world they know. Go over the expectations for the curriculum web and their conduct during it. Discuss with them the timeframe and what to do if they encounter difficulties with any aspect of the curriculum web.
- Consider printing out any truly important web sites or other resources that are necessary for the curriculum web to work successfully. (Be sure to pay attention to copyright issues when you do this! See page 153.) The last thing you will want is to have the Internet go down in the middle of the session, just as students are about to explore a key resources. *Always* have an alternate plan available.
- Consider the questions listed in Table 12.1.

TABLE 12.1   Some Questions to Consider Prior to Implementing a Curriculum Web

Where will I conduct the curriculum web?

Which students are using the curriculum web (class type and grade level)?

How many computers will be used?

What is the computer-to-student ratio?

Who will test my curriculum web?

How will I present the curriculum web to my students?

How will I prepare my students technologically?

What is my back-up plan if I cannot get access to the technology as planned?

Who can I ask for technological assistance?

How will I monitor the students as they use the curriculum web?

What is my plan for students who misbehave?

What follow-up activities will the students perform?

When/where can I get extended computer access?

What are some back-up sites the students can visit, if necessary?

How will I assess student progress?

How will I allow for feedback?

ACTIVITY 12 ■ Writing a Plan for Teaching with Your Curriculum Web

1. Survey your teaching situation in terms of the following elements: people, classrooms, computers, connectivity, and software. List the strengths and weaknesses of each element. Explain how each element will affect your use of curriculum webs.
2. Think about the best ways to group your students, if you have a limited number of computers, or if you have a wide range of computer proficiencies in the class.
3. Think about ways to compensate for technology failure, including some of the strategies discussed in this chapter.
4. Write an implementation plan covering these issues and the questions in Table 12.1. Link the implementation plan to the teaching guide of your curriculum web.

Chapter Summary

This chapter:

- Discusses some factors that will affect how you use curriculum webs in schools, including teacher(s), students, classrooms, computer labs, computers, connectivity, and software

- Suggests some way to work around limitations or barriers presented by such factors
- Presents some issues to consider prior to implementing a curriculum web
- Guides you in developing an implementation plan to link to your teaching guide

Questions For Reflection

David Jonassen (2000, 278) writes, "I believe that computer labs are one of the major impediments to meaningful integration of technology in schools."

Do you agree with Jonassen? Why or why not? Consider the many ways that computer labs are used, from teaching productivity software, to providing a room that can be used on an as-needed basis by whole classes that might not have access to enough computers in their regular classroom. If you are using this book as part of a class, these issues might frame a useful discussion.

Your Next Step

Download Hands-On Lesson 12 to learn about extending the capabilities of your software. After completing Lesson 12, please take the time to fill out the feedback form at *curriculumwebs.com.*

Congratulations! You are as close to done as it is possible to be. All that is left at this point is to implement or use your curriculum web, continually reflect on how it inspires learning, and modify or update your site as you learn about its effectiveness or about new resources, activities, or design principles. The truth is, if you have taken our book seriously, you have now become not only someone who has developed a curriculum web, but someone who will never think about teaching and learning, or utilize technology, in the same way again.

For Further Learning

- See *curriculumwebs.com* for some links pertinent to the topics in this chapter.
- An excellent comprehensive book on using the Internet with students is Grabe and Grabe 2000.
- Good resources on teaching students with special needs include Brett and Provenzo 1995 and Male 1994.
- An overview of ways to use technology in schools is provided by Schwartz and Beichner 1999.
- Leu, Leu and Coiro 2004 contains much good advice from teachers who have used the Internet in schools.

APPENDIX

■ ■ ■ ■ ■ ■ ■ ■ ■ ■

AN OVERVIEW OF
WEB TECHNOLOGIES

Overview

In this appendix we discuss some of the technologies that make up the Internet and particularly the World Wide Web. An understanding of the underlying organization will make the Internet and the World Wide Web less mystifying. As Arthur C. Clark said, "Any significantly advanced technology is indistinguishable from magic." It is our aim in this section to advance your technological understanding to allow you to more easily use and control the Internet. In addition, what follows will introduce you to terminology that is referred to elsewhere in the book.

WEB SERVERS, CLIENTS, AND BROWSERS

A *server* is a computer that stores files as a central resource. It is an information provider.

A *client* is an information consumer, a computer (or a piece of software on a computer) that requests and receives information from a server. The computer you use to surf the Web is a client.

A *web server* is a computer that is hooked to the Internet that stores and delivers web pages for other computers to access.

A *web browser* is a computer program that runs on a client machine and requests web pages from a server. Examples of web browsers are Internet Explorer, Mozilla, Firefox, Opera, and Safari.

How Do Servers Work?

A web server "listens" to the Internet for requests for web pages that are stored on that server. As requests are submitted from **clients,** the web server locates files and sends them over the Internet to the client.

How Do Web Browsers Work?

A sequence of events takes place when a web browser **downloads** a web page. First, the web browser determines what page it should display to the user. Either the user has typed in a URL (a web address—more on that in a minute) or has clicked on a link that specifies a URL. The browser then sends a request out to the Internet for that page. Next, the web **server** whose address was specified in the URL sends to the **client** computer an HTML file containing all the information that the browser needs to correctly display the web page. Finally, the browser interprets the file, formats it, and displays it to the user.

In the client–server relationship the user does not necessarily know just what the server has provided and what the browser has interpreted. Let us examine a sample web page to see what is going on behind the scenes. Assume that a web page contains some large, red text. The server does not send large letters or the color red over the Internet; rather it tells the browser what words make up the text and specifies that they should be displayed in a large-size **font** and should be colored red. The browser then displays the text as large and red because it received that formatting information from the server along with the text itself.

However, the user can set web browser options or preferences that override the formatting information that comes from the server. A user may set the font size of the browser to always show font size 24, for example, perhaps so students can clearly see the page as it is displayed by an overhead projector. Or perhaps the user finds it difficult to read colored text against a colored background and so may specify, via the browser's preference settings, to always show text in black against a white background. Note that the server—and the web page designer—knows nothing about the browser's preference settings; they have no way of knowing how the client handles the information that the server is sending it. This is both a limitation and a strength of web-based design.

Caching

As users are browsing the Web they often return to recently visited pages, usually by pushing the "Back" button. Web browsers are normally configured (again through preference settings) to cache pages. A cache is a storage area on the client machine's hard drive that temporarily saves web pages that may be revisited shortly. When a browser downloads a web page from a server it stores that web page on the client computer's hard drive, interprets the information, and displays it on the monitor. When the user goes to another web page, the original web page's information is erased from the monitor but remains on the client's hard drive, in the cache. If the user then chooses to go back to the original web page, the client computer does not have to download the page again over the Internet; it is already on the local hard drive. This *caching* results in a significant timesaving for the user; the same page does not have to download over and over again.

Some issues do arise with caching:

- Cached pages take up room on the client computer's hard drive. The browser preferences can be set to limit the amount of disk space used up by the cache.
- What happens if a web page has changed since the user last looked at it? This is a common occurrence, especially in interactive web pages that are used in business,

for price quotes, or in auctions. This problem is solved by having the browser contact the web server and ask only for the date and time that the page was last changed. If the web page has not changed since the browser downloaded it, then the cached version is displayed. Otherwise the updated web page is again downloaded over the Internet and displayed. Again, browser preferences may affect this process.

BANDWIDTH

Bandwidth refers to how much data can be moved over a network per unit of time, measured in bits per second. It is often compared to a water pipe: the larger the diameter of the pipe, the more water that can flow through it. Bandwidth is the speed at which your web browser can get web pages from a server. It is limited by that part of the connection between the client and server that has the lowest bandwidth, just as the water that comes out of a faucet is limited by the smallest pipe it must go through as it travels from the water purification plant to your kitchen sink.

The bottleneck in a typical user's Internet connection lies in the telephone line and modem. See Figure A.1.

Web servers can usually communicate to the rest of the Internet at a speed above 3 million **bits** per second. If your computer is limited by a modem that receives data from the Internet at 56k (roughly 56 thousand bits per second), then you can only download web pages at that rate, no matter how fast or slow the server is, or how far away. This is why it makes very little difference to the end user if a web page resides on a server in the user's hometown or across an ocean. What makes the most difference to the user is whether he or she is connecting to the Internet via a 56k modem (56 thousand bits per second) from home or via a **T-1** line (3 million bits per second) from school.

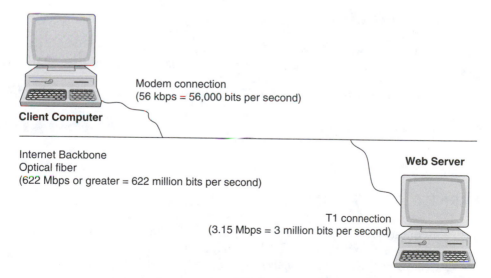

Modem connection
(56 kbps = 56,000 bits per second)

Client Computer

Internet Backbone
Optical fiber
(622 Mbps or greater = 622 million bits per second)

Web Server

T1 connection
(3.15 Mbps = 3 million bits per second)

FIGURE A.1 **Relative bandwidths of different parts of the Internet.**

A NOTE ON BITS AND BYTES

Bits and **bytes,** kilobytes (KB), megabytes (MB), gigabytes (GB), and so on refer to the amount of information that can be stored in computer memory. The smallest unit is a *bit*, which is essentially an on/off switch. It can represent only two numbers: one (on) and zero (off). When eight of these are put together into a *byte*, 2^8 or 256 different numbers can be represented. This is enough to encode all the letters of the alphabet in lower and uppercase, plus some special characters and codes. (**ASCII** is an encoding scheme that represents the alphabet in a standard way so that computers can exchange textual information.) So, roughly, eight bits or one byte equals one character of the alphabet. The text in this book contains approximately 100,000 words, or 500,000 characters, and so would occupy 500,000 bytes on a computer. If you had a 56k modem linked to the Internet, you could download this entire book—minus the graphics—in about 70 seconds.

A picture is worth considerably more than a thousand words—at least in terms of computer memory. Graphics, sound, and especially video files are typically much larger than text files and so download more slowly over the Internet. As discussed in Chapter Nine, limiting download times by making file sizes as small as possible is a significant aspect of web design. A couple of examples will demonstrate the importance of optimizing images and movies:

- A $4'' \times 6''$ photo saved at 300 dpi (dots per inch), which is roughly what a standard digital camera would produce, will take 170 seconds to download over a 56k modem. The same $4'' \times 6''$ photo reduced to 72 dpi, which will look exactly the same on a computer monitor as the higher resolution photo, will download in about 13 seconds.
- A one-minute-long movie with full-quality DVD formatting will take over eight hours to download over a 56k modem. The same movie, saved for the web at 12 frames per second with medium-quality stereo sound, will download in less than eight minutes.

Some of the words used to measure file sizes are:

A **kilobyte** (1 K) is approximately 1,000 bytes. (Actually, it is 2^{10} or 1,024 bytes.)
A **megabyte** (1 MB) is approximately 1,000 K. (Actually, it is 2^{20} or 1,048,576 bytes.)
A **gigabyte** (1 GB) is approximately 1,000 MB. (Actually, it is 2^{30} or 1,073,741,824 bytes.)

INTERNET NAMES AND URLS

Requests for web pages are made by specifying the page's address or URL (Universal Resource Locator). Each URL is unique and consists of four parts. Examine the following URL: *http://cuip.uchicago.edu/cw/WhoAmI/TeachingGuide.htm*. This "web address" can be broken down into several parts. See Figure A.2.

FIGURE A.2   The parts of a URL.

Communications Protocol

http://cuip.uchicago.edu/cw/WhoAmI/TeachingGuide.htm

The communications **protocol** indicates what "language" is needed to access the resource. Http stands for **HyperText Transfer Protocol,** the language of the World Wide Web, and tells your web browser that the file is of a type that it can interpret and display. There are other protocols, some of which your web browser may understand, including https (secure HyperText Transfer Protocol), FTP (**File Transfer Protocol,** used to transfer files of almost any sort), and telnet (used to open a **command-line** terminal window to another computer on the Internet).

Host Name

http://cuip.uchicago.edu/cw/WhoAmI/TeachingGuide.htm

The host name is the Internet address of the web server. Every computer on the Internet has an address that uniquely identifies it, called an Internet Protocol (IP) number. Servers have permanent **IP addresses,** whereas clients that connect to the Internet for a short time, such as a PC **dialing up** an Internet Service Provider (ISP), are given temporary IP addresses.

Most permanent Internet hosts have a name associated with its IP address, which is called a **Domain Name Service** (DNS) address. This was set up for human ease of use. After all, it is much easier to remember "*amazon.com*" than something like 207.171.183.16.

A DNS address can be further broken down into its constituent parts: the *machine name* and the *domain name*.

Machine name: *cuip.uchicago.edu*

The machine name is simply a name given to a computer that is functioning as a server. This is the server used by the University of Chicago-Chicago Public Schools Internet Project.

Domain name: *cuip.uchicago.edu*

The domain name is hierarchical in structure and represents an institution or organization to which the machine belongs. As you read from left to right you move from the most specific to the most general, just as street addresses do. This server is based at the University of Chicago.

The right-most part of the domain name is the top-level domain and can give you a clue as to what type of organization the server belongs to:

> .edu = an educational institution (usually within North America)
> .com = a commercial organization
> .gov = a U.S. government agency
> .mil = a U.S. military site
> .org = formerly a not-for-profit organization; now a catchall category

Some relatively new domains that are available include:

> .net (typically used for international commercial sites)
> .biz (businesses)
> .info (could be almost anything)
> .tv (related to television)
> .name (usually for personal web sites)

Other top-level domain names are geographically rather than logically organized:

> .de = Germany
> .ch = Switzerland
> .au = Australia
> .gb = Great Britain

Path

http://cuip.uchicago.edu/cw/WhoAmI/TeachingGuide.htm

Files reside on a server's hard drive. They are usually arranged logically in a hierarchical grouping for the convenience of the humans who create and update these files. The computer does not "care" where the files are stored, as long as someone remembers where they are. *Directories*, which are known as "folders" on personal computers, are used to keep the files stored in an organized fashion. A complete file name includes the directory **path,** which indicates exactly where the file is located on the server within the computer's hierarchical file system. See Figure A.3.

CUIP's web server contains the "Who Am I?" and "Our United States" curriculum webs. Both units incorporate several activities and have other related files. Because of the hierarchical nature of the file system, it does not matter whether files within different curricular areas have the same filenames; the path will indicate exactly which file is being accessed at any given time.

Filename

http://cuip.uchicago.edu/cw/Whoami/TeachingGuide.htm

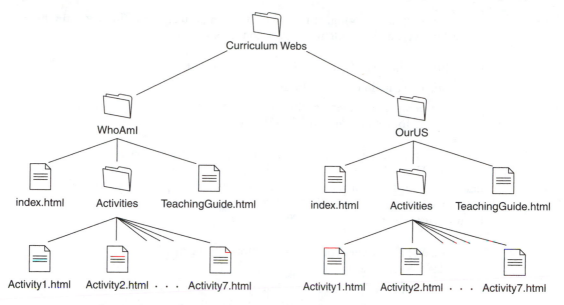

FIGURE A.3   A hierarchical file system on a server.

Because computers are very exact devices, every letter of a URL must be typed exactly so a web browser can locate a web page. You, as the curriculum web designer, will be choosing filenames for your web pages. As you have seen, these names make up part of the URL of the web page. Here are some rules to follow in picking filenames:

Case matters. The file named "`TeacherPage.htm`" is not the same as "`teacherpage.htm`".

No spaces. Files that are accessible via the Web should not have blank spaces in their names. If they do, you will end up creating links with inscrutable codes like "%20" within them. Some web designers choose filenames that are more readable to the human eye by using capital letters or an underscore to separate words, resulting in filenames like "`TeachingGuide.htm`" or "`teaching_guide.html`". The only drawback to this scheme is that it is easy to forget exactly which letters of the filename you capitalized—remember: case matters!

No punctuation marks other than an underscore (_) or dash (-). A name such as "`Teachers'sPage.html`" may result in problems when the web server tries to retrieve the file.

Remember, filenames and directory names (paths) are for human readability, to help you keep your work organized in a logical manner. Name your files descriptively.

Filename Extension

http://cuip.uchicago.edu/cw/WhoamI/TeachingGuide.htm

Filename **extensions,** sometimes called suffixes, are the letters to the right of a dot in a filename. The extension is used to tell the web browser exactly what kind of file the web server is delivering. It is then up to your web server to interpret the file correctly. Some examples of filename extensions are:

.htm or .html: a HyperText Markup Language file

.gif: a picture in Graphics Interchange Format

.jpg or .jpeg: another graphics format, primarily used for photographs (named for the Joint Photographic Experts Group)

Almost all browsers have the built-in capability to correctly display the file types mentioned here. For other kinds of files, a plug-in may be required. Your browser may have come with several plug-ins already installed; if you come across a file type that your browser doesn't recognize, you can often download a plug-in to augment your browser's capabilities. Some other file types are:

.au: Mu Law, a very common sound format. It provides only mono sound, but the files are very small

.aiff or .aif: Audio Interchange File Format, a sound format for the Macintosh.

.wav: Wave, the PC standard for audio

.ram: Real Audio, similar to aiff or wav

.mpg or .mpeg: a sound and video file format, named after the Moving Pictures Expert Group.

.avi: video format for Windows

.mov: QuickTime movie format, the most commonly used video format.

.wma: Windows media audio

.wmv: Windows media video

We hope that this appendix has demystified the World Wide Web somewhat.

GLOSSARY

Acceptable Use Policy (AUP) A document produced by schools or school districts and approved by the school board outlining what is and what is not appropriate Internet-related conduct by teachers and students.

aim The overall purpose of a given **curriculum** unit.

alignment The degree to which the **curriculum** addresses the same knowledge or skills that is covered in various **assessments,** especially standardized tests. Also refers to relationship between the various subjects in a grade level.

animation A sequence of images displayed in such a way as to simulate movement.

applet A small **application,** usually embedded in a web page and written in **java.**

application A piece of software designed to foster productivity on the computer.

articulation The interrelationship of different activities or curriculum units within the whole curriculum.

ASCII The American Standard Code for Information Interchange, pronounced "as-key." Allows computers to communicate with one another by creating a standard for the digital sequences that refer to letters, numbers, and common symbols. There are 128 ASCII codes. Data files that contain only ASCII codes are referred to as ASCII files (or "text files"), and can generally be interpreted by any computer regardless of what programs are available on the computer.

assessment The process of determining what students have learned from a given activity or unit. See also **evaluation.**

attitude Feelings and emotions that affect a learner's readiness to learn. May be the outcome of, or a **prerequisite** to, a set of **learning activities.**

attribute An addition to an **HTML tag** that qualifies or extends the meaning.

audience The **users,** from the web designer's perspective. For a curriculum web, the audience is generally the same as the set of **learners** who will be using the curriculum web.

authentic assessment A method of determining whether **learning objectives** have been met in which learners engage in activities similar to those that might take place in the real world outside of formal schooling.

balance When referring to curriculum, the quality that results from addressing all aspects of students—intellectual, physical, social, emotional, and spiritual—or including a broad range of **learning activities.**

bandwidth The quantity of data that can be moved over a **network** per unit of time.

benchmark A definition of what a student should be able to do at the conclusion of a grade or course. Benchmarks are often more specific than **standards,** but less detailed than **performance criteria.**

bit Binary digIT. The smallest piece of digital information. One bit is one "switch" that can either be on (1) or off (0). All **digital** information is made up of sequences of bits containing 1s and 0s.

bitmap A graphic that is defined **pixel** by pixel, in terms of a specification of each pixel's color and brightness. Bitmaps are larger and slower to download than comparable **vector** graphics.

blog Web log, or journal that is available on the Web. Blogging has become a new form of expressive communication.

breadcrumbs A method used to help the user keep track of where he or she is within your curriculum web by showing current page's location within the structure of the web site, for example: "Home | Chapters | Chapter 6 | Copyright."

byte Eight **bits** of data. It takes 8 bits of data to represent one letter, number, or symbol in **digital** format.

cable modem A device for connecting a computer to the Internet via cables that also deliver TV signals.

cache A storage area on the client machine's hard drive that temporarily saves web pages that may be revisited shortly.

cascading style sheet (CSS) A document that controls the appearance of many web pages at once. By creating a cascading style sheet (CSS), the web designer can easily manage text and paragraph styles such as fonts, headings, bullets, lists, paragraphs, and page margins. CSS styles can also be **embedded** in a **web page.** Only **web browsers** produced after about 2000 can use CSSs.

CGI   See **common gateway interface.**

chunking   The process of breaking information into "bite-size" pieces, that can easily be digested by the user. An important part of web site design.

clearinghouse   A web site providing access to numerous other web sites, usually categorized by topics. Similar to a directory, except clearinghouses are usually devoted to one or more related topics.

clickable   Something that responds somehow when a user clicks on it with the mouse. If the response is appropriate (for example, the user is taken to another page) we say the **link** is "live."

client   A computer that is used to display information or programs generated by a **server,** which is generally in a remote location from the user.

clipboard   An area of a computer's memory used for temporarily storing text or graphics to be pasted into another document.

command line   A method of communicating with a computer in which users must type specific commands, and therefore must know the **syntax** of those commands. Often used for interacting directly with an **operating system** such as Unix or Linux.

common gateway interface (CGI)   A standard for implementing **interactivity** through scripts to control server-based processing of information generated by web pages.

computer lab   A room with many computers devoted exclusively to teaching and learning with computers. Often used in schools for prepackaged educational software (such as Compass Learning) or for teaching about computers (computer literacy class). May also be very useful for teaching in a subject area when learning requires an entire class to use computers at once.

computer platform   The computer's basic technology, including **operating system** and hardware. Different computer platforms are Mac, PC, Unix, Linux, and SunOS.

computerize   To implement computers to assist in tasks that would otherwise be done (or not done) without the computer. Can be taken pejoratively if

used to refer to teaching or learning or other human activities. We cannot really computerize teaching or learning, although we certainly can computerize many tasks that are associated with teaching and learning.

continuity   The ways that curriculum activities relate to prior and subsequent activities. Related to **sequence.**

cookie   A small file that is placed on the user's computer for a specific purpose when the user visits a web site. The file may contain information about the user that is useful to the web site, such as the user's geographical location or shopping preferences (generally determined by the user's own input or actions). Users can set their browser NOT to accept cookies, although in so doing they may lose out on some interactive features of the Web.

cooperative learning   A form of **grouping** in which small teams of learners work together to complete tasks in a noncompetitive environment.

criterion or criteria   A standard on which an assessment or evaluation will be made. Represents the answer to questions such as: "Why do you say this work is excellent?"

culminating activity   A final activity in a **curriculum** that serves to integrate a sequence of **learning activities,** helping students to organize the new knowledge, skills, and attitudes gained through the curriculum.

curriculum   A plan for a sustained process of teaching and learning.

curriculum plan   A written document describing the goals, audience, and activities of a sustained process of teaching and learning. Serves as a blueprint for the design of the curriculum web and is later repurposed as the teaching guide.

curriculum web   A web site or collection of pages designed to support a plan for a sustained process of teaching (or **instruction**) and **learning.**

design   The product of, or a process of, **development.**

development   The process of building a **curriculum** or web site, based on a plan.

dial-up   A connection to a computer network through plain-old telephone service (**POTS**), requiring a modem.

differentiation   The process of structuring a curriculum to provide different learning activities to each learner or group of learners. Similar to individualization.

digital Information that is stored as a sequence of 1s and 0s. See **bit.**

digitize To convert a picture or other document from paper or **analog** form into a sequence of 1s and 0s through scanning or other means.

digital subscriber line (DSL) A specific type of connection to a computer network that uses regular telephone lines but transfers information in digital format, so that a **modem** is not required.

direct instruction An approach to teaching that is highly structured and includes teacher delivery of content and step-by-step instructions; didactic teaching.

directory On a server, a directory is another name for a folder that contains files. Also used to refer to a listing of the files in a folder along with their properties.

distance education An approach to teaching and learning that uses the Internet or other technologies to overcome the physical separation of teachers from learners or learners from each other.

domain name server A computer specifically dedicated to locating the correct **IP address** for any given **URL.**

download To transfer a file from a **server** to a **client** computer.

educative experience Experience that leads toward further growth. The opposite of a miseducative experience.

element (1) A piece or feature of a curriculum plan or teaching guide. We refer to the **aim, rationale, subject matter description,** and so on as elements.

element (2) The basic unit of **HTML.** An element consists of the **tags, attributes,** and content associated with a given piece of a web page, such as a paragraph, heading, table, or image.

e-mail Also email. Short for electronic mail. A form of asynchronous communication in which typed messages are routed over the Internet.

embedded assessment Methods of determining the extent of student learning that are part of learning activities, rather than separate from them. Includes products, performances, rubrics, and self-tests. See **assessment.**

engaged learning A recently popular phrase for learning in which students really care about the outcome of a learning activity. Students tend to learn more and enjoy themselves more when they are engaged in **learning.**

entry-point A page within a web site designed to welcome or orient a new user. May contain a sequence of pages to simulate the feeling of "entering" the site.

environment May refer to the operating system or other parameters in which a computer program functions, or more generally to the entire context or surroundings of a situation.

essential question A provocative and multilayered question that serves as an inspirational starting point for an inquiry or educational investigation.

evaluation The process of determining the success or value of an inanimate object, program, or institution. We do not use this term to refer to judgments made about students or teachers. See **assessment.**

exit-point A page in a web site designed to be the last page seen by the site's users. Often contains "good-bye" message or links to further resources.

extension The part of the filename at the end, after the last period (dot) in the filename. Indicates what kind of file it is. ".exe" indicates executable, ".htm" or ".html" indicates **HyperText Markup Language** file, ".gif" equals Graphic Interlaced Format, and so on. Also called a suffix.

extracurricular The part of a school day that is optional, or ungraded. Generally includes clubs and team sports.

file The basic unit of information on a computer. May be copied, moved, deleted, transferred, opened, or (in the case of an executable file) run.

file path See **path.**

file server A computer that holds files and software accessed by other computers via a network. Generally, these computers have large disk drives and powerful processors. See **server.**

File Transfer Protocol (FTP) An industry standard for sharing files between computers over the Internet.

font A size and style for a given **font family.** For example, Arial 10 pt. is a font within the Arial font family.

formative evaluation A process of determining the quality or qualities of a curriculum web or other product, process, or institution while that product is still under development.

frame A **web page** that contains or displays another web page within it.

frameset   A grouping of **frames** on a web page. Also, the file that sets up the grouping of frames on a web page.

FTP   See **File Transfer Protocol.**

gigabytes (GB)   A unit for measuring memory. 1 gigabyte = 1 billion bytes, or the capacity to hold about 100,000,000 words. See **byte.**

GIF   Graphic Interchange Format, a format used for image files, especially those not needing more than 256 colors. GIF files generally have a .gif **extension.** Pronounced with a hard "g" as in "gift."

grouping   The process of structuring learning activities so that learners work together on some or all learning tasks.

habit   An acquired continuity of response, learned and maintained over time.

heuristic   A concentual tool for understanding complex situations, often involving simplifications or assumptions helpful for solving problems.

heuristic evaluation   A technique that relies on a well-developed list of **criteria** for evaluating a web site or other product.

hierarchical   When referring to a web site, implies a structure in which more general pages provide links to increasingly specific pages.

higher-order thinking   Thinking that requires students to go beyond given information or facts and analyze, synthesize, or evalutate information, forming judgments that often can be applied to new situations or issues.

HTTP   See **HyperText Transfer Protocol.**

hyperlink   Text or picture that the user can click on to browse to another page on the Web.

hypertext   A body of text, graphic material, and so on stored in a machine-readable form and structured in such a way that a reader can cross-refer between related items of information.

hypertext markup language (HTML)   A language, or code for creating web pages. Based on an older language called Standard Generalized Markup Language. Consists of **tags, attributes,** and **content.** A page written in HTML is a text file that includes tags in angle brackets that control the fonts and type sizes, insertion of graphics, layout of tables and frames, paragraphing, calls to short executable programs, and hypertext links to other pages. Files written in HTML generally use an .html or .htm **extension.**

HyperText Transfer Protocol (HTTP)   The underlying **protocol** by which WWW **clients** and **servers** communicate.

hypertextual   Containing many internal links, allowing for navigation in a nonlinear or free-association manner.

IMAP   Internet Message Access Protocol. A protocol that makes it easy to manage your e-mail on a remote server. It allows the user to manipulate messages without downloading them. A newer alternative to **POP3.**

individuation   The formation of individual persons through the lifelong interaction of capacities and habits with opportunities and values. Can be seen as more important for education than that students achieve specific, predefined knowledge or skills.

information granularity   The idea that all sets of information can be broken into pieces that can be easily and quickly grasped. See **chunking.**

inquiry   The process of resolving a problem or difficult situation.

inquiry-based learning   An approach to teaching in which students engage in hands-on activities and construct their own learning.

instruction   The process of guiding students through a sequence of **learning** activities.

instructional supports   Features of curriculum webs explicitly designed to help learners to complete learning activities, often for the purpose of replacing the assistance that might be provided by a teacher in more traditional learning environments.

instructor station   A computer in a classroom used by the instructor or teacher while teaching. Often, an instructor station will have a **projector** that can show what is on the instructor's screen. This allows the instructor to demonstrate how to do certain procedures on the computer.

interactive   Allowing for back-and-forth communication between the **user** and the computer.

interactivity   The principle that every experience results from a combination of factors found in both the **learning environment** and the learner.

Internet   The global network of computers or smaller networks that communicate through a common protocol, TCP/IP. Developed originally as ARPANET by the U.S. Defense Department in the 1960s.

Internet connection (or Internet access)   A computer's link to the Internet, the worldwide network of networks that includes the World

Wide Web. An Internet connection can be direct (as in a computer linked to a schoolwide network connected to the Internet via a T-1 or T-3 line), or through **dial-up** (telephone) access.

Internet Service Provider (ISP) Provider of connections to the Internet, usually via **dial-up, digital subscriber lines,** or **cable modem.**

intranet A **TCP/IP network** that can be connected to the Internet but is usually protected by a firewall or other device.

IP address The unique, four-number address of any computer linked into the Internet. Example IP address: 123.76.89.0. Computers that are permanently linked to the Internet have permanent IP addresses, whereas computers that link only temporarily to the Internet (for example, via dial-up access) are assigned temporary or dynamic IP addresses.

iterative Describes a process in which repetition of a cycle of procedures gradually produces better and better results. We think of building curriculum webs as an iterative process.

java A highly structured computer programming language. Not related to JavaScript.

JavaScript A highly structured scripting language used by web developers to allow greater degrees of control of the user interface. JavaScript **applets** are embedded in the HTML of the web page and run on the **client** machine, rather than the **server.** Not directly related to java.

JPEG Pronounced "Jay-peg," stands for Joint Photographic Experts Group, and represents a type of image file, generally with a .jpg **extension.** JPEGs (also abbreviated JPGs) are ideal for containing photographs.

Kilobyte (KB) 1,000 **bytes** of data. One kilobyte can hold about 200 words or a very small picture.

learner Someone who is seeking growth, or an increase in the capacity for further learning.

learner description A written outline of the target **audience** of the curriculum web, including a description of their **needs.** Generally includes information about the learner's age and grade and may also include information about their interests, background, or goals.

learning An enduring change in an individual's thoughts or actions, caused by experience.

learning activity A task that has been carefully designed to lead learners toward one or more **learning objectives.**

learning objective A desired change in students' skills, knowledge, or **attitudes.**

learning theory A model or concept that explains observed or desired relations between experience and **learning.**

link See **hyperlink.**

local-area network (LAN) A group of computers linked by **network cable** (or wireless LAN) that can share data, files, and peripherals.

lossless A compression process that compresses files without discarding any of the information in the file. The reexpanded file will contain exactly the same information as the original. See **lossy.**

lossy A compression process in which the quality of the image is irretrievably decreased. See **lossless.**

MB See **megabytes.**

medium (plural: media) A substance or material through which information is transmitted; examples include radio, television, audio, video, print, and the Web.

megabytes A unit for measuring of memory. Abbreviated MB. One megabyte = 1,000,000 **bytes,** or the capacity to store about 100,000 words (2,000 pages) or one fairly large image.

megahertz A unit for measuring processing speed. Abbreviated MHz. One megahertz = 1,000,000 cycles of a process per second. Imagine a turnstile in a subway station: each time the turnstile rotates, it processes one rider. Your computer's central processing unit processes one instruction each cycle; so one megahertz means that it processes one million instructions per second.

menu A listing of possible topics, functions, or categories of information, allowing the user to select the next step in his or her interaction with the computer.

Microsoft Exchange A **proprietary** e-mail protocol used by Microsoft's Outlook e-mail software. Generally, e-mail accounts on Microsoft Exchange servers are not accessible outside a school's local-area network.

modem Short for modulator/demodulator. Converts **digital** to **analog** data and vice versa. Allows digital devices like computers to communicate over analog phone lines, or **POTS.**

multimedia The combination of data, images, and sound in a computerized **environment** or program.

MHz. See **megahertz.**

named anchor   A special use of the <A> **tag** with the NAME **attribute** that allows a link to take the user to a specific point within a web page.

navigation   The process of moving around in a computerized (or real) environment.

need   The gap between a current and a desired state of affairs.

network   A set of computers that communicate with one another, and the hardware and software that link them.

network drive   A drive on another computer or the **server.** On a Windows machine, network drives often are named with letters such as f:, h:, p:, or s:, to distinguish them from local drives a: through d:. You can find these drives by clicking on Network Neighborhood. On a Mac you can access file servers by going through the Chooser (which is found under the Apple Menu). Once you log in to the server, its hard drive will be seen as an icon on your desktop and you can access it just as you would any other disk.

node   Refers to either (1) one of the devices that can communicate on a **network** or (2) the point of intersection in a complex web of relationships. An individual web page can be considered a "node" in a **web site** or in the **World Wide Web** at large.

nonpreordinate objective   **Objective** that does not specify what the students' behaviors, skills, or attitudes will be at the conclusion of a curriculum, but rather leaves outcomes open-ended.

objective   A desired outcome pursued through planning or design. See **learning objective.**

online assessment   Methods for determining whether learning objectives have been met that involve learners completing tasks at their computer and submitting the results without resorting to paper.

operating system   The computer program or collection of programs that provides for the basic operations of a computer, including communications between mouse, keyboard, peripherals, display, and network. On a Windows-based computer, the operating system may be Windows 95, Windows 98, Windows 2000, or Windows NT. Other operating systems include DOS (Disk Operating System), MacOS, Unix, and Linux.

open system   The opposite of a **proprietary** system. Open systems allow any user or developer unlimited access to the way the system functions, enabling anyone to produce applications or modifications to the system. HTML and Linux are open systems.

path, or file path   A way of specifying the exact location of a file on a server or other computer. Each element of the path indicates a directory or folder.

PDF   See **Portable Document Format.**

Pentium   A class of central processing unit, or "chip" in a computer. This class came after the class known as the **486.** After Pentiums have come Pentium IIs, IIIs, and IVs.

performance criterion, description, or indicator   A statement of the evidence that will be used to evaluate whether a learner has successfully mastered a specific **learning objective.**

PHP   Short for PHP: Hypertext Preprocessor, a scripting language that is used to create dynamic Web pages. Often, files containing PHP scripts need to have the extension .php. (Note that the long form of the PHP abbreviation also contains, "PHP". This is an example of a self-referential abbreviation, very commonly used by computer professionals.)

pixel   Short for "picture element," the smallest unit on a computer screen. Each pixel can be a different color. The number of pixels per row and per column on a screen indicates the **resolution.**

planning   To create (in advance of implementation) a scheme or method for the accomplishment of an **objective** or set of objectives.

platform   See **computer platform.**

plug-in   A small program that can be added to a browser or other program to extend its capabilities.

POP3   Post Office Protocol, version 3. A standard form of communication between e-mail servers and clients.

portable document format (PDF)   A proprietary format for distributing formatted documents over the Internet. The format can be read on most **platforms,** using the Acrobat Reader **plug-in** available from adobe.com.

portal   A web site considered as an **entry-point** to other web sites, often by providing access to a search engine or directory.

preassessment   An activity that takes place at the beginning of a curriculum unit to find out if the learner has mastered the unit's **prerequisites** or to determine which learning path is most appropriate for that learner.

preordinate objectives   **Objectives** that imply a precise specification of what successful learners can or will be able to do at the conclusion of a curriculum or lesson.

prerequisite   Prior learning outcomes or experiences that are necessary in order for some later activity to take place.

problem-based learning (PBL)   A type of **learning** activity in which students work together to solve real-world problems, and learn as they figure out how to solve the real-world problem. Thought to be more engaging than more traditional forms of academic learning such as memorization or rote learning.

projector   A device for displaying the output from a computer on a screen so everyone in a room can see it. Every **instructor station** should have a projector, so that the teacher can demonstrate the actual steps in a computer application, or can display images, data, or student work so everyone in the classroom can see it. (An alternative is the capacity to control all the computers in the lab so that they all show what is on the instructor station, when this is helpful to the lesson.)

proprietary   A computer program, system, or protocol that is tightly controlled by the company that produces it, such that users and developers must rely on the company for information about how to access or utilize the program, system, or protocol. Windows and MacOS are proprietary systems. See **open system.**

protocol   A standard for communication. Different computers can communicate with one another over the Internet because they use standard protocols.

public domain   Materials that are not **copyrighted** are in the public domain, meaning that anyone can use them for legal purposes. Do not assume that something is in the public domain simply because there is no explicit copyright statement.

publish to web server   To "publish" a web page to a **server** is equivalent to saving it to a directory on the web server. Sometimes, the **web server** is within the **local area network,** and so a user simply needs to choose a network drive when saving a web file. If that **network drive** is accessible via the Web, the mere act of saving the file "publishes" it to the Web. But if the web server is not part of the local area network, it is necessary to "publish" the web page by sending it, usually via **FTP,** across the **Internet** to the server. Also known as **uploading.**

random-access memory, or RAM   The primary memory used to store programs and information that a computer is processing. The contents of RAM disappear when the computer is turned off, as opposed to read-only memory (ROM) which usually holds the memory when the computer is turned off.

rationale   A reason or reasons that something is worth doing; in a **curriculum plan,** a short essay justifying the activities and structure of the curriculum or its inclusion in a course of study.

RealAudio   A proprietary protocol for transmitting streaming audio or video, produced by RealNetworks.

reflection   The process of considering whether selected actions have led to desired consequences, and what to do about that.

resolution   A measure of how densely packed a picture or computer screen is. Usually measured as the number of **pixels** across by the number of pixels down. Higher resolutions allow for more information to be displayed on the same size of screen.

rubric   A chart listing evidence that will support claims about student learning and showing a developmental sequence from beginner to expert in achievement of learning objectives. See **assessment.**

scaffolding   Supporting learning through providing the **instructional supports** and conceptual frameworks that help the learner to successfully learn difficult concepts or skills.

scalable   Capable of being scaled, or having its size changed without loss of appearance or resolution. Flash animations have the quality of being scalable to fit the resolution of the user's computer screen. Some fonts are scalable, meaning they can be changed in size without becoming fuzzy as they get bigger.

scope   Refers to a curriculum's breadth and depth of subject matter coverage. See **subject matter description.**

search engine   A web site that allows the user to search an index of web pages according to keywords. The index is created by a computer program that crawls the Web and logs the words on each page.

self-regulated learner   A learner who decides in a reasonable and effective manner what activities are necessary in order to reach learning goals.

sequence   Refers to the way that activities are organized over time; sequence can be rigidly controlled, resulting in a linear structure, or left up to student interest or choice, in a **hypertextual** or nonlinear structure.

server   A computer designed to store and deliver information for multiple **client** computers.

splash page   A web page that loads first when the user first enters the web site, but then disappears automatically as it is replaced by the site's home page.

site map   On a web site, provides a visual overview of the structure of the web site, showing major links and groupings of pages. Web designers can create paper-based prototype site maps at an early stage in the design process, or include a final site map in the web itself.

source code, or source   The **HTML** in a **web page** that is interpreted by the web **browser** when the browser displays the page.

standard(s)   A description of what students should learn in school, often the result of a process of building consensus across multiple stakeholders.

status bar   A section of an application's window that gives information about the state of the application. In browsers, the status bar can display the **URL** of a link that the user is pointing to, or the web-page designer can use **JavaScript** to change the content of the status bar.

streaming   Process by which a video or audio file is transmitted from a web **server** to a **client** and played on the client as it is received, as opposed to waiting until the entire file has been downloaded.

subject matter description   An outline or other description of a curriculum's topics or content.

surfing   Browsing around on the Web without any particular purpose.

summative evaluation   A process of determining the quality or qualities of a curriculum web or other product, process, or institution after it has been completed.

table   A rectangular arrangement of rows and columns into which text, graphics, links, and other elements can be placed.

table cell   The space in a **table** that results from the intersection of one row with one column. In HTML, each cell of a table can have its own background color but all the cells in a table share certain formatting properties such as whether their borders are visible.

tag   The basic unit in which **HTML** marks up the content of a web page. Always contained within brackets <thus>. Most—but not all—tags have a

start tag <H1> and a corresponding end tag </H1>. Tags may also contain **attributes.**

task analysis   The process of determining every specific action or skill that must be performed or mastered in order to complete a more complicated task. Sometimes used to determine the best way to teach or learn the complicated task.

T-1   A **digital** communications line that transmits at about 1.5 megabits per second.

teacher   The most important person in a classroom, responsible for managing the **learning environment.**

teaching   The process of trying to influence student **learning** through the creation and manipulation of the **learning environment.**

teaching guide   A document that lists a curriculum's **aim, rationale, subject matter description,** description of **learners** and their **needs,** expected **prerequisites, materials, instructional plan,** and **plan for assessment and evaluation,** and provides advice to teachers and learners about how to use a **curriculum.**

template   A document that contains some content and/or formatting that can serve as the basis for creating multiple documents with the same content and/or formatting.

uniform resource locator (URL)   A naming convention that uniquely identifies the location of a computer, directory, or file on the **Internet.** The URL also specifies the appropriate Internet **protocol,** such as gopher, **HTTP,** and so on.

uploading   The process of transferring a file from the user's computer to a server. See **publish to web server.**

URL   See **uniform resource locator.**

vector   A line or movement defined by its end-points. Vector graphics are smaller and faster than **bitmaps,** which are defined by each **pixel.**

wayfinding elements   Used on web pages to communicate to the user where they are within a web site's overall structure.

web   With lowercase w, "a web" refers to a collection of related **web pages** constructed for a specific purpose.

Web   When capitalized, "the Web" is shorthand for the **World Wide Web.** (Note that we do not capitalize "web" when it is used as an adjective, as in web-based, web page, or web design.)

web-based e-mail account   An e-mail account in which access is made through a web browser, by logging into a web page. Available through larger portals such as yahoo.com and hotmail.com. Often allow use of **attachments,** storage of archival messages, and linking to external **POP3** and **IMAP** e-mail servers. Usually supported by advertising.

web browser   A software program, such as Internet Explorer or Safari, that retrieves a document from a **web server,** interprets the HTML codes, and displays the document to the user with as much graphics as the software can supply.

web page   A **World Wide Web** document with a unique **URL.** Pages can contain almost anything, such as news, images, movies, and sounds.

web server   A computer equipped with the **server** software to respond to web **client** requests, such as requests from a web **browser.** A web server uses the Internet **HTTP, FTP,** and gopher protocols to communicate with clients on a TCP/IP network.

web site or website   A collection of **web pages** joined together by a set of links and sharing a common purpose. Generally all the pages on a site are stored on the same **server.**

white space   The portions of a web page that are empty. These are important for "setting off" those sections of the page that are not empty.

wiki   A web site that allows any user to add and edit any content. Also refers to the software that enables such a web site.

World Wide Web (WWW)   The set of **hyperlinked** data, image, sound, and video files that are stored on computers linked to the Internet and are accessible via the **hypertext transfer protocol** (HTTP). In this book, referred to as the Web for short.

WYSIWYG   An acronym for "What You See Is What You Get." Pronounced "whizzy-wig." Refers to a program that shows the page being edited exactly as it will appear when eventually viewed on paper or screen.

zone of proximal development   The difference between what a learner is capable of achieving on his or her own and what the learner can do with proper **instructional support.**

REFERENCES

Abbey, Beverly, ed. 2000. *Instructional and Cognitive Impacts of Web-Based Education.* Hershey, PA: IDEA Group.

Ackermann, Ernest C. and Karen Hartman. 2002. *Searching and Researching on the Internet and World Wide Web.* Wilsonville, OR: Franklin Beedle.

Adobe Creative Team. 2002. *Adobe Photoshop 7.0 Classroom in a Book.* Berkeley, CA: adobepress.

Aggarwal, Anil, ed. 2000. *Web-Based Learning and Teaching Technologies: Opportunities and Challenges.* Hershey, PA: IDEA Group.

Aggarwal, A. K. and Regina Bento. 2000. Web-Based Education. In *Web-Based Learning and Teaching Technologies: Opportunities and Challenges,* edited by Anil Aggarwal, 1–16. Hershey, PA: IDEA Group Publishing.

Alagemalai, Sivakumar, Kok-Aun Toh and Jessie Y. Y. Wong. 2000. Web-Based Assessment: Techniques and Issues. In *Web-Based Learning and Teaching Technologies: Opportunities and Challenges,* edited by Anil Aggarwal, 246–256. IDEA Group.

Apple, Michael W. 1991. The New Technology: Is It Part of the Solution or Part of the Problem in Education? *Computers in Schools* 8(1 /2 /3), 75.

Arter, Judith A. and Jay McTighe. 2000. *Scoring Rubrics in the Classroom: Using Performance Criteria for Assessing and Improving Student Performance.* Thousand Oaks, CA: Corwin.

Bastiaens, Theo J. and Rob L. Martens. 2000. Conditions for Web-Based Learning with Real Events. In *Instructional and Cognitive Impacts of Web-Based Education,* edited by Beverly Abbey, 1–31. Hershey, PA: IDEA Group.

Berger, Pam. 1998. *Internet for Active Learners: Curriculum-Based Strategies for K–12.* Chicago: American Library Association.

Bielefeldt, Talbot. 2001. Technology in Teacher Education: A Closer Look. *Journal of Computing in Teacher Education* 17(4): 4–15.

Bigge, Morris L. and S. Samuel Shermis. 2003. *Learning Theories for Teachers,* 6th ed. Boston: Allyn & Bacon.

Bloom, Benjamin. 1956. *Taxonomy of Educational Objectives.* New York: Longman.

Boisvert, Raymond D. 1998. *John Dewey: Rethinking Our Time.* Albany: State University of New York Press.

Bonk, Curtis J., Jack A. Cummings, Norika Hara, Robert B. Fischler and Sun Myung Lee. 2000. A Ten-Level Web Integration Continuum for Higher Education. In *Instructional and Cognitive Impacts of Web-Based Education,* edited by Beverly Abbey, 56–77. Hershey, PA: IDEA Group.

Brett, A. and Provenzo, E. F., Jr. 1995. *Adaptive Technology for Special Human Needs.* New York: State University of New York Press.

Bruce, Bertram C. 2003. *Literacy in the Information Age: Inquiries into Meaning Making with New Technologies.* Newark, DE: International Reading Association.

Bruner, J. S., et al. 1957. *Contemporary Approaches to Cognition: A Symposium Held at the University of Colorado.* Cambridge, MA: Harvard University Press.

Brunner, Cornelia and William Tally. 1999. *The New Media Literacy Handbook: An Educator's Guide to Bringing New Media into the Classroom.* New York: Anchor Books/Doubleday.

Burbules, Nicholas. 2004. Ways of Thinking about Educational Quality. *Educational Researcher* 33(6): 4–10. (Available online at http://www.aera.net/pubs/er/pdf/vol33_06/03ERv33n6-Burbules.pdf; last accessed October 2004.)

Caine, R. N., and Caine, G. 1991. *Making Connections: Teaching and the Human Brain.* Alexandria, VA: Association for Supervision and Curriculum Development.

Capraro, Michelangelo, et al. 2004. *Macromedia Flash MX 2004 Magic.* Berkeley, CA: Peachpit.

CEO Forum. 2001. School Technology and Readiness Report: Key Building Blocks for Student Acheivement in the 21st Century. Washington DC: CEO Forum on Education and Technology. (Available online at http://www.ceoforum.org/downloads/report4.pdf; last accessed October 2004.)

Clandinin, D. Jean and F. Michael Connelly. 1992. Teacher as Curriculum Maker. In *Handbook of Research on Curriculum,* edited by Philip W. Jackson, 363–401. New York: Macmillan.

Crotchett, Kevin R. 1997. *A Teacher's Project Guide to the Internet.* Portsmouth, NH: Heineman.

CPS. 2000. Evaluating Rubrics. *Instructional Intranet.* Chicago: Chicago Public Schools. (Available online at http://intranet.cps.k12.il.us/Assessments/

Ideas_and_Rubrics/Intro_Scoring/Eval_Rubrics/
eval_rubrics.html; last accessed October 2004.)

Cuban, Larry. 1986. *Teachers and Machines: The Classroom Use of Technology since 1920*. New York: Teachers College Press.

Cucchiarelli, Alessandro, Maurizio Panti and Salvatore Valente. 2000. Web-Based Assessment in Student Learning. In *Web-Based Learning and Teaching Technologies: Opportunities and Challenges*, edited by Anil Aggarwal, 175–197. Hershey, PA: IDEA Group.

Cunningham, Craig A. 2000. Improving Our Nation's Schools through Computers and Connectivity: An Impossible Dream? *Brookings Review* 41–43, Winter.

Cunningham, Craig A. 2003. The Internet as a Tool for Shared Inquiry. *Jewish Educational Leadership* 1(1): 12–14.

Cunningham, Craig A. and Diana Joseph. 2004. Putting Passion On-Line: A Protocol for Building Motivation into Curriculum Webs, a presentation at the Annual Meeting of the Society for Information Technology in Teacher Education, Atlanta.

Cunningham, Ward and Leuf, Bo. 2001. *The Wiki Way: Quick Collaboration on the Web*. Boston: Addison-Wesley.

Dewey, John. 1976 [1899]. *School and Society*. In *The Middle Works of John Dewey*, volume 1, edited by Jo Ann Boydston. Carbondale: Southern Illinois University Press.

Dewey, John. 1985 [1916]. *Democracy and Education*. In *The Middle Works of John Dewey*, volume 9, edited by Jo Ann Boydston. Carbondale: Southern Illinois University Press.

Dewey, John. 1991 [1938]. *Experience and Education*. In *The Later Works of John Dewey*, volume 13, edited by Jo Ann Boydston. Carbondale: Southern Illinois University Press.

Dodge, Bernie 1997. Some Thoughts about WebQuests. (Available online at http://edweb. sdsu.edu/courses/edtec596/about_webquests.html; last accessed October 2004.)

Dodge, Bernie. 1999. *WebQuest Taskonomy: A Taxonomy of Tasks*. (Available online at http://edweb.sdsu.edu/webquest/Process/WebQuestDesignProcess.html; last accessed October 2004.)

Dodge, Bernie. 2001. FOCUS: Five Rules for Writing a Great WebQuest. *Learning and Leading with Technology*, 28(8, May): 6–9.

Druin, Allison and Cynthia Solomon. 1996. *Designing Multimedia Environments for Children*. New York: John Wiley and Sons.

Duchastel P. 1978. Illustrating instructional texts. *Educational Technology*, 18(11): 3–3.

Eisner, Elliot. 1985. *The Educational Imagination: On the Design and Evaluation of School Programs*, 2nd ed. New York: Macmillan.

Elliott, Stephen N. 1995. Creating Meaningful Performance Assessments. ERIC Digest E531. (Available online at http://www.ed.gov/databases/ ERIC_Digests/ed381985.html; last accessed October 2004.)

Flanagan, David. 2001. *JavaScript, The Definitive Guide*, 4th ed. Sebastopol, CA: O'Reilly & Associates, Inc.

Fogg, B. J., Cathy Soohoo and David Danielson. 2002. How Do People Evaluate a Web Site's Credibility? Results from a Large Study. *Consumer Web Watch*. (Available online at http://www.consumerwebwatch.org/news/report3_credibilityresearch/stanfordPTL_abstract.htm; last accessed October 2004.)

Gagne, Robert M. 1985. *The Conditions of Learning*, 4th ed. New York: Holt, Reinhart and Winston.

Gagne, Robert M. and Robert Glaser. 1987. Foundations in Learning Research. In *Instructional Technology: Foundations*, edited by Robert M. Gagne, 49–84. Mahwah, NJ: Lawrence Erlbaum Associates.

Gardner, Howard. 1983. *Frames of Mind*. New York: Basic Books.

Glavac, Marjan. 1998. *The Busy Educator's Guide to the World Wide Web*. London, ON: NIMA Systems.

Gooden, Andrea R. 1996. *Computers in the Classroom: How Teachers and Students Are Using Technology to Transform Learning*. San Francisco: Jossey-Bass.

Grabe, Mark and Cindy Grabe. 1998. *Integrating Technology for Meaningful Learning*. Boston: Houghton Mifflin.

Grabe, Mark and Cindy Grabe. 2000. *Integrating the Internet for Meaningful Learning*. Boston: Houghton Mifflin.

Gray, Sharon. 1997. Training Teachers, Faculty Members, and Staff. In *Web-Based Instruction*, edited by Badrul H. Khan, 329–332. Englewood Cliffs, NJ: Educational Technology.

Green, Garo. 2003. *Macromedia Dreamweaver MX 2004 Hands-on Training*. Indianapolis, IN: Peachpit.

Greenaway, Robert. 2004. Facilitation and Reviewing in Outdoor Education. In Barnes, P. and Sharp, R. (Eds) *The RHP Companion to Outdoor Education*. Dorsett, UK: Russell House. (Available online at http://reviewing.co.uk/articles/facilitating-outdoor-education.htm; last accessed October 2004.)

Hackbarth, Steve. 1997. Web-Based Learning Activities for Children. In *Web-Based Instruction*, edited by Badrul Khan, 191–212. Englewood Cliffs, NJ: Educational Technology.

Harris, Judi. 1998. *Virtual Architecture: Designing and Directing Curriculum-Based Telecomputing.* Eugene, OR: International Society for Technology in Education.

Harris, Susan and Zee, Natalie. 2002. *HTML & Web Artistry 2 More Than Code.* Berkeley, CA: Peachpit.

Hativa, Nira and Alan Lesgold. 1996. Situational Effects in Classroom Technology Implementations: Unfulfilled Expectations and Unexpected Outcomes. In *Technology and the Future of Schooling,* NSSE 95th Yearbook, edited by Stephen Kerr, 131–171. Chicago: NSSE.

Healy, Jane. 1998. *Failure to Connect: How Computers Affect our Children's Minds, For Better and Worse.* New York: Simon and Schuster.

Hill, Brad. 1997. *World Wide Web Searching for Dummies.* Foster City, CA: IDG Books.

Hixson, Susan and Kathleen Schrock. 2003. *Developing Web Pages for School and Classroom.* Westminster, CA: Teacher Created Materials.

Hogan, K. and Pressley, M., eds. 1998. *Scaffolding Student Learning: Instructional Approaches and Issues.* New York: University of Albany, State University of New York.

Huitt, W. 1997. Cognitive Development: Applications. *Educational Psychology Interactive.* Valdosta, GA: Valdosta State University. (Available online at http://chiron.valdosta.edu/whuitt/col/cogsys/piagtuse.html; last accessed October 2004.)

International Society for Technology in Education (ISTE). 2000a. *National Educational Technology Standards for Students: Connecting Curriculum and Technology.* Eugene, OR: ISTE. (Available online at http://cnets.iste.org/students/; last accessed October 2004.)

International Society for Technology in Education (ISTE). 2000b. *National Educational Technology Standards for Teachers.* Eugene, OR: ISTE. (Available online at http://cnets.iste.org/teachers/; last accessed October 2004.)

Jackson, Philip W., ed. 1992. *The Handbook of Research on Curriculum.* A Project of the American Educational Research Association. New York: Macmillan.

Jonassen, David H. 2000. *Computers as Mindtools for Schools: Engaging Critical Thinking.* Upper Saddle River, NJ: Prentice Hall.

Jones, Beau, Gilbert Valdez, Jeri Nowakowski and Claudette Rasmussen. 1994. *Designing Learning and Technology for Educational Reform.* Oak Brook, IL: North Central Regional Educational Laboratory.

Joseph, Linda C. 1999. *Net Curriculum: An Educator's Guide to Using the Internet.* Medford, NJ: CyberAge Books.

Kapoun, Jim. 1998. Teaching Undergrads WEB Evaluation: A Guide for Library Instruction. *College and Research Libraries News* 59(7).

Khan, Badrul H., ed. 1997. *Web-Based Instruction.* Englewood Cliffs, NJ: Educational Technology.

Kerr, Stephen. 1996. Visions of Sugarplums: The Future of Technology, Education, and the Schools. In *Technology and the Future of Schooling,* NSSE 95th Yearbook, edited by Stephen Kerr, 1–27. Chicago: NSSE.

Krough, Suzanne Lowell. 1990. *Integrated Early Childhood Curriculum.* New York: McGraw Hill.

Lachs, Vivi. 2000. *Making Multimedia in the Classroom: A Teachers' Guide.* London: Routledge and Falmer.

Lazear, David. 1991. *Seven Ways of Knowing: Teaching for Multiple Intelligences.* Palatine, IL: IRI/Skylight.

Leebow, Ken. 1999. *300 Incredible Things for Kids on the Internet.* Marietta, GA: VIP.

Leshin, Cynthia B. 1998. *Internet Adventures: Step-by-Step Guide to Finding and Using Educational Resources.* Boston: Allyn & Bacon.

Leu, Donald J., Deborah Diadiun Leu and Julie Coiro. 2004. *Teaching with the Internet: New Literacies for New Times,* 4th ed. Norwood MA: Christopher-Gordon.

Lie, Hakon Wium. 2005. *Cascading Style Sheets,* 3rd ed. San Francisco: Addison Wesley.

Lundsten, Apryl and David Spencer. 2001. *Streaming Media Clearly Explained.* San Diego: Academic Press.

Madaus, George F. and Thomas Kellaghan. 1992. Curriculum Evaluation and Assessment. In *Handbook of Research on Curriculum,* edited by Philip W. Jackson, 119–154. New York: Macmillan.

Male, M. 1994. *Technology for Inclusion.* Boston: Allyn & Bacon.

March, Tom. 1998a. Why WebQuests? An Introduction. *Ozline.com.* (Available online at http://www.ozline.com/webquests/intro.html; last accessed October 2004.)

March, Tom. 1998b. The WebQuest Design Process. *Ozline.com.* (Available online at http://www.ozline.com/webquests/design.html; last accessed October 2004.)

March, Tom. 2000. WebQuests 101: Tips on Choosing and Assessing WebQuests. *Multimedia Schools,* October. (Available online at http://www.infotoday.com/MMSchools/oct00/march.htm; last accessed October 2004.)

March, Tom. 2001. Theory and Practice on Working the Web for Education. *Ozline.com.* (Available online at http://www.ozline.com/learning/theory.html; last accessed October 2004.)

Merrill, Paul. 1987. Job and Task Analysis. In *Instructional Technology: Foundations*, edited by Robert M. Gagne, 141–174. Hillsdale, NJ: Lawrence Erlbaum Associates.

Meyer, Eric. 2002. *Eric Meyer on CSS*. Indianapolis, IN: New Riders.

Moursund, D. and Bielefeldt, T. 1999. *Will New Teachers be Prepared to Teach in a Digital Age? A National Survey on Information in Teacher Education*. Santa Monica, CA: Milliken Exchange for Information Technology. (Available online at http: //www. mff.org/publications/publications.taf?page= 154; last accessed October 2004.)

Musciano, Chuck and Kennedy, Bill. 2002. *HTML & XHTML: The Definitive Guide*. 5th ed. Stanispol, CA: O'Reilly & Associates.

National Society for the Study of Education. 1996. *Technology and the Future of Schooling*. Ninety-fifth Yearbook of the National Society for the Study of Education, Part II, edited by Stephen T. Kerr. Chicago: NSSE.

Navarro, Ann. 2001. *Effective Web Design*. Alameda, CA: Sybex.

Nielsen, Jacob. 1994. Heuristic Evaluation. In *Usability Inspection Methods*, edited by J. Nielsen and R. L. Mack, 25–64. New York: John Wiley.

Nielsen, Jacob. Undated. Severity Ratings for Usability Problems. (Available online at http:// www. useit.com/papers/heuristic/severityrating. html; last accessed October 2004.)

Oakes, Jeanine. 1985. *Keeping Track: How Schools Structure Inequality*. New Haven, CT: Yale University Press.

Ornstein, A. C. and F. P. Hunkins. 1998. *Curriculum: Foundations, Principles, and Issues*, 3rd ed. Boston: Allyn & Bacon.

Pirouz, Raymond. 1998. *HTML Web Magic*. Indianapolis, IN: New Riders.

Piper, Paul S. 2000. Better Read that Again: Web Hoaxes and Misinformation. *Searcher*, 8(8; September). (Available online: http://www.infotoday. com/searcher/sep00/piper.htm; last accessed October 2004.)

Pratt, David. 1994. *Curriculum Planning: A Handbook for Professionals*. Belmont, CA: Wadsworth.

Provenzo, Eugene F., Jr., Arlene Brett and Gary N. McCloskey, O. S. A. 1999. *Computers, Curriculum, and Cultural Change: An Introduction for Teachers*. Mahwah, NJ: Lawrence Erlbaum.

Rebenschied, Shane. 2004. *Macromedia Flash MX 2004 Beyond the Basics Hands-On Training*. Indianapolis, IN: Peachpit.

Robinson, Paulette and Ellen Yu Borkowski. 2000. Faculty Development for Web-Based Teaching: Weaving Pedagogy with Skills Training. In *Web-Based Learning and Teaching Technologies: Opportunities and Challenges*, edited by Anil Aggarwal, 216–226. Hershey, PA: IDEA Group.

Roblyer, M. D. 2004. *Integrating Educational Technology into Teaching*, 3rd ed. (2004 Update). Columbus, OH: Merrill.

Rubin, Andee. 1996. Educational Technology: Support for Inquiry-Based Learning, in *Technology Infusion and School Change: Perspectives and Practices* (Cambridge MA: TERC). (Available online: http:// ra.terc.edu/publications/terc_pubs/tech-infusion/ ed_ tech /ed_tech_frame.html; last accessed October 2004.)

Sather, Andrew, Ardith, Gañez, and Bernie DeChant. 1997. *Creating Killer Interactive Web Sites*. Indianapolis: Hayden Books.

SBC Filamentality. 2003. Activity Formats. *Filamentality Online Support*. (Available online: http://www.kn. pacbell.com/wired/fil/formats.html; last accessed September 2004.)

Schmidt, William H. and Curtis C. McKnight. 1998. What Can We Really Learn from TIMSS? *Science*, 282, 1830–1831.

Schofeld, Janet Ward and Ann Locke Davidson. 2002. *Bringing the Internet to School: Lessons from an Urban District*. San Francisco: Jossey-Bass.

Schön, Donald. 1983. *The Reflective Practitioner: How Professionals Think in Action*. New York: Basic Books.

Schwartz, James E. and Robert J. Beichner. 1999. *Essentials of Educational Technology*. Essentials of Classroom Teaching Series. Boston: Allyn & Bacon.

Serim, Ferdi and Melissa Koch. 1996. *NetLearning: Why Teachers Use the Internet*. Sebastopol, CA: O'Reilly.

Sharan, Shlomo. 1999. *Handbook of Cooperative Learning Methods*. Westport, CT: Praeger.

Shedroff, Nathan. 2001. *Experience Design*. Indianapolis, IN: New Riders.

Sherman, Chris and Gary Price. 2001. *The Invisible Web: Uncovering Information Sources Search Engines Can't See*. Medford, NJ: CyberAge Books.

Siegel, David. 1997. *Creating Killer Web Sites, The Art of Third-Generation Site Design*, 2nd ed. Indianapolis, IN: Hayden Books.

Siegel, Martin A. and Sonny Kirkley. 1997. Moving Toward the Digital Learning Environment: The Future of Web-Based Instruction. In *Web-Based Instruction*, edited by Badrul Khan, 263–270. Englewood Cliffs, NJ: Educational Technology.

Siegler, Robert S. and Martha W. Alibali. 2005. *Children's Thinking*, 4th ed. Upper Saddle River, NJ: Prentice Hall.

Sizer, Theodore R. 1992. *Horace's School: Redesigning the American High School.* Boston: Houghton Mifflin.

Skomars, Nancy. 1998. *Educating with the Internet.* Rockland, MA: Charles River Media, Inc.

Slavin, Robert E. 1994. *Cooperative Learning: Theory, Research, and Practice.* Needham MA: Allyn & Bacon.

Spainhour, Stephen and Robert Eckstein. 2002. *Webmaster in a Nutshell*, 3rd ed. CA: O'Reilly & Associates.

Sprague, Debra, Kimberly Kopfman and Sandi de Levante Dorsey. 1998. Faculty Development in the Integration of Technology in Teacher Education Courses. *Journal of Computing in Teacher Education*, 14(2), 24–28.

Stepien, W. and Gallagher, S. A. 1993. Problem-Based Learning: As Authentic as It Gets. *Educational Leadership*, 50(7), 25–28.

Stigler, James W. and James Hiebert. Winter 1998. Teaching As a Cultural Activity. *American Educator* 4–11.

Tanner, Daniel and Laurel Tanner. 1985. *Curriculum Development: Theory into Practice*, 3rd ed. Englewood Cliffs, NJ: Merrill.

Tetiwat, Orasa and Magid Igbaria. 2000. Opportunities in Web-Based Teaching: The Future of Education. In *Web-Based Learning and Teaching Technologies: Opportunities and Challenges*, edited by Anil Aggarwal, 17–32. Hershey, PA: IDEA Group.

Tognazzini, Bruce. 2003. First Principles of Interaction Design. *AskTOG.* Nielsen Norman Group.

(Available online at http://www.asktog.com/basics/firstPrinciples.html; last accessed October 2004.)

Tyler, Ralph. 1949. *Basic Principles of Curriculum and Instruction.* Chicago: University of Chicago Press.

U.S. Department of Labor. 1991. *What Work Requires of Schools: A SCANS Report for America 2000.* Washington, DC: US Department of Labor. (Available online at http://wdr.doleta.gov/SCANS/what work/whatwork.pdf; last accessed October 2004.)

Veen, Jeffery. 2000. *The Art and Science of Web Design.* Indianapolis, IN: New Riders.

Warlick, David. 1998. *Raw Materials for the Mind: Teaching and Learning in Information and Technology Rich Schools.* Raleigh, NC: Landmark Project.

Weinman, Lynda. 2003. *Design Web Graphics 4.* Indianapolis, IN: New Riders.

Wiggins, Grant and Jay McTighe. 2000. *Understanding by Design.* Upper Saddle River, NJ: Prentice Hall.

Wiles, John W. 1999. *Curriculum Essentials: A Resource for Educators.* Boston: Allyn & Bacon.

Williams, Robin, John Tollett and Dave Rohr. 2001. *Robin Williams Web Design Workshop.* Berkeley, CA: Peachpit.

Williams, Robin and John Tollett. 2000. *The Non-Designer's Web Book*, 2nd ed. Berkeley, CA: Peachpit.

Yeung, Rosanna. 2004. *Macromedia Flash MX 2004 Hands-On Training.* Indianapolis: Peachpit.

Zeldman, Jeffrey. 2003. *Designing with Web Standards.* Indianapolis, IN: New Riders.